CHILDREN IN THE PREHISTORIC

PUEBLOAN SOUTHWEST

Children in the Prehistoric Puebloan Southwest

Edited by

KATHRYN A. KAMP

THE UNIVERSITY OF UTAH PRESS

Salt Lake City

The Defiance House Man colophon is a registered trademark
of the University of Utah Press. It is based on a four-foot-tall
Ancient Pueblo pictograph (late PIII) near Glen Canyon, Utah.

18 17 16 15 14   1 2 3 4 5

LIBRARY OF CONGRESS CATALOGING-IN-PUBLICATION DATA

Children in the prehistoric Puebloan Southwest / edited by Kathryn A. Kamp.
  p. cm.
Chiefly papers presented at a symposium organized for the Society for American Archaeology
meeting held in Philadelphia in April 2000.
Includes bibliographical references and index.

  ISBN 978-1-60781-361-3 (pbk. : alk paper)

1. Pueblo children—Material culture. 2. Pueblo children—Anthropometry. 3. Pueblo
Indians—Antiquities. 4. Pueblo pottery. 5. Human remains (Archaeology)—Southwest,
New. 6. Southwest, New—Antiquities.
I. Kamp, Kathryn Ann. II. Society for American Archaeology. Meeting
(65th : 2000 : Philadelphia, Pa.)

  E99.P9C485 2002
  305.23'0979'0902—dc21

                                    2002003440

Contents

Preface

The time seems ripe for the discussion of age as a critical variable in archaeology. Scholars in a number of areas have been investigating children, so this group makes a logical starting point. Clearly, the elderly should be a focus of future research.

When I first began teaching courses on gender in prehistory in the mid-1980s, my students and I were very frustrated because the temporal and areal focuses of existing resources were so scattered that it was difficult to obtain any sense of the dynamics of gender relations in a particular setting. Since then some excellent volumes have begun to fill the gap in a general fashion. Here it is my hope that by focusing on children in a delineated time and place, we can illuminate the relevant details of prehistory and show some of the promise of this area of study.

Most of the chapters in this book originated in a symposium with the same title, organized for the Society for American Archaeology meetings in Philadelphia in April 2000. Nan Rothschild, one of the discussants, kindly undertook the challenging task of providing an introductory chapter that both comments on the chapters and puts them in a broader context. At the suggestion of Jeff Grathwohl, of the University of Utah Press, John Whittaker and I added a chapter comparing artistic images of Pueblo childhood with the archaeological vision described in the other chapters.

I would like to thank all the contributors for being cooperative, organized, and fun to work with. Jeff Grathwohl was, as always, a supportive

editor, and Michelle Hegmon and an anonymous reviewer for the Press offered constructive comments for both individual authors and the volume
as a whole. Robyn Wingerter, secretary for the Grinnell College Anthropology Department, provided valuable clerical assistance.

Kathryn A. Kamp

1

Introduction

NAN A. ROTHSCHILD

Children are missing from most archaeological accounts. This neglect has been noticed only recently, one scholar suggesting that dogs have been studied with greater archaeological attention than children (Moore 1997). The lack of information on children is closely linked to the previous neglect of women, an assumption that a single genderless past could be written from a male perspective, focusing on men's activities. The archaeology of women's lives is now an important part of the field, but children are still mostly absent, with some very recent exceptions (Deverenski, ed. 2000; Kamp 2001b). Their skeletal remains have been noted and analyzed, but there has been little discussion of their activities or their place in social life, except in formulae that consider child care a task for women (Surovell 2000). An even greater gap in archaeological discourse concerns the lack of focus on the interesting question how (and whether) cultures construct and mark the state of childhood. This oversight is perplexing because all societies structure lives by gender and age to some degree, and ritual is universally involved in the transition from one culturally defined life period to another. Perhaps the lack of interest derives from the fact that children, like women, exist at the weaker end of the dichotomized dimensions of male/female, adult/child. They are feminized, in the sense of being other-than-male and other-than-powerful, and they exist in a category that includes the elderly, the enslaved, and other weak, muted, and marginalized groups. Many forms of analysis have reinforced this problem by focusing on the activities of adults and situating agency exclusively in adult hands, ignoring the power available to children and youth.

Childhood is a sociocultural construct. There is, to be sure, a biological definition of adulthood based on the ability to procreate, but that is only one of the attributes cultures note in defining age-based status. Initial awareness of the variability constructed in childhood came from two anthropologists, both women, Margaret Mead and Ruth Bunzel, who looked at child-rearing practices as sources of cultural difference. Mead also used Samoan adolescence to suggest that not all societies were marked by the turmoil found in American adolescents. Philippe Ariès went beyond Mead to consider the relative recency of the modern Western view of childhood, suggesting that it emerged between the fifteenth and eighteenth centuries in Europe (Stephens 1998). During the medieval period, childhood was a rehearsal for adulthood. This well-documented model suggests that children were apprenticed early and expected to perform adult tasks from early ages, perhaps 6 or 7. Even later, in seventeenth-century paintings, children are portrayed as small adults, wearing adult clothing in miniature. The prescription for children's training varied with rank or class and with gender: elite children (both females and males) learned special skills they would need for their adult roles whereas peasants and children from lower social ranks began a more physical kind of work at an early age. Elements of this lifestyle were still visible in the preindustrial period in the West, when the artisanal labor system incorporated men and women, adults and children, into the production process.

The idea of a separate phase of life developed gradually, as capitalism did, until by the eighteenth century childhood had been conceptualized as a distinct stage marked by particular emotional and educational needs. Originally, this conception was restricted to the elite, but gradually it spread throughout society as the ideal, although it was not achieved at all socioeconomic levels. The contemporary Western life cycle structures life by different rules, depending on class. For the middle class and elite, the period of childhood and adolescence is long. Adulthood begins around age 21 to 25 or even later, depending on the extent of education. For the working class and the poor, childhood can end as early as 14 to 16, and contributions to household economy may begin earlier. Sharon Stephens suggests an association between the development of the idea of childhood and bourgeois notions of family, home, individuality, and privacy (1998:4–5). The increased distinction between male/female and adult/child corresponds to the growing gap between private and public domains and to economic distinctions between production and consumption associated with the development of industrial capitalism. These binary divisions were also linked to concepts of "civilization" and the required control of instincts suggested by Norbert Elias and taken up by Ariès (Cunningham 1995:5–6). Children were constructed in contrast to adults: as savages by E. B. Tylor and as irrational by Jean Piaget (Prout and James 1990:11–12).

The Western concept of a proper childhood has been exported as part of the global and transnational processes currently dominant today. It implies a romanticized and mythical idea of a period of safety and innocence, a happy carefree life, a protected and idyllic time. As prolonged by continuing education, youth is a cultural moratorium, a time out from adulthood (Wulff 1995:7). During this period there is little expectation that the child will make a meaningful contribution to family labor, but she or he is expected to "play" and receive schooling and training for adulthood. The failure to achieve this kind of life introduces the concept of dangerous and deviant children, those who behave in what adults see as inappropriate and frightening ways (Stephens 1998:15; Wulff 1995). A number of phenomena correlate with the definition of the special state of childhood: there are special personnel (experts) trained in a range of aspects, special places for recreation (such as Disneyland), and special equipment. Contemporary children would be relatively easy to identify from the material record because of the vast and expensive array of equipment, from elaborate clothing and furniture, to special foods and eating paraphernalia, to toys of every description.

Considerable attention has been paid in the literature to descriptions and definitions of childhood, but children themselves do not appear to have acquired power as a result of this recognition. Their value has shifted from economic importance to psychological significance, from workers to "priceless" objects. Nevertheless, they are seen as incomplete by adults (Wulff 1995) and are ignored in official records and statistics, even when the goal of data collection is the improvement of children's lives (Qvortup 1990). Several observers note that children and youth are agents in the construction of their own lives, that they are not simply "empty vessels" waiting to receive adult instructions but actively negotiate their childhood (Stephens 1998; Wulff 1995), sometimes in ways that are not understood by adults. There are often special badges or uniforms, language, and behavior that code their status for one another.

CHILDREN OF THE PAST

In exporting ideas about modern lives to the examination of the past, it is crucial to recognize our own biases and not impose modern expectations on the lives of the past, whether derived from ethnography or history.

Specifically, in terms of the lives of past children we must make certain that we are not creating a marked stage where none existed. An objective reality of a phase of physiological immaturity is a constant, but the social or cultural reaction to the shift from immature to mature is handled variably and defined differently. These are two separate dimensions and do not necessarily coincide temporally. Within the period defined as "non-adult" there are often substages, which may be marked by a number of criteria. These criteria exist in contrast to stages defined by physiological analysis of skeletal remains. A recent article suggests that the number of identifiable stages is important in the classification of human ancestors: Bruce Bower reports on a study that determined that *H. sapiens* goes through five stages of growth after birth—infant, child, juvenile, adolescent, and adult; two of the stages—childhood and adolescence—don't appear in other species. Adolescence is visible in the skeleton because it is marked by a sudden growth spurt (Bower 2001).

Another physical reality is the high rate of infant mortality in some cultures of the past. It is unclear how societies handled this sad condition. One coping mechanism could have been to invest little (emotionally) in infants. Evidence bearing on this idea comes from census data and the practice of giving a series of infants the same name. In medieval times the same name was often given to two living children with the assumption that only one would survive, and as late as the eighteenth century it is reported that a newborn infant would receive the same name as a recently deceased child (Stone 1979:57). In nineteenth-century New York City, in another high-infant-mortality population (Seneca Village), census data show more than one child in a family with the same name (New York State 1855).

Information on how childhood is defined may come from autobiographies, ethnographically recorded societies, or past cultures with pictorial or written records. The construction of childhood as a category is part of the overall patterning of society, and many of these categories are marked by ritual and material associations, particularly at points of transition. Sometimes children are treated as incomplete adults, and at other times they hold a special and highly marked status. Some cultures have clearly marked age classes, although cultures vary in terms of what age categories exist, what attributes and activities are assigned to each, and how each is valued. Societies with well-defined age grading (such as the Nuer of East Africa) have several age classes that progress through life together, based on the age at which initiation takes place (Evans-Pritchard 1936). There is also variability in how gender differences are signified among children and how these differ between children and adults. Some information on this subject comes from mortuary data (Deverenski 2000; Lillie 1997; Sillar 1994; Stoodley 2000) and from Aztec documentary sources (Joyce 2000), correlating particular objects with individuals of certain ages; many of these objects are gender-specific, once a given age has been attained. As R. A. Joyce notes, Aztec children and their bodies were marked according to their age, gender, achievements, and status; and material culture, including clothing and hairstyle, was an active socialization mechanism. Some variability was structured by social factors but some by individual circumstances. The rich information available from societies with written accounts and images as well as material and skeletal remains indicates the subtleties that elude much of archaeology that doesn't have these sources. Egyptian (Meskell 1994, 1999) and Aztec (Joyce 2000) accounts of children's lives and deaths reveal an amazing wealth of detail about perceptions and expectations of the normal life cycle.

THE ARCHAEOLOGICAL AND MATERIAL APPROACH TO CHILDREN

The consideration of children's physical lives is usually addressed through skeletal collections, a practice that, incidentally, demonstrates the significance of mortuary analysis involving human bone. Questions of overall health involve the analysis of age at death, indicators of childhood nutritional stress, bone chemical analysis showing diet composition, evidence of specific epidemic diseases, and evidence of the effects of transition from a broad-spectrum food base to a narrower one, usually linked to the development of food production. Analyses of this sort are always implicitly comparative, with adults or other communities of children used for contrast. It is important to remember that the class of children who died young represents a stressed group and only one component of the entire population, as the others survived childhood intact to die later.

The social aspects of children's lives include considerations of social structure and the activities they undertook. Information on these subjects may also be derived from mortuary analysis, examining how children's bodies were treated at death, where they were buried, and whether they received the same kinds of graves, ritual, and grave offerings as adults. Grave goods can offer information on their social standing and their normal tasks. One of the few instances of attention classically paid to children involves the analysis of children's grave goods to consider whether rank positions were inherited in specific Precolumbian societies. As DNA analysis proceeds, it will be possible to establish the sex of child burials and thus look at the continuity of children's labor and status into adulthood. There may also be the potential for understanding the work effort of children by examining skeletal muscle attachments, although that has not yet been done. Assigning productive tasks to children on the basis of grave goods is difficult because of the frequent paucity of tools associated with children's burials (Meskell 1994; Rothschild 1990; Stoodley 2000).

A brief analysis of a series of Precolumbian mortuary sites from the midwestern and southeastern United States, ranging from the Archaic to Mississippian periods, reveals that children received grave goods thought to signify social importance, such as shell beads, copper ornaments, pipes, flutes and rattles, and red ocher. One child was buried with a medicine bag, and several had worked mandibles. Most children were not buried with tools, although it is unclear what the mandibles were used for. These practices imply that some children held high social ranks or perhaps simply that their parents chose to send them to the afterlife equipped with these goods. During the Archaic many of these artifacts were found in the graves of both adults and children, but in the Mississippian sites there seem to have been some objects specifically associated with either adults or children, implying a greater marking of the difference between adults and children at that time (Rothschild 1990). There do not appear to be particular items used across the board to signal an age-related status; the choice of which objects served that function was made locally.

The analysis of artifacts that are not linked to burials is problematic because it is difficult to ascertain which ones were designated for, made by, or used by children (Marango 1991). The idea that amusement is reserved for children (Deverenski 1994) is a modern one and is not borne out in daily practice. The other category of objects routinely assigned to children are crudely made things, which may have been produced by children or others who are not as competent as adults at "normal" skill levels, but these distinctions are difficult to make. Some archaeologists have been able to identify "novice" manufacturers of certain tool classes (Finlay 1997; Sillar 1994; Crown, this volume; Bagwell, this volume). This identification is worthwhile, although if childhood is an apprenticeship (Deverenski 1997), the transition will often be quite gradual.

THE CHAPTERS

The chapters in this volume represent a good beginning in remedying the neglect of Precolumbian children. Although the contributions focus on the southwestern United States, the issues raised apply to many contexts. The

Southwest is an ideal setting in which to discuss these questions because of the wealth of archaeological information about the region and the long, continuous period of settlement, even though one cannot assume identical cultural meanings or behavior during the extended period of occupation. The many interesting questions raised in this book fall into two classes. One set considers what children's lives were like, and the other addresses the cultural construction of childhood. Included in the first set are studies of children's physical condition—their mortality rates, nutrition, and health—and their sociocultural situation—their activities and social status. The other focuses on a specific society's perception of a subadult or the point of transition from child to adult—how are these conceptions defined and marked? What are children's expectations, rights, and obligations? Some studies combine elements of both approaches. The ability to answer any of these questions depends on the kinds of information available as well as how the questions are structured.

The chapters as a group are excellent examples of the use of multiple kinds of information, from ethnography to rock art, from museum collections—an underused and important resource—to recently excavated sites, with theoretical insights drawn from psychology and cognitive studies as well as anthropology and archaeology. The chapters interconnect in significant ways. Several of them use information from skeletal analysis, and two are primarily concerned with the physical aspects of childhood in the Southwest. Kristin Sobolik's and Stephanie Whittlesey's contributions make an excellent complementary pair, overlapping in their concerns but quite distinctive: one approaches the entire Prehispanic past known from archaeological sites in the Southwest, and the other examines a single site, Grasshopper Pueblo. The analysis of skeletal collections is extremely important, especially when the samples are large and well excavated and recorded, although the kinds of information recovered are very specific and limited to certain subjects. There is always a concern about sampling in the analysis of cemetery data and the possible random or systematic exclusion of certain individuals who died elsewhere or of particular causes. Age has been recorded as a significant factor in burial placement and treatment; a number of anthropologists note groups of children who are buried in specific contexts. At Deir el Medina in Egypt, for example, burial location was highly segregated by age (Meskell 1999); among the Lodagaa, children who were not yet weaned and could neither walk nor talk were buried at a crossroads (Goody 1962:149); unbaptized children in Ireland were buried outside church graveyards (Finlay 2000); and as-yet-unnamed children in the Andes are buried far from the village (Sillar 1994).

Sobolik examines more than 7,300 burials from at least 40 sites whose subsistence is based on food production, grouped into five time periods and four cultural traditions. Almost all the sites are precontact, ruling out the possibility of death from European diseases or conflict. She characterizes the entire collection as revealing high infant mortality, ill health, chronic malnutrition, and a high infectious disease rate for children in this area, regardless of time or culture. There are some statistically relevant differences regarding site size—small Anasazi sites show a higher mortality rate than large ones—and time—there seems to be a somewhat lower mortality rate in the later Pueblo periods than in the earlier ones, although another way to interpret this finding is that more adults were dying during Pueblo IV times. The issue of infant and child mortality rates is an important one and must be addressed comparatively. Another shockingly high rate of death at an early age has been recorded at the African Burial Ground, an eighteenth-century site in New York City, where half the almost 400 sets of human remains were of children under the age of 12, and half of those had died in infancy (Mack 1995). Sobolik's interest in the effects of agriculture and sedentism on childhood health calls for comparison with nonagricultural populations, but as she notes, there are none of any size available for analysis.

Whittlesey's in-depth examination of one of the sites Sobolik uses leads to some interesting suggestions, one of them being that children's poor health is dependent on poor maternal health, indicated by possible prenatal effects, and reinforcing the suggestion that men had better access to protein than women. I would argue that the high rate of female deaths may mean that some men were buried elsewhere, unless a disproportionate number of the infants and children were male. She also suggests the presence of two populations at Grasshopper, one an immigrant Anasazi group and the other a Mogollon one. Her analysis of mortuary practices is quite revealing and bears on the construction of childhood. The greater variation in children's treatment (grave type or position of the body) along with the small quantity and lack of variability of grave goods compared with adults, suggests that children had a different status than their elders. If grave goods are derived from the group participating in the mortuary ritual, there is likely to have been a smaller group involved in a child's funeral than an adult one. Whittlesey suggests, based on a combination of place of burial and quantity of artifacts in graves, that there was a culturally marked difference between an infant and a child of more than one year. This finding is supported by data I collected from a series of eastern North American sites, whose analysis led me to the conclusion that infants were regarded as extensions of their parents whereas children above a year or so in age were seen as separate individuals, having their own, inevitably lower, status (Rothschild 1990). It would be informative if Whittlesey's analysis could be applied to the remaining categories of society. Her data suggest that rank at Grasshopper was not passed on through inheritance to children, although a conclusive statement would require the examination of the entire population.

Claudette Piper's chapter is an intriguing one, as it uses physical data (head deformation in children) as well as artifacts to infer social behavior. In this case the behavior inferred is maternal and is presumably related to subsistence practices; its consequences appear in infants. Hers is a diachronic study, beginning with Basketmaker populations and progressing to Pueblo ones, mostly from the southern Colorado Plateau. It involves intensive use of museum collections, ethnography, and skeletal data. She believes that increased head flattening after Basketmaker III (seen in skeletal material) derives from the practice of placing children in cradleboards in a supine position, convenient for leaving a child while the mother did horticultural tasks. This contrasts with the previous, prehorticultural and less sedentary lifestyle in which children were carried on their mothers' backs, placing less pressure on the back of the head and resulting in little deformation. Piper also notes reduced effort expended on Pueblo cradleboards, in comparison with Basketmaker ones, and suggests that child-care practices are a good marker of cultural differences.

Kathryn Kamp, Elizabeth Bagwell, and Patricia Crown are all concerned with social aspects of childhood, with particular reference to children's labor. Kamp's chapter is a broad consideration from many cultures of the possible range of activities that children may usefully participate in, applied to the Sinagua, whereas Bagwell and Crown focus on ceramic behavior and production. Kamp relies on ethnographic information, acknowledging that there is little archaeological support for her inferences (but see Kamp et al. 1999). Although there are no definite tasks that are specifically assigned exclusively to children, she finds ethnographic descriptions of a wide range of activities they participate in, from child and animal care to foraging, food preparation, and housework, to herding and farming. The underrecognition of children's contributions seems to derive from the modern perspective that children require labor rather than perform it and perhaps also from the fact that the activities they do perform are little valued. The tasks themselves often require extensive time but not intensive concentration and are clearly demarcated by gender once boys are considered old enough to leave their mothers.

A second chapter by Kamp with John Whittaker considers contemporary images depicting Pueblo children. The authors discuss the idealized and romanticized views projected by modern artists in portraying the lives of these children—for example, showing them as consistently healthy and cheerful. Kamp's ideas about the present-day view that children require labor rather than contribute labor are also reflected, as only limited activities and play are depicted in spite of the range of tasks ethnographically known to have been performed by subadults. Further distortions in the images studied pertain to family composition—families are typically drawn as the nuclear unit—and gender roles, with women often passive.

There is no doubt that children have been—and in many cultural settings are—productive members of society. The problem is finding evidence of their activities. If the society is one in which there are few meaningful distinctions in terms of age-graded labor responsibilities, then the contributions of children will increase gradually and be relatively unmarked. Perhaps an analysis of specific tool or task production, dividing it into components and considering what the requirements for performance of each one might be, could suggest work components that would be possible for children, the elderly, or disabled to participate in. This, in effect, is what both Bagwell and Crown undertake for ceramic production, with reinforcement from Kamp et al.'s study of fingerprint size (1999).

Bagwell addresses children's ability to form vessels, and Crown examines the painting of pots. Both approaches involve the inevitable (and probably mostly valid) assumption that skill increases with age, an assumption supported by developmental and learning studies of children. Bagwell is concerned with standardization, as she discusses the definition of skill levels by age, although these levels are also affected by cultural notions of appropriateness and the degree to which children of certain ages get to practice their skills. Her identification of criteria for assessing the competence of vessel form manufacture are quite useful, as is the idea that the ability to manufacture vessels of a recognizable type is a significant one. She applies these ideas to a group of pots from Pecos. The most important element of her study is the recognition of two different classes of small vessels, one crude group presumably made by children and one set made by competent potters. Another interesting point is the comment that few of the small crude pots had come from children's graves but were mostly from trash deposits. I have suggested elsewhere that goods found in children's graves would have been contributed by others and were unlikely to have been their own possessions (Rothschild 1990).

Crown's important study builds on her earlier work and that of W. R. DeBoer (1990) and others in deconstructing the means by which knowledge is transmitted as children learn to perform certain tasks. After suggesting several mechanisms, she focuses on the differences between observation/imitation and directed learning, in which a skilled person instructs an unskilled one. In a painstaking analysis of more than 700 museum-collected decorated pots, she identifies a group made or decorated wholly or in part by unskilled or incompetent individuals, most likely children. Combinations of skill visible in some efforts suggest that adults and children participated variably: sometimes one age group made a vessel that the other painted, and sometimes both adult and child decorated a vessel that one or the other had made. Her analysis suggests that teaching craft skills varied by cultural region, time period, and ware type. She finds that adults were more involved with the production of polychrome vessels than with black-on-white ones, and she further hypothesizes that after A.D. 1100, in the Reserve, New Mexico, area, black-on-white craft techniques were taught to children before polychrome ones.

The chapters by Kamp, Bagwell, and Crown all contain information pertaining to the cultural construction of age-related work efforts, but other kinds of status distinctions are more typically signaled and may be easier to recover from the past. Kelley Hays-Gilpin explicitly addresses the structuring of social categories of age—in her case, among young Hopi women. She suggests that the contemporary Pueblo identify an age class of physiologically adult, unmarried, eligible young women by a distinctive hairstyle, and she speculates that this period of "maidenhood," existing between childhood and adulthood, has persisted as a category for as long as 1,500 years. She uses rock art and pottery images as evidence that the hairstyle, involving spiral whorls of hair over each ear, was culturally significant over this time span. She relies on a combination of ethnographic information and archaeological data, and she plans to add oral-history interviews with Hopi elders in the future, showing them images in rock art and pottery of maidens, birthing mothers, and phallic flute players to gain insight into age and sex identities and how they may have changed over time. This is an imaginative study, bearing directly on cultural perceptions of various age-states. The hair whorls would have been a clear signal of eligibility, visible at some distance, and may have served several cultural purposes, regulating the movements of young women as well as those who interacted with them. The work resonates with Joyce's discussion of Aztec hairstyles and their significance in identifying life transitions and an "insistently stable gendered materiality that had the power to impose particular ways of being adult" (2000:479).

Cynthia Bradley's chapter focuses on linking ideology to child-rearing

practices as seen in skeletal remains and their location at Sand Canyon
Pueblo, a ritual center and habitation site. Sand Canyon burials show that
the population was relatively well nourished, with few of the indicators of
childhood stress seen at Grasshopper Pueblo, which Bradley uses for comparative purposes. Bradley believes Sand Canyon's ritual role and associated feasting led to its members' good health. The total burial sample
available for analysis consists of 29 individuals, with 9 burials recovered
from room fill and other, more usual contexts. Her most interesting material focuses on an age grade similar to that examined by Hays-Gilpin, a
group of adolescents, defined as between 12 and 20 years of age (a somewhat longer interval than that used in some definitions of adolescence), recovered from Sand Canyon Pueblo. Bradley suggests that both male and
female adolescents are likely to be involved in situations of physical conflict, often for idealistic reasons. Nine of the 20 individuals found un-
buried, in and around kivas, on roofs and courtyard floors, were in this
age class, and some show evidence of trauma around the time of death;
these individuals presumably died during an attack on the pueblo just
prior to abandonment.

It is interesting to compare Bradley's data with those reported by
Whittlesey, who finds the lowest death rate at between 10 and 15 years at
Grasshopper. This represents a more typical age-at-death profile, and the
factors affecting the Sand Canyon population, including a physical attack
on the pueblo, were not relevant at Grasshopper. The category of adolescent is a particularly interesting one in many societies, as it mediates the
transition from the status of child to that of adult. It is likely to be quite
different for males and females, in terms of both the activities and requirements that mark it and the actual biological age at which it occurs. Lynn
Meskell suggests that girls become sexual beings earlier than boys but that
the male transition is more marked (2000). Cross-cultural research
demonstrates that there is often a more dramatic transition for a male than
for a female, as he moves from childhood (where he is closely tied to his
mother's activities) to a specifically masculine definition and behavior.

CONCLUSION

This book raises important questions about the lives of children in the
past. Children's skeletons provide direct glimpses of their lives but offer
little of what may have been strong emotional reactions to their deaths. As
Meskell (1999) notes, these reactions pay little heed to the fact that children lack power; moreover, the idea that societies with high infant and

childhood mortality rates are universally indifferent to an individual death is contradicted by the great investment and care taken with burial. The activities that occupied children on a daily basis are difficult to discern archaeologically. Some progress is being made in this endeavor, however, especially in ceramic and lithic production. Such areas, in which skill is difficult to attain and requires practice, are more likely to yield to archaeological investigation than other areas, although it is mostly not yet possible to separate children's products from objects made by unskilled individuals of other ages. Social status is accessible through mortuary behavior, and some age-group distinctions may be discerned through an analysis of artifacts, images, and documents, with the understanding that material culture is actively used to construct identity. I hope that in the future greater attention is paid to the fascinating question of the age structure of past societies, which should be considered along with gender, class, rank, and the other categories that divide and define human groups. The transition to adulthood, which may or may not be marked and associated with a defined stage of adolescence, may be particularly productive as a way to understand how childhood was constructed in a given society. In any case, it is long past time to pay attention to children, to see what we already know about them and what we can learn. The subject is important not only because it provides data about children themselves but also because it offers significant information about society as a whole.

ACKNOWLEDGMENTS

I would like to thank Kathy Kamp for the invitation to be involved in this project and for her constructive approach to the entire process, and I am grateful as well to the contributors for their willing cooperation. I also thank Lynn Meskell and Lesley Sharp for alerting me to recent interesting literature on children, and I appreciate the helpful suggestions of two anonymous reviewers. The ideas and interpretations are my own.

2

Prehistoric
Puebloan Children
in Archaeology and Art

KATHRYN A. KAMP AND

JOHN C. WHITTAKER

As Nan Rothschild so aptly points out in the introduction to this volume, archaeologists in general and Southwestern archaeologists in
particular have paid scant attention to children. Although since about
1990 an increasing literature on prehistoric Puebloan women has begun to
accumulate, children remain at best shadowy figures, either linked to abstract concepts such as birthrates or surfacing as a necessary component of
the analysis of mortuary remains. Nevertheless, it is clear that a complete
picture of the dynamics of any society must include an understanding of
the position of children. The importance of children has not been trans-
parent to archaeologists, but artists, novelists, and museum curators have
long realized that no depiction of any time period is complete with only
adult actors. Thus, because they have been obliged to include children in
their prehistoric scenarios, artists have by default become forerunners in
thinking about the children of the prehistoric past.

The goals of the archaeologist and the artist may not be identical. While
realizing that no archaeology is value-free (Shanks and Tilley 1987 and
others), most archaeologists claim some sort of accuracy as an ultimate
goal. Authors of popular works, especially fictional ones, and the artists
who illustrate them may wish to make broader statements about the na-

ture of the human condition. The sources for interpretation available to archaeologists and artists are very similar, however, although the degree to which they are consulted varies considerably. Thus, artists, like archaeologists, can use archaeological data to inform them about what the landscape, dwellings, and possessions looked like in a particular time and place and can supplement this base with the available information on subsistence systems, manufacturing sequences, and so forth. The second major source of information for both archaeologists and artists is ethnographic: descriptions of modern and historic Pueblo groups and general cross-cultural data. Finally, both artists and archaeologists are potentially prey to ethnocentric biases, which may influence their interpretations. Although one hopes that the anthropological training of the archaeologist would promote greater vigilance, this may not always be the case.

Artistic depictions of prehistoric life reflect both scholarship and the biases impinging on archaeologists, artists, and the public. Because artists must make interpretive decisions and tell a story whereas the scholarly tradition attempts to rein in imagination, some of what we really believe about prehistoric people (and ourselves), and the spheres of life we consider most important, may be less ambiguously displayed in art than when hedged with academic caution. How do artistic depictions of prehistoric southwestern children compare with current scholarship as reflected in this volume?

We examined a sample of more than 340 images from 68 sources (Table 2.1). Some illustrations were duplications of previous images or included only people too indistinct for detailed analysis, so we recorded information on 1,583 individual figures from 63 different sources (Table 2.2). Because adult fiction is not normally well illustrated, we did not include any examples of this genre. We emphasized adult and children's nonfiction sources primarily because of the difficulty of locating appropriate children's fiction and the reluctance of libraries to lend some of the examples we could find. In the case of fiction, we had a high standard for inclusion: although the work had to be fictional, we demanded that it explicitly portray ancient puebloan life. This criterion excluded both stories based on more modern pueblos and those recounting traditional Puebloan myths and other tales, unless they claimed to provide images of a real prehistoric past.

Because children's books tend to be more lavishly illustrated than adult books and children's fiction is by far the most well illustrated of any category, the underrepresentation of children's fiction in the number of sources was not true in terms of the total number of images analyzed (Table 2.2).

TABLE 2.1. SOURCES USED IN THE ANALYSIS.

Author	Publication Date	Sources Including Illustrations for Which a Numerical Analysis was Conducted	
		Category of Work	No. of Illustrations Recorded
Arnold	1992	CHILDREN'S NONFICTION	3
Ayer	1993	CHILDREN'S NONFICTION	1
Bairy	1951	CHILDREN'S NONFICTION	3
Baldwin	1963	CHILDREN'S NONFICTION	1
Beem	1999	CHILDREN'S NONFICTION	1
Bird	1993	CHILDREN'S FICTION	10
Brody	1990	ADULT NONFICTION	1
Buff and Buff	1956	CHILDREN'S FICTION	25
Canby	1982	ADULT NONFICTION	1
Cheek	1994	ADULT NONFICTION	1
Colton	1960	ADULT NONFICTION	1
Cordell	1984	ADULT NONFICTION	1
Cordell	1985	ADULT NONFICTION	6
Cordell	1994	ADULT NONFICTION	1
DiPeso	1958	ADULT NONFICTION	18
Elting and Folsom	1963	CHILDREN'S NONFICTION	8
Erdoes	1976	CHILDREN'S NONFICTION	1
Erdoes	1983	CHILDREN'S NONFICTION	1
Fisher	1997	CHILDREN'S NONFICTION	10
Folsom and Folsom	1994	ADULT NONFICTION	1
Frawley	1999	CHILDREN'S NONFICTION	1
Frazier	1986	ADULT NONFICTION	3
Freeman and Freeman	1986	CHILDREN'S NONFICTION	12
Fuller	1991	ADULT NONFICTION	2
Gates	1996	CHILDREN'S FICTION	9
Gladwin	1957	ADULT NONFICTION	1
Gustafson	1997	CHILDREN'S NONFICTION	5
Haas	1986	ADULT NONFICTION	1

TABLE 2.1. SOURCES USED IN THE ANALYSIS. (cont.)

	Sources Including Illustrations for Which a Numerical Analysis was Conducted		
Author	Publication Date	Category of Work	No. of Illustrations Recorded
Hubbard-Brown	1992	CHILDREN'S NONFICTION	6
James	1994	CHILDREN'S FICTION	11
Jennings	1968	ADULT NONFICTION	2
Jones and Cordell	1985	ADULT NONFICTION	1
Jones and Euler	1979	ADULT NONFICTION	1
Kamp	1998	ADULT NONFICTION	10
King	1951	ADULT NONFICTION	3
Lavender	1998	CHILDREN'S NONFICTION	4
Lister and Lister	1987	ADULT NONFICTION	1
Lyon	1993	CHILDREN'S NONFICTION	7
Mails	1983	ADULT NONFICTION	4
Marriott	1952	CHILDREN'S NONFICTION	7
Martell	1993	CHILDREN'S NONFICTION	1
Martin et al.	1947	ADULT NONFICTION	2
McDermott	1974	CHILDREN'S FICTION	27
Mike	1991	CHILDREN'S FICTION	21
National Park Service	1999	ADULT NONFICTION	1
Osborne	1964	ADULT NONFICTION	6
Petersen	1991	CHILDREN'S NONFICTION	2
Petersen	1999	CHILDREN'S NONFICTION	1
Pilles	1993	ADULT NONFICTION	2
Powell	1993	CHILDREN'S NONFICTION	2
Rasmussen	2001	CHILDREN'S NONFICTION	3
Redman	1993	ADULT NONFICTION	2
Rohn	1989	ADULT NONFICTION	4
Sattler	1993	CHILDREN'S NONFICTION	5
Schroeder and Hastings	1958	ADULT NONFICTION	1
Shuter	2000	CHILDREN'S NONFICTION	1

TABLE 2.1. SOURCES USED IN THE ANALYSIS. (cont.)

| | Sources Including Illustrations for Which a Numerical Analysis was Conducted | | |
Author	Publication Date	Category of Work	No. of Illustrations Recorded
Stillman	1993	CHILDREN'S FICTION	9
Trimble	1990	CHILDREN'S FICTION	10
Wenger	1991	ADULT NONFICTION	19
Wetterstrom	1986	ADULT NONFICTION	1
Wilkinson and Pollard	1994	CHILDREN'S NONFICTION	4
Young	1999	CHILDREN'S NONFICTION	6
Yue and Yue	1986	CHILDREN'S NONFICTION	30

Other Sources with Illustrations Consulted but Not Recorded

Ambler	1989
Burby	1994
Crum	1996
Lange	1998
Naranjo	1993

Table 2.2. Characteristics of Analyzed Images.

Type of Literature	No. of Sources	No. of Images	Images per Source	No. of Individuals Represented	No. of Individuals per Image
Adult nonfiction	29 (46%)	92 (27%)	3.2	454 (28.7%)	4.9
Children's nonfiction	26 (41%)	126 (37%)	4.8	805 (50.9)	6.4
Children's fiction	8 (13%)	122 (36%)	15.3	323 (20.4%)	2.6
All	63 (100%)	340 (100%)	5.4	1,582 (100%)	4.7

Children's fiction tends to focus on a few protagonists and have a much lower average number of individuals shown in each illustration. It is not uncommon to have pictures showing just one or two characters. Children's nonfiction, in contrast, tends to include more individual figures than adult nonfiction. Nonfiction sources often attempt to show "life" in general, working many individuals and activities into a single image. Consequently, about half the individual figures analyzed are from nonfiction written for children, and children's fiction accounts for only about 20 percent of the total (Table 2.2).

AN ARCHAEOLOGICAL RECONSTRUCTION OF CHILDHOOD

The chapters in this volume posit that prehistoric Puebloan children would have been very active, visible members of their communities. In the prehistoric pueblos children appear to have worked (Kamp), played (Bagwell; Kamp), learned (Bagwell; Crown; Kamp), and participated in ritual activities (Bradley; Hays-Gilpin). They were valued and cared for by adults (Bradley; Piper; Whittlesey) but may also have acted as caretakers for others (Kamp). Although many aspects of their lives may have been pleasant and fulfilling, they also fell prey to ill health (Sobolik; Whittlesey), died of disease and malnutrition at an alarming rate (Sobolik; Whittlesey), and sometimes even perished as the victims of violence (Bradley).

From birth to full adulthood, children would have progressed through a number of developmental stages. Some or all may have been marked by initiation ceremonies, changes in dress or clothing (Hays-Gilpin), or recognized alterations in responsibilities. There is archaeological evidence for some of the stages. Children are frequently buried in rooms, and their funerals may have been private occasions, in contrast to the more public ceremonies provided adults (Whittlesey). Mortuary treatments indicate two transitions in the early years, one at birth and the second at about a year, perhaps corresponding with naming (Whittlesey). As children became older, their treatment after death suggests that they became more and more public entities. Finally, at the other end of childhood, as in more recent times, a girl's transition to puberty may have been marked by a change in hairstyle, which was altered again at a subsequent life-stage ceremony, marriage (Hays-Gilpin).

Very young children may have been active workers in a variety of tasks, including caring for children, collecting water and firewood, and helping in the fields, while older ones also made crafts, ground corn, hunted, and cooked (Kamp). Learning skills such as the ceramic craft discussed in detail by Elizabeth Bagwell and Patricia Crown was also an important part of the childhood experience, although leisure and play must have had their place in a child's world as well. The three may sometimes be difficult to separate. The production of figurines or miniature pots provides learning opportunities but may also be play, and some early attempts at potting may become part of the household ceramic assemblage, used and valued for their function (Bagwell; Crown; Kamp).

Health and nutrition for Puebloan children was generally poor (Sobolik). Although levels of nutritional and infectious disease were lower in some sites (Bradley; Sobolik; Whittlesey), there was a very high childhood mortality rate (Sobolik; Whittlesey). Women also suffered poor maternal health, as indicated by a high mortality rate, presumably due to the rigors of childbirth and difficulties sustaining pregnancy and lactation when nutrition was poor (Whittlesey). The hoods on cradleboards document adults' attempts to protect children from the flies, dust, and sun that must have posed an endemic problem at many villages (Piper).

It is important to note that the chapters by Cynthia Bradley, Patricia Crown, Kristin Sobolik, and Stephanie Whittlesey all provide evidence that child-raising practices were not static over time or uniform through space. Thus, there was not one prehistoric Puebloan childhood but many. This conclusion should not be unexpected, since the roles of both children and adults would have been reliant on the total sociocultural system. Piper sees changing subsistence systems as a primary causal factor, but it is also possible that changes in child-raising techniques themselves led to alterations in other aspects of the social system.

COMPARING THE ARTISTS' VIEW

Although publications directed primarily at a professional archaeological audience, such as site reports, occasionally include a reconstruction that incorporates people (Wetterstrom 1986), most of the professional archaeological literature restricts illustrations to maps, diagrams, and actual archaeological sites and artifacts.[1] This pattern, which may reflect a desire to avoid unnecessary speculation, is also somewhat characteristic of nonfiction written for adults, in which photographs of archaeological sites tend to replace the line drawings found in site reports. Even some illustrators of children's books prefer to restrict themselves to drawings and photographs of artifacts and sites. Photographs of modern or historic Pueblo scenes may augment the depictions of archaeological remains. Unfortunately, sometimes these illustrations are not labeled historic, and thus the undiscerning reader may well assume that the pictures are simply depictions of the past, or for that matter are images from the present, since the theme of tradition and continuity is strong in many of these works. The best examples make the distinction clear. For example, *Native Americans of the Southwest: A Journey of Discovery*, by Tito Naranjo (1993), includes one chapter (pp. 27–40) that is a fictional tale situated in Puye Pueblo ca. A.D. 1350. The illustrations (not recorded for analysis), which portray women grinding and collecting water and men weaving, hoeing, and participating in a ceremonial race, are photos of the historic past and are clearly labeled as such.

One common method for obtaining an image is to photograph a museum diorama. Dioramas from Mesa Verde (Ambler 1989:3; Arnold 1992:26, 27, 47, 49; Baldwin 1963:88, 134; Beem 1999:12; Crum 1996:14, 47; Hubbard-Brown 1992:cover; Lavender 1998:45), Zion National Park (Folsom and Folsom 1994), the University of Colorado Museum (Lange 1998:26), and Chaco Canyon (Elting and Folsom 1963:cover; Petersen 1999:17) have all been used, some photographed multiple times in the same publication, focusing on different portions of the diorama. As can be seen from the impressive list of publications using them, the dioramas from Mesa Verde are particularly influential. Sometimes close-up photographs are taken, but other times the reproduction of a diorama or mural is so small that the individual figures are almost indiscernible. Under these circumstances, we noted the use of the diorama but did not record the illustration in the data set. A similar situation occurs with an overview of Pueblo Bonito (Cordell 1994:108–109; Canby 1982:556–557; Gates 1996:42–43; Jennings 1968:271; Wilkinson and Pollard 1994:70–71). This appears in various renditions, but commonly the plaza and surround is peopled with tiny, indistinct figures that appear to be standing or walking adult humans but are not further identifiable. They are icons indicating to the viewer that we are looking at a past when people lived in the pueblo, but the people themselves are not really the focus of any attention or interpretation.

The Underrepresentation of Children

Children are visible in images of prehistory, although babies are less so. Using a fairly tough criterion, that an image must clearly either be a child or be identified as such in the caption, we found that about 15 percent of the figures depicted in nonfiction works for either adults or children are children (Table 2.3). Babies are only infrequently pictured in all types of literature. Children's fiction has a significantly higher representation of older children than any nonfiction (chi square of 51.9 with 4 degrees of freedom; $p \leq .0001$), presumably because they are often main characters. The effect is even more dramatic if one examines the age of central figures in an illustration (Table 2.4). The differences between children's fiction and all nonfiction are stark: images in fiction systematically focus on the child, but depictions in nonfiction, even in children's nonfiction, tend to ignore children.

Compared with the actual numbers of children that must have been present in the prehistoric pueblos, subadults are seriously underrepresented in illustrations. Although mortuary data are by no means a direct reflection of population parameters, the high percentage of subadults in burials (as high as 65 percent at Grasshopper, according to Whittlesey) is striking. In general, prehistoric horticulturalists, like their modern analogs, should be expected to have low survivorship into old age and high birthrates balancing high infant mortality (Swedlund and Armelagos 1976; Weiss 1973). The result is a population with a high proportion of children. Reported examples include three Yanomamo villages (Chagnon 1974:159) where 34 to 41 percent of the population is 10 years old or younger, and the Tsembaga of New Guinea, with 26 percent under 10 (Rappaport 1968:16). Prehistoric burial populations in the Southwest pretty unanimously indicate a high proportion of children and high child mortality (Bennett 1975; Kamp and Whittaker 1999; Martin et al. 1991; Palkovich 1980). The demographic structure of historic and modern pueblos cannot be assumed to resemble that of prehistoric ones but is also gen-

TABLE 2.3. NONRANDOM REPRESENTATION OF CHILDREN.

	Adult	Child	Baby	ALL
Adult nonfiction	374 (82%)	66 (15%)	14 (3%)	454 (100%)
Children's nonfiction	660 (82%)	130 (16%)	15 (2%)	805 (100%)
Children's fiction	210 (65%)	106 (33%)	7 (2%)	323 (100%)
TOTAL	1244 (79%)	302 (19%)	36 (2%)	1,582 (100%)

Table 2.4. Nonrandom Representation of Children as a Central Focus.

	Adult	Child or Baby	Both Adult and Child	ALL
Adult nonfiction	80 (87%)	7 (8%)	4 (4%)	92 (99%)
Children's nonfiction	111 (88%)	10 (8%)	5 (4%)	126 (100%)
Children's fiction	57 (47%)	51 (42%)	14 (11%)	122 (100%)
TOTAL	248 (73%)	68 (20%)	23 (7%)	340 (100%)

erally youthful. The Acoma population maintained a stable 37 to 39 percent under 14 between 1967 and 1974 (Garcia-Mason 1979:465), Moenkopi varied from 27 to 36 percent 0–10-year-olds between 1937 and 1962 (Nagata 1970:227), and Bacavi in 1910 was approximately 33 percent 0–10-year-olds, although the proportion of children decreased in later years (Whiteley 1988:132). Thus, at any given time in most prehistoric pueblos, there would have been a lot of children—a much larger percentage than in the imaginative reconstructions of Pueblo life found in nonfiction works.

Interestingly, the relative paucity of women parallels that of children, perhaps demonstrating their symbolic linkage and relative lack of power. In both adult and children's nonfiction, males comprise a higher percentage of the figures than females, although for children's nonfiction the effect is not particularly dramatic (Table 2.5). A study of representations of Cro-Magnon people (Gifford-Gonzalez 1993) discovered a similar underrepresentation of both women and children.

There are also a fairly large number of figures for which no gender could be determined. Some of this indeterminacy is due to large numbers of very small figures in some illustrations (although the effect was reduced since I did not re-record small diorama images multiple times). Some of the effect may be purposeful, however. Some illustrators made no systematic distinctions in either hairstyle or clothing between males and females, making it impossible to distinguish between the two except on the basis of chest anatomy when visible. Illustrators sometimes seem to avoid making a decision about gender roles by intentionally fashioning ambiguous figures—perhaps, at least in recent years, to avoid the accusation of gender stereotyping.

Birth and Infancy

Despite the presence of babies, not a single woman giving birth or even obviously pregnant is pictured. Whether that is due to some outmoded

TABLE 2.5. RELATIONSHIP BETWEEN AGE AND TYPE OF ACTIVITY.

Type of Activity	No. of Children	No. of Adults	Total
Carrying object	15 (11%)	123 (89%)	138 (100%)
Talking	15 (11%)	117 (89%)	132 (100%)
Ceremonial	26 (20%)	104 (80%)	130 (100%)
Building	*3 (2%)*	127 (98%)	130 (100%)
Watching	32 (26%)	93 (74%)	125 (100%)
Locomotion	**31 (32%)**	65 (68%)	96 (100%)
Preparing food	*8 (9%)*	77 (91%)	85 (100%)
Manufacturing	16 (20%)	66 (80%)	82 (100%)
Agricultural work	*6 (8%)*	69 (92%)	75 (100%)
Hunting	15 (20%)	60 (80%)	75 (100%)
Playing	**51 (100%)**	0 (0%)	51 (100%)
Fighting	*0 (0%)*	42 (100%)	42 (100%)
Child Care	4 (14%)	25 (86%)	29 (100%)
Household chores	6 (27%)	16 (73%)	22 (100%)
Listening	**13 (81%)**	3 (19%)	16 (100%)
Miscellaneous	28 (27%)	74 (73%)	102 (100%)
Indeterminate	35 (16%)	183 (84%)	218 (100%)
ALL	304 (20%)	1,244 (80%)	1,548 (100%)

Note: Activities in which children are dramatically overrepresented are in bold.

Activities in which they are dramatically underrepresented are in italics.

notion of propriety or is just an oversight is not clear. Certainly, in the treatment of babies and young children, we found an almost Victorian sensibility. Babies are shown being held, propped in cradle boards, and even crawling on their own, but never breastfeeding. Very young children are sometimes naked, but with the exception of two recent illustrations (Wenger 1991:41, 70) in which a tiny boy's penis clearly dangles, genitals are never clearly portrayed; instead, they are covered, obscured, or averted.

Babies are held in the arms in a variety of positions (48 percent), placed in cloth slings on the back (9 percent), suspended in a cradle (4 percent), and held in cradleboards (39 percent), where Claudette Piper predicts that infants spent a significant portion of their time. There is little consensus about how the cradleboards should look or be placed. Although Piper argues that during Puebloan times cradleboards were often laid flat, only a single illustration with a woman holding a board on her lap shows this stance. More commonly, cradleboards are propped upright or carried on the back exactly in the manner that Piper argues would not be possible with many of the Pueblo-period archaeological examples.

Piper notes that the cranial shaping that occurred because of cradleboard use may have been somewhat intentional. This notion is echoed by Stephen Trimble (1990:23), who comments, "Blue Feather, like all the babies of the village, spent much of his first year bound in a cradleboard. He was wrapped in fine cotton and rabbit fur blankets woven by his father in the kiva, with soft juniper bark under him. He was taken out only for washing and to change the absorbent bark—his 'diapers.' . . . During this time the cradleboard permanently flattened his head, so he would look like all the other villagers." Similarly, Hah-nee of the cliff dwellers is identified by others in the village as an outsider and taunted by his contemporaries because his head is the wrong shape (Buff and Buff 1956). We found it amusing that news sources in 2000 (e.g., Tanner 2000) profiled a new medical syndrome worrying American parents: plagiocephaly. It seems that flattening of the back of the skull has increased dramatically since campaigns against Sudden Infant Death Syndrome taught parents to keep babies sleeping on their backs. Cosmetically concerned and rich Americans can now have their infants fitted with an expensive plastic helmet for several months to prevent this "deformity."

Parenting is overwhelmingly viewed as the task of females, and this is nowhere more true than with babies. The illustrations showed 91 examples of distinct adult-child or child-child interactions that could be interpreted as parenting. These included carrying children, walking with them while holding their hands, working with them or being assisted by them in work, talking to them either individually or as a group, and, in the case of very small children, merely having them crawl or toddle nearby. Sixty (66 percent) of the depictions portrayed females as the primary parental figure, 21 (23 percent) showed males, and the remaining illustrations showed either both or figures of indeterminate gender. In four instances, as suggested by Kamp, female children were shown taking care of babies, generally carrying them on their backs, but no male of any age is shown caring for a baby.

Maturation, Marriage, and Ritual Initiation

The artistic depictions of stages of maturation are amorphous enough that it is difficult to separate one's own cultural expectations from an interpretation of the images. Obviously, this is a confounding factor in all analysis, but it is particularly insidious for discerning age variation. Since age categories are cultural constructs, the definition of stages for ancestral Puebloan groups would probably have been different from the current Western categories or even from more recent Pueblo categories. With these caveats in mind, it seems possible to differentiate infancy, toddlerhood, childhood, and adulthood in many artistic depictions of the prehistoric Pueblos. A teenager or youth category is generally much harder to identify.

From an infancy in which crawling (Figure 2.1), being held, or lying in a cradle or cradleboard appear from the illustrations to be the only options, children progress to being able to walk on their own. Babies are never shown being fed, changed, or bathed. Nor are they depicted in active interaction with adults or older children. One illustration does show an older woman identified in the text as a grandmother conducting a naming ceremony for a new baby, but it was not recorded, because although the text referred to Anasazi, the context was clearly historic with a donkey or mule visible in the street beyond.

"Toddlers" are depicted as very short and quite chubby, a modern Western stereotype. They are generally shown naked, walking in a limited area such as a room or holding an adult's hand. With the exception of close-up head portraits (Trimble 1990:23) and illustrations designed to depict artifacts rather than activities or situations (e.g., Brody 1990:77, illustration of a baby in a cradleboard), babies and toddlers are almost never pictured alone; there is always an older child or adult in the vicinity who appears to be in a caretaking role. An interesting possible exception is Amy Henderson's illustration of a naked child crawling around the corner

Figure 2.1. Two children, one a baby, play near a woman grinding corn. Illustration by Amy Henderson from *Life in the Pueblo* by Kathryn Kamp (1998).

of an exterior pueblo wall (Kamp 1998:frontispiece). The age of this child is a bit ambiguous, however, as it is less plump and slightly larger in scale in comparison with the nearby wall than might be expected for a baby, despite its dress and mode of locomotion.

Slightly older children, who comprise the majority of the figures and the main focus of this analysis, are much more autonomous, found in a wide range of situations and engaging in a variety of activities. Some artists differentiate girls from boys by replicating the clothing styles of adults, but others do not clearly distinguish between genders on the basis of apparel, making the sex of children who are too young to display secondary sexual characteristics impossible to discern. When girls and boys are easily differentiated, girls tend to follow the activity patterns of adult females in the same illustration, and boys follow those of males. There seems to be a mixed message here. On the one hand, children are viewed as asexual beings, and thus boys and girls are much more interchangeable than men and women. On the other hand, especially in some children's books, childhood is viewed as training for adulthood, and a clear subtext is that even in the past, children learned appropriate gender roles by imitating, helping, and learning from same-sex adults.

In general, adolescents are very hard to identify. For males, height is the only clue to youth, but given problems of perspective, it is often impossible to specify the exact height of a figure in the distance. Some artists (see Erdoes 1983:12; Freeman and Freeman 1986:36; Gates 1996:51; King 1951; Martin et al. 1947:133; McDermott 1974; Trimble 1990; Yue and Yue 1986:97) also use hairstyle to indicate age and marital status, following the historic Hopi analogy described by Kelley Hays-Gilpin (this volume) in which puberty is signaled by the adoption of a "butterfly" whorl hairstyle. At marriage the hairstyle is again changed. Though most works use this convention to signal an age/status category and even discuss the Pueblo custom, some seem simply to use whorls as a standard female hairstyle. Thus, Gerald McDermott (1974) shows a woman clearly identified as the hero's mother with her hair in whorls. The text associated with one drawing of a woman's head with hair whorls is decidedly odd. It reads, "The women didn't need to use their hair to make pottery, like they did when they made baskets. They let their hair grow long" (Freeman and Freeman 1986:36).

The Family Unit

Family groupings often imply a nuclear family pattern. In fiction the child's world usually revolves around family. The nuclear family is of paramount importance, but grandparents and often aunts and uncles may extend it. In nonfiction the nuclear family is normally a less overt institution, although the text may mention parents and family. The illustrations themselves sometimes identify an intended family. Thus, a *National Geographic* painting by Peter Bianchi (Osborne 1974:172) shows a close-up of a woman tending a baby while she applies slip to a bowl. A young girl explicitly identified as her daughter helps her by mixing the slip. In the background her son brings wood for a woman identified as "grandmother," who is firing ceramics. Most illustrations do not include such explicit labeling, but the numerous clusters consisting of a male, a female, and either one child (Baity 1951:98; Folsom and Folsom 1994:71; Gates 1996:28; Jennings 1968:275; Wenger 1991:41, 70) or several children (Cordell 1985:35; Martell 1993:26) make it easy for viewers to envision a nuclear family.

Clusters that imply a mother and a child or children are even more common. An illustration in *The Pueblo* (Yue and Yue 1986:52–53) shows a cutout view of a three-story pueblo. Multiple activities are taking place in the rooms and on the rooftops. It seems symbolic rather than coincidental that in the absolute center of the drawing in an otherwise bare room a woman is holding a baby with two playing children, one a girl and the other a boy, at her feet. In the same book another illustration shows a mother teaching a girl (her daughter?) to make a pot while a young boy (brother?) looks on and a baby sleeps peacefully in a suspended cradle.

Within the family and village men seem to take on the traditional role of breadwinner—in this case bringing home the rabbit or deer and working in the cornfield. Women tend children and prepare food. For those shown engaging in child care, the incidence of touching, being helped by, or simply appearing to look after a child in the vicinity (Figure 2.1) was not statistically different for males and females. Parental interactions are somewhat different for males and females, however, in addition to the lack of male interaction with infants mentioned previously. Females are more likely to carry babies but not older children. Men take leadership roles, even when children are involved. Thus, males are more likely to be visibly talking to children (chi square = 20.973 with 2 degrees of freedom; $p \leq .0001$). In the illustrations only men are given the role of speaking to large groups of assembled children, telling them stories and instructing them in cultural lore. This is in spite of the popularity of the ceramic female "storyteller" figures that have achieved near-icon status in southwestern popular culture (Babcock 1986).

Work, Play, and Learning

Table 2.5 shows the relative percentages of adults and children (not including babies) performing a variety of types of activities. Although the range of activities pictured for adults and children is similar, only children are shown clearly playing and only adult males fight. In addition to playing, children are much more likely than adults to be depicted listening or simply moving through space and slightly more likely to be watching or doing household chores. Locomotion is an odd category, since it may simply represent the artist's desire to have a figure in the picture but without the definition to provide a distinct activity. Thus, the person walks, runs (rarely), or climbs a ladder. To some extent, listening and watching may be similarly amorphous. Nevertheless, the large number of children coded as listening is due to small groups of children shown listening to stories, and listening and watching may also both be viewed as components of learning. Crown notes that cross-culturally observation is a common mode of learning for children, and some children are clearly watching the activities of others with rapt attention (Figure 2.2). The household chore category is a bit of a catchall, including such activities as sweeping, making a fire, chopping wood, feeding turkeys, and throwing away trash.

Learning and play, often considered the hallmarks of childhood, are definitely portrayed, but the depiction of work is less clear. Both Bagwell and Kamp suggest that play and learning may have sometimes been combined so that children learned in part by producing toys. Kamp further argues that children performed significant amounts of labor, including the production of ceramics, and that their work formed an important part of the economic strategy. Thus, work, play, and learning are all perceived as components of a childhood existence, but the emphasis may vary and the three may be hard to separate. One book of nonfiction for children (Elting and Folsom 1963:19) echoes the same type of ambiguity, as the authors claim a basic similarity between the types of activities that children engaged in at Pueblo Bonito and those of today's children: "They did what boys and girls still do. They helped their parents. They played games. They learned the skills they would have to know when they grew up." Elting and Folsom explicitly note that a boy shown with a bow and a girl with a miniature pot are not merely playing but learning the skills they will need as adults.

Work, play, and learning are often confounded in illustrations as well. The oft-reproduced Mesa Verde diorama provides several examples. A very young child, toddler age perhaps, hands his mother an ear of corn. Is

Figure 2.2. A young boy watches an older one and a man flintknap, perhaps a father and his two sons. The flintknapping of the older child can be seen as either work or a learning activity, but the younger is clearly gazing in rapt attention. Illustration by Amy Henderson from *Life in the Pueblo* by Kathryn Kamp (1998).

this child helping her process corn or is the woman engaged in child care and simply taking time to divert a youngster, or both? Or, alternatively, should the woman be viewed as teaching the child the appropriate way to process corn? Another toddler holds a bow and arrow. The bow is over twice his height, so actually shooting it would be impossible. Nevertheless, the caption beneath the photograph of the diorama portion reads, "The men and boys were the hunters of the community" (Arnold 1992:47). Analogously, an infant sits at a mano and metate holding the mano as if to grind. Functional grinding seems unlikely, given the extremely small size of the child, yet clearly a relationship to work activity is intended.

In some cases the intent presumably is to demonstrate that children were doing useful activities. *Chana, an Anasazi Girl* (Mike 1991) is a set of paper dolls with an accompanying fictional story that consciously attempts to educate about Anasazi lifeways. Children are pictured as active workers. Chana gathers wild plants for her mother to cook and firewood to keep the family warm. She makes a pot to give a much older brother, who plans to marry soon. It is referred to as a learner's attempt but also as an appropriate gift. Chana's younger sister makes a corncake and cares for their baby sister. Their youngest brother plays but also chases the turkeys away from the stored corn. Another brother hunts and helps fix the check dam.

In many of the activities normally perceived as work, children are underrepresented. Thus, far fewer than expected children are involved in building, preparing food, or agricultural work (Table 2.5). The actual roles undertaken in these arenas are illuminating. In construction activities, adults carry on a range of activities. Males are frequently shown transporting logs and repairing roofs; women, in contrast, spend their time mainly plastering floors and walls, but adults also engage in other activities such as chinking, digging, cutting trees, carrying stones, preparing mortar, and passing building materials. Children generally carry stones or help mix mortar, but the limited scope of their activities is no surprise, given the low number of children participating in construction. In the agricultural realm (Figure 2.3), while most adults hoe, three of the six children engaged in

Figure 2.3. Children chase birds from fields of corn. Note the dog in the background. Dogs are illustrated with children at a higher rate than would be expected. Illustration by Robert Greisen from *Exploring Bandelier National Monument* by Sarah Gustafson. Copyright 1997 by Sarah Gustafson.

agricultural work chase birds (an activity suggested by Kamp, this volume, on the basis of ethnographic materials).

Children engage in manufacturing activities at about the expected rate (Table 2.5). According to the chapters in this volume, children may learn ceramics at a fairly young age, painting (Crown) and forming small vessels (Bagwell; Kamp), possibly aided in their efforts by adults. Making ceramics is by far the most illustrated craft activity. Of the 82 individuals engaging in craft production, 35 (43 percent) are making pots and an additional 4 form figurines or miniatures. Six of the potters and all the miniature and figurine makers are children. Almost always women and girls are the ceramicists, although sometimes gender is not attributable. Trimble (1990:15) explains the picture of a woman and a younger woman with her hair in whorls: "Her daughter followed her movements. Only after Dragonfly had done each step once on her own did the mother correct her." Similarly, Charlotte Yue and David Yue (1986:72) have a "daughter" plainly watching and imitating a woman coiling a pot. Lisa Ferguson (Rohn 1989:14) shows a child helping a woman by making a small pot. Though the clothing leaves the gender of the child somewhat ambiguous, so we recorded it as indeterminate, the fine features of the depiction are certainly conventional for the way a girl, rather than a boy, would be indicated.

Presumably, children were also learning a variety of other skills, some less amenable to archaeological investigation and others simply not yet the subject of research. Although ceramic manufacture is by far the most frequently portrayed example of craft production, weaving (8 individuals), making baskets (6), spinning (3), hide working (3), sewing and embroidery (3), and stone tool production (3) are all pictured more than twice. Most of these are solely adult activities, however. Although two children are shown making baskets and one flint knapping (Figure 2.2), children are not shown doing any of the other manufacturing activities.

Ritual Participation

C. A. Lutz and J. L. Collins (1993:90) calculate that almost 20 percent of *National Geographic*'s depictions of the developing world center on ritual. They suggest that this is part of a trend to exoticize rather than an unbiased representation. We find it hard to assess the appropriate proportional representation for religious activities, but it is interesting that the percentage of images classed as ceremonial was much lower for the illustrations of the prehistoric Puebloan world, ranging from 12 percent for children's fiction to only 6 percent for children's nonfiction. The numerical representation of children parallels their overall representation, but the exact nature of their participation is different from that of male adults and also varies between children's fiction and both adult and children's nonfiction. All the nonfiction shows children attending ceremonies rather than actively participating in them. The same is true for women. Except for one illustration of a marriage ceremony and a second of a ceremony associated with house construction (Yue and Yue 1986:30), both rituals in the realm of the domestic, females are shown only in passive roles. Fictional depictions, however, include both boys and girls as dancers. Interestingly, adult women remain observers. The more active participation of children in children's fiction may simply be a result of the tendency to make them the heroes of the tale, a phenomenon discussed in more detail below.

Ceremonial activities are primarily shown either in kivas or in plaza areas, although this is not invariable. For example, an illustration in Mails 1983:174 shows a male in clearly ceremonial garb, holding an abundantly feathered prayer stick. At his feet are two ceramic vessels, a palette, and possibly tubes of pigments and a pipe. He is standing with one foot raised, perhaps dancing. In the background are mesas, and the illustration is labeled, "Chaco Canyon and Fajada Butte," referring to a particular site in Chaco Canyon that has been recently popularized as a ritual solar marker (e.g., Frazier 1986). Plazas are generally the site for dances, but some depictions make determination of an exact locale problematic. The single wedding recorded was in an unidentifiable room, perhaps emphasizing a domestic rather than ceremonial aspect.

Paralleling ethnographic accounts, kivas are depicted as the site for rituals involving smaller groups and are often interpreted as sacred spaces, but they are also the realm of a wide range of other activities, including weaving, spinning, knapping, trading, and simply talking. In all the illustrations they are the domain of adult males; only rarely are either women or children admitted. When they are (in this sample two children and one adult female), the intruders are placed in a rather liminal position on the ladder, either entering or exiting the room.

Idealizing the Past: Depicting Beauty, Health, and Conflict

Many of the illustrations idealize the past. Ancient Puebloans are pictured as beautiful and healthy. Just as they never give birth, they rarely seem to become ill or die. Obviously, this would make for an interesting demographic structure. Just as the people are beautiful and healthy, so are their surroundings. Dirt, insects, and disorder are remarkably absent. Rooms are generally tidy and strikingly bare, often almost devoid of objects.

People in the illustrations are generally attractive. Men have good musculature, often but not always exposed by scant clothing. Women are frequently bare-breasted. Most are young, neither fat nor thin, and have breasts that don't droop. The notion that Puebloan people are uniformly fairly attractive by current Western ideals is so standard that a painting by Peter Bianchi, in a *National Geographic* article lavishly illustrated by him, which shows rather coarsely featured individuals greeting a returning hunter, seems almost jarring (Osborne 1964:178–179). One of us commented that it almost seemed like the stereotypic depiction of Paleolithic cave dwellers.

Despite the fact that it is well attested that Puebloan health was fairly poor and infant mortality was high, this is not obvious in illustrations. Not a single death was shown in any of the pictures in the initial sample analyzed.[2] Later we did find one depiction of a burial (Powell and Gumerman 1987:107) in a nonfiction popular work written for an adult audience. The message about death is softened somewhat, however, since the deceased is shown as an elderly woman and identified in the caption as "the grandmother." Thus, the high death rate among the very young is still ignored.

Malnutrition was evident in a number of depictions, however, and is usually associated in the text with droughts and agricultural failure. Generally, it is adults and old people who, with thin limbs and torsos and visible ribs, show the effects of scarcity; children in the same work or even the same illustration may appear well fed. In a world populated by plump and healthy children, women, and men, Charles DiPeso (1958:143) shows a single very thin and toothless elderly male. In *Hah-Nee of the Cliff Dwellers* the protagonist, a young boy, interacts extensively with his grandfather, who is described as toothless and with a stiff back and "skinny fingers" (Buff and Buff 1956:8–9). The old man is pictured frequently, and two other emaciated elderly individuals are shown departing from the village with the aid of walking sticks, driven away because they were suspected of causing drought. Hah-nee himself is shown as plump and healthy, as are other younger adults in the story. Even as people are depicted abandoning their pueblo in the face of subsistence difficulties, they may appear well fed (Lyon 1993).

Illustrations drawn by Betsy James for a book chapter by Linda Cordell (1985) provide an interesting counter to the general trends. One picture (Figure 2.4), labeled simply "Malnutrition," shows an emaciated child in the foreground eating an ear of corn. His ribs show, his limbs are thin, and his face is gaunt, but his belly is distended. In the background a woman grinds. Her arms also seem prominent, suggesting that she too is suffering the effects of a poor diet. In another picture an ill adult is shown being tended by two women, one elderly. The caption is simply "Epidemics." Similarly, an earlier article by D. King (1951:6) includes a Paul Coze illustration showing both children and adults of all ages with prominent ribs; the caption proclaims, "Drought forced abandonment of pueblos."

In addition to virtually ignoring malnutrition and disease, pictures of the Puebloan past generally idealize it by presenting a clean and orderly living environment. A similar phenomenon has been noted for living-history museums (Gable and Handler 1993; Jameson and Hunt 1999; West 1988). A striking example of this "sterilization" of the past occurs in a children's book on Mesa Verde. Under the bold heading "Health hazards," the text reads: "Although the Anasazi spent a lot of time outside, the air they breathed was not always good for them. Garbage was dumped in front of the village and left to rot. If someone died in the winter when the ground was too hard to dig a grave, the body might be buried in the garbage. Some bodies were also placed in empty rooms near the back of the pueblo, while other empty rooms were used as toilets" (Martell 1993:27).

Figure 2.4. In an illustration entitled "Malnutrition" an emaciated child eats an ear of corn while a woman grinds in the background. Drawing by Betsey James from "Why Did They Leave and Where Did They Go?" by Linda S. Cordell. Reprinted by permission from *Understanding the Anasazi of Mesa Verde and Hovenweep*, edited by David Grant Noble. Copyright 1985 by the School of American Research, Santa Fe.

The accompanying illustration shows no evidence of any of these horrors. Adults work and children play, but no garbage is visible and the swarms of flies that surely must have followed concentrations of human refuse and inspired the Puebloan people to put hoods on their cradleboards to protect their infants' faces (Piper) do not appear to pester the inhabitants.

The treatment of violence also contributes to the somewhat unrealistic and idealized picture of the Puebloan past. Though a number of texts both fictional and nonfictional acknowledge that violence existed, generally it is an external force, either Spanish or Athapascan. It is the rare illustration, such as Cordell's (1985:39) "Factionalism," that shows internal dissension. As Bradley (this volume) points out, children were certainly sometimes the victims of aggression and perhaps even combatants themselves under some circumstances, but this is never depicted. Children are not even shown being punished, although some ethnographic sources (Talayesva and Simmons 1942) recall rather harsh discipline.

Idealizing the Child

Just as Puebloan conditions are idealized and sanitized in most illustrations, children themselves and the very institution of childhood are idealized and even in some cases valorized. Whereas adult nonfiction sometimes simply ignores children, perhaps because they are seen as irrelevant to the important, adult aspects of life, most children's books include some emphasis on children and the roles they played in prehistory.

Often the intention seems to be to create empathy, demonstrating that these children, though from another culture and time, were no different from the children of today. Thus, both the text and the illustrations emphasize perceived parallels. This tendency may account for both the prevalence of play and the frequent presence of dogs (child's "best friend") in illustrations. An additional common message is a moral one. The children of prehistory are viewed as role models, helping parents by working, learning, and playing with siblings. They are not disobedient, they get along well with one another, and they do not cry. The proper behavior of children is natural and timeless.

Children's fiction tends to have children, rather than adults, as main characters. Sometimes the story merely acts as a vehicle for explaining the prehistoric pueblos, using named characters but having little in the way of a plot. Blythe Roveland (1992) has noted that in fictional depictions of the Paleolithic written for children, boys and girls are often shown as the creators of culture. For the prehistoric Pueblos, continuity, not change, is the emphasis, so culture creator is not a usual role for characters. Instead, stories frequently show the child as hero or heroine. Details vary, but drought and enemy attack are common villains. Heroes warn of attack, helping the village prepare to fend off the enemy (Buff and Buff 1956; Stillman 1993), or help the village in time of drought. For example, in *The Mud Family* (James 1994), when drought threatens a pueblo, the young heroine is told that she should play with her mud dolls because she is too young to help by dancing for rain. After she conducts her own private ceremony with her dolls, however, rain comes and the family is again happy. In a slightly different twist, Hah-nee is given a map by an old man he has befriended and leads his family away from both the famine and the dissension it has caused (Buff and Buff 1956).

THE UNEMOTIONAL PAST

Artistic reconstructions attempt to help audiences visualize the human dimensions of the past, adding depictions of people and activities to those of artifacts and structures. Being openly imaginative, they are released from some of the restraints that keep scholarly writing fact-based and distant. Nevertheless, most artistic depictions of the past lack the emotional content, the human, storytelling warmth, that one might expect. This is particularly true of "serious" nonfictional portrayals, in which perhaps the artistic spirit has been bled dry by the attempt to incorporate accurate archaeology.

Humans are not all alike, yet one of the things we can know with certainty about the past is that people then, as now, had strong feelings about their lives. What does it mean to you to bury your child, to know that the rains did not come and you will be hungry this winter, to face an enemy intent on your death, to believe that the darkness outside the pueblo is inhabited by inimical beings over which humans have no power? Did the ancients not express love for their spouses, cuddle their children, roar with laughter at a dirty joke, exult when the footrace was won or the rival discomfited? Very little of the vivid fire of life animates the attempts of artists to show the past, even when they depict events that must have stirred the heart. In a rare burial scene two mourners sit by the corpse of an elder, laid in her pit. Their faces are lined but bland, perhaps sad, perhaps just old, but the bereaved are not sobbing, or praying, or sunk in sorrow with their faces in their hands. The malnourished child gnawing an ear of corn (Figure 2.4) looks sickly but not particularly depressed. The occasional battle scene shows fighting at a distance but rarely faces contorted with rage and fear. Of course, many emotional events are avoided in the first place—as we have shown, death, disease, hunger, and violence are rare in reconstructive art.

In most depictions life goes placidly on, with calm, normal daily activities the focus. That is realistic as far as it goes: the great dramas of life are rare. Even in daily life, however, people laugh, play, quarrel, and weep, but in most of the depictions we saw, very little of these common emotions was visible. Several possible explanations come to mind. Most prosaically, lively and emotive faces are more difficult to portray, but many of the artists seem quite capable. It could be that the stoicism with which "Indians" are sometimes stereotyped affects some depictions, but in our experience, lack of emotion characterizes modern depictions of the past everywhere, from the Paleolithic to the medieval. Most likely, the artist is simply imitating the archaeologist in not imagining too deeply. We visualize artifacts, structures, and activities, and of course people were involved in all, but they remain strangely shadowy. We can see them, and draw them, but not feel them. We use depictions to indicate a living past, and to explain artifacts, structures, and activities, but only a few reach beneath the skin to make the viewer say, "That looks like fun" or "Gosh, how awful!"

CONCLUSIONS

It may be argued that the impact of the artist's reconstruction is as pervasive as the text that accompanies it or even more. Over the years numerous Americans, primarily of the middle class, have been educated about the so-called third and fourth worlds by the National Geographic magazine (Lutz and Collins 1993). The illustrations in adult and children's books, especially nonfiction works, and the museum dioramas from which many of them are taken, have fulfilled a similar role for prehistory, providing a visual window into the past, entertaining while informing, and claiming to provide a general description and explanation rather than capture a specific historic moment. Lutz and Collins (1993) argue that National Geographic's photographs exoticized, idealized, sexualized, and by removing cultures from a historic context, naturalized the developing world. Similar statements could be made for the presentation of the Puebloan past in general, and specifically for the children who inhabited it.

The illustrations from nonfiction tend to deemphasize children but also to romanticize them. Ethnographic materials from the modern and historic pueblos shaped the portrayal of children, but there is simultaneously a tendency to slip into a stereotypic Western model of the child, living in a small, happy, nuclear family consisting of parents with one boy, one girl, and perhaps an additional infant, spending considerable amounts of time playing but also helping parents and learning the skills of adulthood. Although children may well have spent a considerable portion of their time doing useful work, the pictures emphasize play more than work, and almost all the depictions of children working seem ambiguous. In other words, it is often unclear to what extent the children and adults consider the activity learning or play rather than work.

In modern Western culture, youth is viewed as synonymous with health and beauty. Accordingly, prehistoric children are pictured as healthy, despite the archaeological evidence that they were often ill, and plump, despite the archaeological evidence that they were often malnourished. The surroundings in which they live are picturesque and clean, lacking flies, dirt, and excrement. Death, like pregnancy, is omitted from images, and when violence occurs, only adult males, never children or even women, are the victims. We know there were children in the past but show fewer of them than there must have been. Both artists and archaeologists assign them a few tasks but assume that children played and learned while adults did the really important stuff, the activities that need explanation because they are obvious in the archaeological evidence.

Most parents will tell you that their children are the most important things in their lives, but our understanding of the past short-changes them because archaeologists have tended to ignore them in our research and because both we and the artists who use our findings rarely allow themselves an involved, emotional visualization that goes beyond furnishing a site with mannequins.

ACKNOWLEDGMENTS

We would like to thank Dani Long, a Grinnell graduate, anthropology student, and artist, who worked on an initial investigation of depictions of the Puebloan Southwest for a summer research project under Kathy's direction. Grinnell College provided funds to support her in this endeavor. Her work convinced us of the productivity of the project and made us aware of a number of sources for illustrations. We would also like to thank the staff of Grinnell's interlibrary loan department, who ordered innumerable books and journals for us. Over the years conversations with

Amy Henderson, an archaeologist and artist who illustrated Kathy's book *Life in the Pueblo*, alerted us to the complex issues involved in crafting an image when so many variables are not precisely known.

NOTES

1. Charles DiPeso's field reports are notable exceptions. For example, the Reeve Ruin report (DiPeso 1958) includes numerous drawings of people building houses, using and making artifacts, and so forth.

2. We are continuing to collect, record, and analyze images.

3

The Morphology of Prehispanic Cradleboards

Form Follows Function

CLAUDETTE PIPER

Archaeologists have noted the necessity for the care of infants (Bolen 1992; Surovell 2000; Zeller 1987) but have not spent much effort studying the specifics of child care. For the American Southwest, concrete archaeological evidence for child-care practices is preserved in the form of both cradling devices and the cranial deformations that sometimes occurred as a result of their use. My examination of cradleboards from the Colorado Plateau region demonstrates that as labor is reorganized with the adoption of agriculture as a major subsistence strategy, practices for the care of infants and young children change. This shift is reflected in the appearance of cranial deformation and in changes in the use and morphology of cradleboards.

A number of examples of Basketmaker Period cradleboards are preserved in dry contexts, but no unbroken line of cradling evidence exists for the American Southwest. I have been unable to locate any cradleboards discarded between about A.D. 750 and about A.D. 1100, probably because lifestyles during this time span did not encourage disposal of perishables in dry contexts. Because cradling devices used between Basketmaker II and Pueblo III times were not preserved, patterns of cranial deformation, not the remains of the cradleboards themselves, provide the major evidence for cradling techniques during this hiatus. At the transition from Basketmaker III times to Pueblo I times, as agriculture and a more sedentary lifestyle become characteristic of the area, flattened heads became so common that the Pecos Conference called cranial deformation a Pueblo I diagnostic (Kidder 1927).

In the past, archaeologists have assumed that harder cradleboards caused flattened crania (Reed 2000; Roberts 1931; Rohn 1971; Steward 1933; Stewart 1940; Watson 1961). My research, however, suggests that the method of use of the cradleboards, not their form, induced cranial deformation. When the cradleboard is used primarily in an upright position, the infant's head is more mobile and flattening is less likely to occur. Thus, as the archaeological evidence shows, the early Basketmakers used cradleboards, but the manner of their use did not induce cranial flattening. In contrast, later occupants of the plateau region habitually rested their cradleboards in a more level position, causing the infants' skulls to flatten in distinctive patterns.

That cranial deformation first appears in Pueblo I skeletal material suggests that changes in child-care practices were concurrent with those in settlement and subsistence patterns, the organization of labor, and other cultural practices. During the Basketmaker Period, child care was probably combined with work such as gathering that required considerable mobility. Cradleboard construction and the absence of cranial deformation show that children were habitually carried on the back. Since ethnographic evidence suggests that children were cradleboarded only until about six months to a year old (Beaglehole and Beaglehole 1935; Dennis 1940), presumably the infants would still have been nursing. In order to have left their babies in camp while doing tasks away from camp, the mothers could have been absent for no more than five or six hours, unless a surrogate mother nursed all children left in camp or a substitute food was available. Thus, it is likely that an emphasis on gathering would make it advantageous to devise a means of keeping children who were still nursing with their mothers, at the same time retaining a high degree of mobility for the mother.

Later, during Pueblo times, women may have been able to do more of their work in a restricted location fairly near camp. Cradleboards were not abandoned, however; their mode of usage was simply altered. Instead of being carried upright, babies were laid flat or propped against a rock or wall or tree while parents tended crops, ground corn, or did other tasks in the vicinity. Alternatively, perhaps the babies were left in the care of older children but in close enough proximity to the mother to allow her to nurse when necessary. As usage patterns evolved, so did the form of the cradles. Some of the features such as footrests that were useful for carrying a child upright were no longer necessary and were frequently omitted.

CRANIAL DEFORMATION IN THE AMERICAN SOUTHWEST

Two types of deformation, occipital and lambdoidal, often are geographically bounded. As defined by E. K. Reed (1949), occipital deformation flattens the back of the skull almost straight at close to 90 degrees from the Frankfort plane. Lambdoidally deformed crania are flattened on the upper part of the occiput at an angle of 50 to 60 degrees. Figure 3.1 illustrates the difference between these types of deformation in comparison with an undeformed cranium.

Early southwestern anthropologists (Hewett 1906; Kidder 1924; Morris 1925; Morss 1927; Pepper 1902; Roberts 1929) suggested that deformed crania belonged to a different "race" that had invaded the Southwest and defeated or displaced Basketmaker peoples. By comparing Hawikuh Zuni with southern Utah Basketmaker crania, T. D. Stewart (1940) and C. C. Seltzer (1944) dispelled that notion. Many archaeologists (Rohn 1971, 1977; Stewart 1936, 1940; von Bonin 1936) have commented on the two different styles of cranial deformation. At Grasshopper Pueblo E. S. Cassels (1972) found no correlation between class and type of cranial deformation. Using a limited data set, Reed (1949) attempted to correlate deformation style with inhumation practice; further inquiry might inform this research question. To date, however, I have not located publications on either the implications of the sudden appearance of cranial deformation or the significance of different child-care practices.

Although deliberate cranial deformation occurs in other parts of the world (Dorsey 1899; Gerszten 1993; Hoshower et al. 1995; Rogers 1975), in the Southwest both lambdoidal and occipital deformation have been

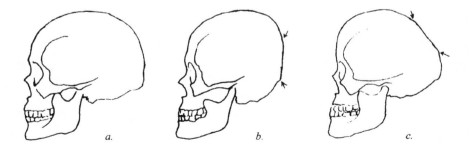

Figure 3.1. Types of crania in the Southwest: *a.* undeformed; *b.* occipitally deformed; *c.* lambdoidally deformed. Redrawn from Reed 1949, courtesy of *El Palacio*, Museum of New Mexico. Original drawing by Erik K. Reed.

interpreted as unintentional and largely accidental. In the "Anasazi" region a hooded cradleboard used with a wooden wedge or cedar bark pillow to prop up the head probably caused lambdoidal deformation. Ethnographic sources suggest that this wedge, which inadvertently caused the lambdoidal deformation, may have been used to prevent the child from growing with a short neck. Thus, I argue that the lambdoidal deformations may be the result of a deliberate aesthetic choice, although producing the deformation was unlikely to have been the focus of the practice.

CRADLEBOARDS: AN OVERVIEW

All over the world people use implements to spread the weight of an infant who cannot yet walk as far as one might want to travel. As a young mother around the house, I most often used a woven cotton sling, bright orange, slung on the opposite shoulder. This device left my right arm totally free, and I could wash dishes, cook, and talk on the phone. For longer jaunts, I, like many of my friends, used a Gerry pack in which the child sat upright, facing forward.

Probably the most common image of cradleboards in the northern Southwest is that of Navajo cradleboards made of wooden planks with attached hoods. The child is strapped in tightly, faces backward, and can be rested or transported in any number of ways, including on horseback. A traveling exhibit of Kiowa cradleboards (Hail 2000) includes photographs of cradleboards made with foot supports carried in the arms, propped against a building or tree, and carried on the back or on horseback. When the cradle is carried on the back or on a horse, the baby is positioned facing backward.

There were no horses in the Prehispanic Southwest. Agriculture in one form or another, supplemented with gathering and hunting, was the primary means of economic subsistence. Cradleboards during the earliest periods, when presumably foraging was more important, were designed to be carried on an adult back with the child facing backward. By Pueblo III times, most cradleboards could no longer be easily slung on the back and carried for any distance. It follows that people who farmed needed cradling devices that provided security for sedentary children but did not need to be carried as frequently.

CRADLEBOARDS ON THE COLORADO PLATEAU

Archaeologists often look at old questions with new data; here, like other researchers (Kehoe 1991; Spector 1993), I am trying to look at new questions with old data. My evidence consists of about 50 "cradleboards" and many other accessories used for infant care.[1] The cradleboards I describe are from dry sites such as sheltered caves or burned, collapsed, and buried structures in arid locations. Nearly all these data are from collections made before 1960, but I believe this is the first attempt to compare these artifacts across time and through space and place them in social context.

In cradleboards used between about 200 B.C. or older and A.D. 1200 certain themes recur, and to some extent the style or form of a cradleboard can be used to assign it to a specific temporal space. One difficulty in assigning affiliation is that most of the cradleboards excavated in the early part of the last century are not securely provenienced, nor have they been radiocarbon dated.

Historic Cradles

Before examining the artifactual evidence from prehistoric times, it is useful to look at historic cradleboards and compare them with those from the distant past.[2] W. Dennis and M. G. Dennis (1940) describe cradles from southwestern pueblos. Wicker was most commonly used in Hopi, although by 1940 many cradles were made of single boards because they were easier to construct. These cradles normally are used for only one child and then destroyed; occasionally, a second, larger cradle is made as the child grows. An infant is placed on the cradle the first day of life (Dennis and Dennis 1940:109; Thompson and Joseph 1944:51). Except for "changing the soiled clothes and for bathing," children are cradle-boarded at all times for the first three months of life, but the cradle is not used at all after six months to a year (Dennis 1940:32; Thompson and Joseph 1944).

Figure 3.2 (Mason 1889:192–193 and Figure 26) illustrates two wicker "Moki [Hopi] cradle-frames," recorded before 1887, and Figure 3.3 (Mason 1889:193 and Figure 27) shows a Zuni "cradle-board" made of a rough-hewn board, three feet by one foot, with a collapsible hood. Side loops hold crisscross lashing that secures the child to the board. No footrests are present on any of these examples, and O. T. Mason noted that children in cradles are always provided a soft pillow.

The use of a similar cradleboard from "Oraibi Pueblo," acquired from Geo. A. Dorsey after an expedition in 1897, is described in the records of the Chicago Field Museum: "Over the bottom of the cradle for three-fourths of its length is spread a cedar bark mat, and over this are several thicknesses of a blanket. No pillow is used and the head is usually lower than the body. The cradle is often held in the mother's arms but it generally

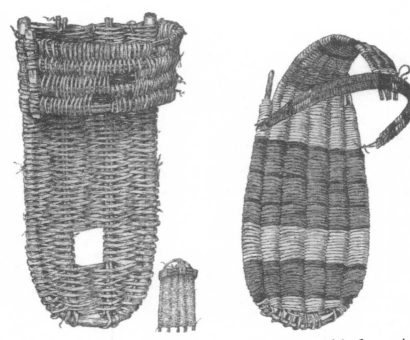

Figure 3.2. "Moki" cradleboards, wicker devices consisting of the floor and the awning (Mason 1889:192–193 and Figure 26). O. T. Mason suggested that the hole on the left cradle was used "for cleansing purposes," but any parent would find that explanation improbable. More likely, lashing went around the infant and through the back, allowing the carrier to be securely strapped to a tree.

lies on the floor by her side as she works or in some secluded corner. The specimen has seen much service and has been repaired." Dorsey (1899:743) added that the cradleboard is "not often strapped to the back." Dennis and Dennis (1940:109) confirmed that observation: "The cradle is never carried on a person's back and is never placed vertically." "Swinging the cradle from the rafters is not a Hopi custom," but "the Tewa at Hano formerly used swinging cradles and occasionally do so today." In pueblos on the Rio Grande, cradles are suspended in a horizontal position, but not in Zuni. A Zuni cradle is made of a single board with a collapsible hood; beneath the infant's neck a piece of turquoise is buried in the wood. At Acoma, Laguna, and Isleta, lightning-struck wood is the preferred material for cradleboard construction (Dennis and Dennis 1940:110–112).

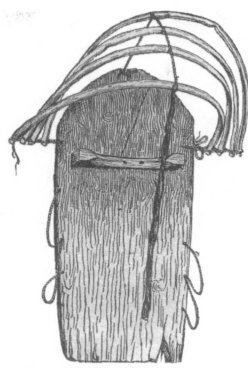

Figure 3.3. Historic Zuni cradleboard (Mason 1889:193 and Figure 27). A permanent neckrest is attached to this cradleboard. Uniquely, Zuni cradleboards are made with collapsible hoods. Side lashings would have secured infant and bedding.

Basketmaker (Anasazi) and Prepottery (Mogollon) Cradles

Rigid Cradles. Basketmaker cradles, as described by the earliest southwestern archaeologists, fall into two general categories, "rigid" and "flexible" (Kidder and Guernsey 1919), although I believe only the "rigid" type was used to carry an infant upright. These cradleboards were as strong and serviceable as a modern Kelty child backpack, the makers caring about appearance as well as functionality. Generally, they include features such as footrests and appear to have been designed to allow the infant to be placed or carried in an upright posture.

The cradleboard in Figure 3.4 is an example of the most common rigid type. Similar cradleboards have been excavated from the Middle Chinle, Arizona (Morss 1927:36 and Plate V), from White Dog Cave in northeastern Arizona (Smithsonian Institution catalog no. 349189), and from Betatakin

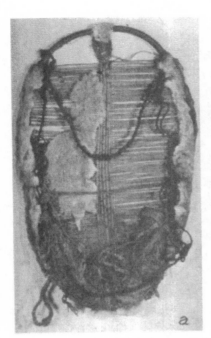 

Figure 3.4. "The handsomest cradle" from White Dog Cave, Arizona, Cist 35. The strap toward the top would allow the cradle to be carried or hung. The wad of cedar at the bottom would have provided support for an upright infant. Plate 20 from Samuel James Guernsey and Alfred Vincent Kidder, *Basket-Maker Caves of Northeastern Arizona*, 1921. Reprinted courtesy of the Peabody Museum, Harvard University.

Canyon, northeastern Arizona (Smithsonian catalog no. 303275). Its two-piece bentwood frame is lashed into an oval that is padded to a thickness of 1.5 cm and covered with hide so that the edges are completely smooth. From top to bottom a transverse platform of willow twigs is lashed to the frame. Bound to the transverse with human hair, yucca twine, or sinew, a set of longitudinal willow twigs adds stability and strength. This pattern created a "decoration" that might signal cultural affiliation (Wobst 1977) and would have been immediately identifiable, except, as in the case of Basketmaker sandals (Hays-Gilpin et al. 1998), the design would not have been visible. Only when the child had been removed from the adult back could the design be seen.

Although in this example only five rods run longitudinally and are perpendicular to the cross rods, other cradles are made with many longitudinal twigs, sometimes arranged in a V pattern. This type of frame is most commonly larger at the top but occasionally is a true oval. Rarely is the

Figure 3.5. Footrest from a cave in Cave Lake Canyon, vicinity of Kanab, Kane County, Utah (Nusbaum 1922:Plate XLI). Courtesy of the National Museum of the American Indian, Smithsonian Institution, negative no. NO7329. Photograph by Jesse Nusbaum.

frame larger at the bottom, so rarely that such an anomaly, I suspect, is mistaken orientation, as I discuss and illustrate later in this chapter.

All these boards have some device, usually loops, through which a binding cord would lace to secure baby and bedding to the frame. Near the top and bottom of the cradleboards are longer loops that may have been used to suspend the cradle in a horizontal position. About one-third the way up the platform is a yucca string stained with excreta, apparently used to hold cedar-bark diaper bundles (Guernsey and Kidder 1921:56–58 and Plate 21b).

Also near the bottom of this cradle, as on virtually all Basketmaker II cradles, is a pad or platform that Guernsey described this way: "Tied around the bottom of the hoop there is a horse-shoe shaped roll of cedar bark, which must have formed a kind of soft platform for the baby's feet to rest against when the cradle was held upright" (Guernsey and Kidder 1921:56). Illustrated in Figure 3.5 is a footrest excavated from Cave du Pont near Kanab, Utah.

Two other rigid cradleboard types must be discussed as separate entities. A cradle from Falls Creek on the Animas River north of Durango, Colorado (Figure 3.6), nearly contemporaneous with those from more westerly regions, is more solidly constructed with both vertical and horizontal rods that fill the frame. These rods are lashed together "with a binding of sinew, so laid out that they provided a decoration of large

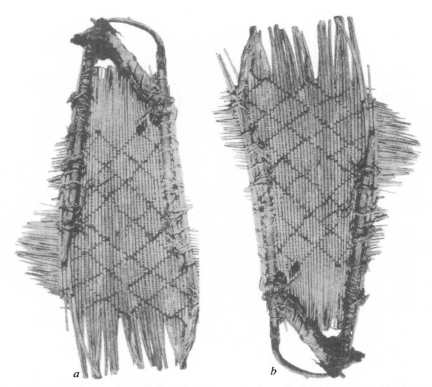

Figure 3.6. Falls Creek cradleboard. Figure 88-2 from Earl H. Morris and Robert F. Burgh, *Basket Maker II Sites near Durango, Colorado*, 1954; *a*. as hung and illustrated; *b*. the more likely orientation. One of the most obvious differences between this Animas River board and those from the Utah San Juan is the method by which the two frame pieces are lashed together and their lack of twill weaving. Such differences, as R. G. Matson suggested (2001), may strengthen his contention that Basketmaker groups developed from different populations. Photograph copyright I. M. (Zeke) Flores. Reprinted courtesy of the Carnegie Institution of Washington.

diamond-shaped units" (Morris and Burgh 1954:69). The remaining end of the frame was "wrapped with fiber cord and reinforced with animal hide bearing short reddish hair." Because I have not been able to locate this artifact to examine and photograph, I must rely on more subjective impressions created by the photographic image and my own memory.[3] This cradleboard is one that I believe has always been illustrated upside-down. One end of the bentwood frame had broken away, and that end had frayed, probably the reason this board was hung with the small end at the top. Earl Morris and Robert Burgh (1954:69) also illustrated the

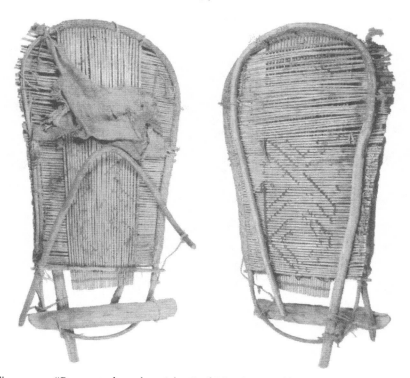

Figure 3.7. "Pappoose board—wicker" of "Ancient Pueblo" people, collected by
G. H. Green and acquired by the Chicago Field Museum on April 28, 1894.
Although many of the transverse rods have been lost and the longitudinal rods
disturbed, exquisite twill weaving decorates and softens the frame, none the
worse for 2,000 years of wear. On this board, 68.5 cm tall, the material that
lashed longitudinal to transverse rods has disintegrated, leaving only the design
in the original pale color, the remainder of the exposed rods weathered to a warm
tan color outlining the nested diamond pattern. The arced wooden piece originally may have lashed in a different position as a carrying handle. Alternatively,
it may have been a precursor to the arced bedding holders as in Figure 3.16. The
top outer frame had been repaired with what appeared to be pitch resin.
Courtesy of the Chicago Field Museum (Accession no. 21530). Digitally enhanced photo by Claudette Piper.

board with this orientation. Were one to reverse the illustration, however,
the shape would more nearly conform to the ubiquitous style in other
northern regions near the San Juan River and Basin. In addition, when the
picture is rotated, the sinew-wrapped stick becomes a functional footrest.

Conforming to this general type of "rigid cradleboard," but stronger,
are boards from the Grand Gulch area in Utah (Figures 3.7 and 3.8).

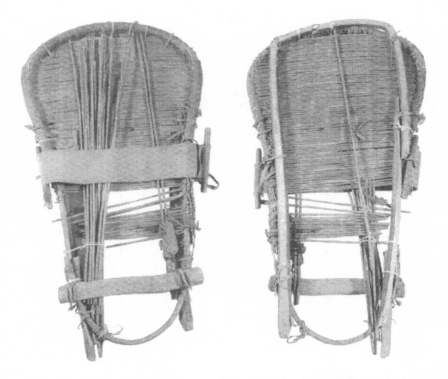

Figure 3.8. This cradleboard, 60 cm tall, is a near duplicate of the one in Figure 3.7 although it lacks the bentwood arc and retains a toggled strap. Lashed to the larger, inside frame were 28 longitudinal and 91 transverse twigs, bound with human hair in a nested diamond design. At one time finely woven cloth covered the entire inside of the bed. Courtesy of the Chicago Field Museum (Accession no. 21533). Digitally enhanced photo by Claudette Piper.

Apparently, they are very rare because I am aware of no literature that illustrates, discusses, or references similar cradleboards. Three construction details differentiate Grand Gulch cradleboards from other rigid cradleboards. First, these boards had both an inner and an outer frame, unlike the frames described earlier that were constructed of a single support frame made of two pieces of bentwood lashed together. The inner frame had been encased in a finely twilled binding. The other frame, on the outside, or backside, of the board, was smaller in diameter, was left bare, and would have provided structural support. It would seem also to be a practical device to raise the cradle a bit to keep the bedding off the ground when the child was off the mother's back.

The second difference is found in the materials used to construct the

Figure 3.9. Footrests, or structural braces, on Grand Gulch cradleboards. Digitally enhanced photo by Claudette Piper.

footrests.[4] Rather than formed of rolled cedar bark, they were carved of wood in a shallow S shape. The outward curve of the S, on both boards, projected on the right side so that the right foot would have led the left (Figure 3.9). I cannot discern any reason why an S shape would be more functional than a straight piece, and as it required more labor to manufacture, I wonder if the shape might have symbolic meaning. Kelley Hays-Gilpin (personal communication 2000) noted the similarity between this shape and that of fending sticks and the similarity in shape between fending sticks and rock art representations (Geib 1990).

The third difference between these boards and those common in the Kayenta–San Juan areas is that, at least on one board (Figure 3.8), the child would not have been lashed with the typical crisscrossed binding of a fur-covered cord (Kidder and Guernsey 1919; Nusbaum 1922). Instead, ingenious toggles were attached to the ends of a broad strap that would have secured both baby and bedding to the frame with a design that allowed quick, easy release (Figure 3.10). Toggles appear to be a vast technological improvement over lashing, but they were not imitated in Basketmaker cradleboards from other localities. They appear again in a Pueblo III cradleboard from the other side of the San Juan River.

Flexible Cradles. Flexible cradles are much rarer and take two forms. It is not clear that either type actually functioned as a cradleboard. The first type is made of a piece of bentwood or firmly rolled grass rim formed into a teardrop shape and filled with yucca-string netting (Figure 3.11). I know of only two examples, one a "toy" from Kane County, Utah (Nusbaum 1922:Plate XLII), and the other quite large at 84 cm in length (Kidder and Guernsey 1919:Plate 71b). Kidder and Guernsey questioned whether they

Figure 3.10. Toggled belt on Grand Gulch Cradleboard. Digitally enhanced photo by Claudette Piper.

were in fact cradles but noted that they were "assumed to be such" because of their shape, because they often were padded inside with grass and shredded bark (1919:165), and because they were too flimsy to be used for transporting. If these items were used as "cradles" of any kind, I believe that they would better be called "hammocks," as they might have served to keep an infant or stores off the ground.

Kidder and Guernsey (1919:165–166 and Plate 72) also described a second "flexible" style, termed a "flexible cedar bark cradle" (Figure 3.12), and noted that Byron Cummings (1910:10) described these from "Sagiotsosi," as did Walter Hough (1907:21) from Tularosa Cave. The Kidder and Guernsey cradle is 76 cm long, constructed of thick strips of cedar bark running lengthwise, and twined together with twisted yucca strips; it contained "a number of piñon nuts." Elizabeth Morris (1980:122 and Plate 81d) described a similar bag, containing sunflower seeds, which she believed was a container.

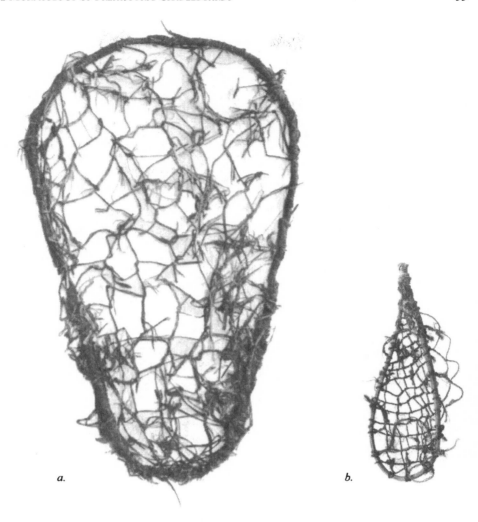

a.   *b.*

Figure 3.11. Variability in the size of flexible cradles. *a.* "Flexible grass cradle" with flimsy construction and great size, 83.8 cm long, would not be suitable for carrying even the lightest infant on one's back. Plate 71b from Samuel James Guernsey and Alfred Vincent Kidder, *Basket-Maker Caves of Northeastern Arizona,* 1921. Reprinted courtesy of the Peabody Museum, Harvard University. *b.* The "toy cradle," found in the burial of a young girl, is 38.1 cm long and made with the two bands near the top and bottom typical of Basketmaker cradles. Loops at the sides also are similar to those on cradles (Nusbaum 1922:Plate XLI). Courtesy of the National Museum of the American Indian, Smithsonian Institution, negative no. NO7317. Photo by Jesse Nusbaum.

Figure 3.12. "Flexible cedar bark cradle," 82 cm by 32.5 cm, from "Kin Boo Koo" Canyon, Marsh Pass, Arizona. Collected by S. J. Guernsey and R. G. Fuller in 1915. Courtesy of the Smithsonian Institution (Accession no. 349219). Digitally enhanced photo by Claudette Piper.

A similar cedar-bark bag, excavated by P. S. Martin et al. (1952:316–318 and Figure 122) from Tularosa Cave, is curated at the Field Museum and identified as from the Prepottery phase (Figure 3.13). Although this object is not from the Colorado Plateau, I include it because it has been widely reproduced and may be an important reason most archaeologists assume that harder cradleboards caused cranial deformation. Both more sophisticated in construction technique and in a far better state of preservation, this bag is constructed of "bear grass fiber twined with yucca fiber" and filled with grass. Both top and bottom are tied shut, the top more tightly, so that an "egg shaped cradle" is created. One side is open, held together across the lower half and the upper quarter with a loose netting of yucca strips. In each of these bags, one side opens, bound so that it could be tied closed. Kidder and Guernsey (1919:Figure 78) illustrated a similar edge binding.

Whether any of these articles was associated with sleeping or cradling is an open question. Padded inside with grass and as narrow as they are, they would have had little room inside for a child's body and would have been far longer than necessary. Of possible importance is the fact that three similar cedar bags from the Pine Lawn phase, from the same expedition (No. 260869, No. 26082, and No. 261083), were originally identified as "carrying baskets." At some later date that description was crossed out and re-

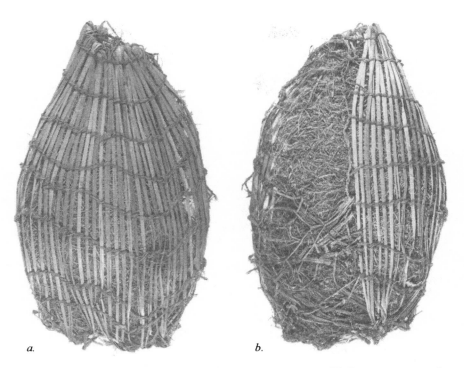

a.   *b.*

Figure 3.13. "Flexible cradle, 84 cm by 47 cm, is grass filled, Prepottery" phase. Photograph shows front and back. Both this "cradle" and the one in Figure 3.12 are so narrow that they seem too small to enclose a child, although they would have provided warmth if opened and used as a covering. Courtesy of the Chicago Field Museum (Accession no. 260868). Digitally enhanced photo by Claudette Piper.

placed with "cradle" in the case of No. 261083 and "flexible cradle?" in the case of No. 260860. These articles may have been used for winter warmth as well as containers, as Morris believed (1980:122 and Plate 81d). Perhaps the presence of piñon nuts indicates that the bags were used to transport trade items, the seeds and nuts being travel food or items for exchange.

Basketmaker Bedding. Archaeologists have recovered well-preserved bedding used with Basketmaker II cradleboards. People from Tsegi Canyon, as well as from the Glen Canyon area, used the same kind of bedding. On the Colorado Plateau a rigorous climate required warm garments in the winter, and Basketmaker II people devised a practical layette (Guernsey and Kidder 1921:54 and Plate 4). An almost identical set of Basketmaker bedding was recovered from the Glen Canyon area. The

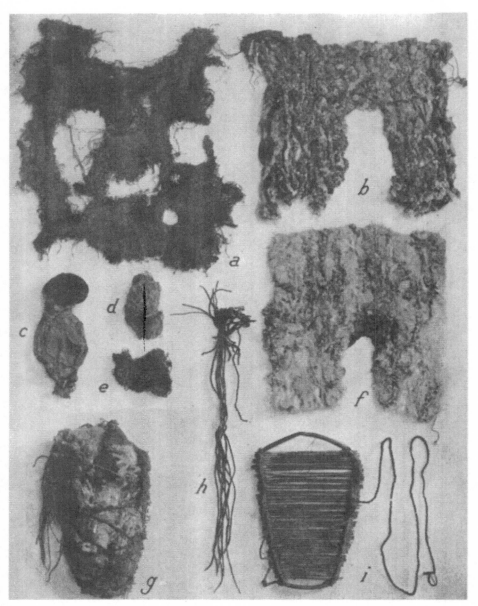

Figure 3.14. Bedding used for Basketmaker infants. "*g*, Cradle bundle as found. The other figures show cradle and contents unwrapped. *a*, Woven cloth; *b, f,* Fur cloth blankets; *d*, Umbilical pad; *e*, Absorbent bark; *i*, Cradle." The outermost blanket is woven cloth, and the next cover is a square fur-string blanket. The innermost blanket is of the same size and shape, made of string "wound with strips of fluffy white fur from the bellies of rabbits." The dried umbilical cord was attached to a corner of the outer blanket. Plate 4 from Samuel James Guernsey and Alfred Vincent Kidder, *Basket-Maker Caves of Northeastern Arizona,* 1921. Reprinted courtesy of the Peabody Museum, Harvard.

child lay on wrapping of hide with the hair still attached, the edges of which were gathered around the outside of the arms and over the chest. The back of the wrapping didn't extend below the buttocks of the child, but the extensions at each side partially wrapped the child's legs. Between the legs was a "diaper" of grass padding (Figure 3.14). In the Glen Canyon burial the child wore a feather necklace and its blanket was stained with red ochre (Lipe 1960:222).

Many umbilical pads, tied over the navel of infants to prevent hernias, have been found in mortuary context with the typical rigid cradle. Made of several small corncobs tied, a piece of sandstone, or whittled pine bark, these pads most often were covered with a prairie-dog skin turned inside-out (Guernsey and Kidder 1921:58–59, Plates 22 and 31; Lipe 1960:222 and Figure 69f). J. L. Nusbaum (1922:Plate XLII) described a more simple pad from the Glen Canyon area made of a skin cover stuffed with grass and hair.

Pueblo III Cradleboards

Cradleboard design changed radically between the end of the Basketmaker period and Pueblo times. In comparison with earlier times when only one clear example of cradleboard design exists, many forms are present by Pueblo III. Some are almost identical to those of Basketmaker times and may in fact have been passed down through time; radiocarbon dating should answer that question. Many are made with hoods, but few footrests are present, suggesting that the cradles may not have habitually been used in an upright position. A much greater variety of materials are used in construction, including twilled yucca weaving, wooden planks, and cottonwood bark. Unlike earlier times, Pueblo III has no prototype design. Most important, in almost all cases expediency of manufacture seems to have been of paramount importance.

Rigid Cradleboards. The "rigid" cradleboard typical of Basketmaker II times continued to be manufactured, with adaptations, in Pueblo III times. For example, a cradle from a midden near Ruin 7 (Guernsey and Kidder 1921:108 and Plate 42) is "battered from use and probably discarded as worn out, [but] this cradle still shows the excellence of its construction." The longitudinal and transverse rods are lashed together with fine human-hair cord, fashioned into a design of large diamonds.

Other rigid cradles, but with woven yucca leaves rather than a tied-rod base, were in use during Pueblo III times. One example (Figure 3.15) is from Iceburg Canyon (Site NA10,555) in the Glen Canyon area (Reiley 1969). The two-piece bentwood frame, 61.2 cm long, is similar to those of

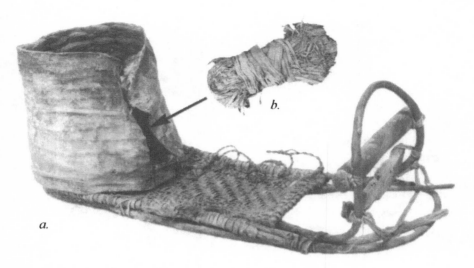

Figure 3.15. Pueblo III cradle from the Glen Canyon Recreation Area, Site NA10,555. The juniper bark pad may have been propped against the hood, producing lambdoidal deformation. Courtesy of the Museum of Northern Arizona Photo Archives, Catalog no. NA10555.B1.11. This cradle is very similar to the one illustrated in Guernsey 1931. Side loops would have been used to secure the child to the bed. When originally unwrapped, the bark pad rested on the base of the hood on the wooden frame, just below a wooden dowel probably used to support the neck. The bark may have been used to support the head, producing slight lambdoidal deformation.

earlier boards, although it is constructed with a bark hood and a bowed bottom to hold bedding in place. A dowel and a piece of worked wood lashed to the bottom of the frame would have provided support for an upright infant. The cottonwood hood is 21.6 cm high with a maximum diameter of 25.5 cm, awkward to carry on one's back. At the base of the hood was a wooden dowel that may have been used as a neckrest. With the cradle backing was a juniper-bark pad that perhaps supported the infant's head, which was slightly deformed on the lambda (Birkby 1969).

Guernsey (1931:105 and Plate 64) described a Pueblo III cradleboard from Cave 8 in Adugegi Canyon. This cradle's backing was twilled weaving of whole yucca leaves. Found with the cradleboard was a toggle stick attached to a feather-string band that secured bedding in place. This toggle is very similar to that described in association with a Grand Gulch cradleboard (Figure 3.10), although the woven band is finer in Grand Gulch. In addition, a headboard, 17 cm by 11 cm by 1.5 cm thick, was found with the cradle. Such "pillows" are found only in association with Kayenta

Anasazi burials. Were this board to be propped at an angle against the hood, an infant's head would be in position to be lambdoidally deformed (Figure 3.16). I am unaware of any other reference to a headboard causing lambdoidal deformation, but Hopi ethnography hints at a motive for the resulting deformation: "A small pad of folded cloth is placed under the head to ease the discomfort of the hard board. A roll of cloth is placed under the neck to keep the child from becoming short-necked or 'bull-necked'" (Dennis 1940:31). If the aesthetic sensibility of presumed Hopi ancestors preferred long necks, the logical consequence would be lambdoidal deformation.

As mentioned previously, two kinds of cranial deformation (Figure 3.1) occur in the American Southwest and indicate two distinct styles of child-care techniques. Occipital deformation, found throughout most of the Southwest, occurs on the back of the cranium, the consequence of lying in one position most of the day (Dennis and Dennis 1940:32; Thompson and Joseph 1944:51). The configuration of this cranial shape implies that the baby rested on its back. The lack of footrests in many late cradleboards and the unsuitability of many specimens for carrying on the back suggest that a common practice at this time was to rest cradleboards in a fairly flat position.

A similar artificial cranial deformation, termed *deformational plagio-cephaly*, has occurred in contemporary times since health practitioners began promoting the "Back to Sleep" campaign to prevent sudden infant deaths. Physicians have compared an infant cranium to a water-filled balloon that flattens when laid on a table. Deformation requires several months to become apparent, 3.6 months on the average, according to modern researchers (Turk et al. 1996).

Figure 3.16. How a headrest might produce lambdoidal deformation. Redrawn, with wooden wedge in place, from Guernsey 1931:Plate 64. Drawing by Ron Redsteer.

Figure 3.17. Wood plank cradle from Canyon de Chelly. Courtesy of the Chicago Field Museum (Accession no. 42342). The holes at the bottom and the sides of the boards would have been lashed to secure side pieces in a vertical position. Digitally enhanced photo by Claudette Piper.

Lambdoidal deformation, with certain exceptions that may indicate migration in the Mogollon area (Bennett 1975; Cassels 1972; Stewart 1973) and others, or co-residence (Reid and Whittlesey 1997; Whittlesey and Reid 2001), is found exclusively in the "Anasazi" region. This form of deformation, occurring close to the crown of the head, cannot be explained in the same way as occipital deformation. Stewart (1940:163–164) ques-

tioned a popular assumption of the time that deformation was entirely accidental, "due to the weight of the head on a hard cradleboard." He added
that the "predominance of lambdoid deformation (unexplainable on the
basis simply of head weight)" in those areas where it is found, "lends force
to the view that in general among the Pueblos deformation was more than
accidental" (1940:163–164). Although artifactual evidence is meager, the
cause of lambdoidal deformation must be attributed to either pillowing or
positioning.

Wood Plank Cradles. Other cradleboards from all around the Four
Corners area are much like an early version of the historic Zuni board
(Figure 3.3). These rigid cradles were commonly used during Pueblo III
times and were found in many areas, including Canyon del Muerto (Field
Museum no. 42342), Grand Gulch (Field Museum no. 21527), and Mesa
Verde (Rohn 1971:233 and Figure 275; Watson 1961:175). This is the
type of cradle, I believe, that led most early archaeologists to assume that
harder cradleboards caused cranial deformation. Although the plank cradle is firm, relatively speaking, the willow-backed cradleboards of Basketmaker II times are not much "softer." Furthermore, we must assume that
no less bedding or padding was used on this type of board. A far more important aspect of this cradle is the expedient nature of its construction.
One bottom and two side pieces are carved, a few holes are drilled in the
inner edges so that the pieces may be tied together, and very quickly a serviceable cradleboard is ready for use.

A wood plank cradleboard from Canyon de Chelly (Figure 3.17), collected sometime before 1906 by Stewart Culin, consists of three smoothed
planks: a base plank (20 cm by 47.5 cm) to which two side pieces (8 cm
wide) were tied to form a shallow cradle into which a child could have
been strapped. Although shorter and narrower than most cradles, it certainly is wide enough for a baby and bedding. A fecal stain on the cradleboard allows an examiner to determine the orientation of use.

The cedar bark cradle from Grand Gulch illustrated in Figure 3.18 still
has the leather thongs that attached the 6-cm wooden sides to the 64.5-
cm-by-24-cm base. The smoothed wooden arc may be the remnant of a
collapsible hood, very similar to that with the Zuni cradle in Figure 3.3.
The bottom of the base is covered with padded leather.

Before moving to the next type of Pueblo III cradle, I reproduce in
Figure 3.19 what I believe to be the photograph that codified the notion of
"hard vs. soft" (Watson 1961:174–175). After examining the cradleboards illustrated throughout this chapter, I hope the reader will be as
puzzled as I was about this photograph. These two cradleboards did not fit

Figure 3.18. Cedar bark cradle from Grand Gulch. The carved wooden arc probably was a carrying handle. Courtesy of the Chicago Field Museum (Accession no. 21527). Digitally enhanced photo by Claudette Piper.

any typology I had developed as I examined the data set. The "Basket Maker cradle" was smaller at the top than the bottom, and the strap that allowed the cradle to be hung was at the wrong end. The cord at the top right *might* have served to lash the child to the cradle, but it looked more like a "diaper string." Likewise, the "Pueblo cradleboard" did not look right. But when I turned the photo upside-down, suddenly these two boards fit within the range of variability I had previously established. I am almost certain that, like the Falls Creek cradleboard (Figure 3.6), these cradleboards are illustrated upside-down, most likely because of an error by the publisher. The round object thus would be a footrest, not the headrest Morris (1980:122 and Figure 81) had identified in other contexts. It might serve either function, but in any case would have been unusual.

Cottonwood Bark Cradles. One other common type of Pueblo III cradle, again of extremely expedient manufacture, is made of cottonwood bark and found in sites as diverse as Mesa Verde (Rohn 1977:225–226 and Plate 80) and Canyon de Chelly (Morris 1925:298). Described by A. H. Rohn as "a rectangular piece of bark" 58 cm by 40.5 cm, it was

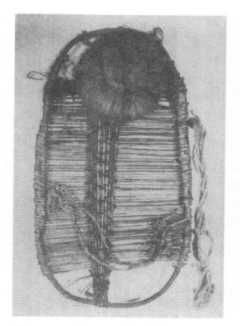 

Figure 3.19. What's wrong with this picture? This illustration, from *Indians of the Mesa Verde* (Watson 1961), reprinted courtesy of the Mesa Verde Museum Association, probably was published in an inverted position. When the page is turned upside-down, these cradles closely resemble the Basketmaker and Pueblo cradles illustrated in this chapter. As A. B. Kehoe (1991) demonstrated, orientation must be considered when analyzing the function of an artifact.

"formed into an apparent cradle by curling the two long sides over about 5 inches on the smooth inner side of the bark. The two ends were then tipped upward slightly and an arc of oak was attached to one end." Rohn notes that it was nearly the size of other "wooden cliff dweller cradles" and that a lengthwise split had been repaired with split yucca strips.

TEMPORAL CHANGES IN CRADLEBOARDS

Despite the almost universal assumption that harder cradleboards caused cranial deformation (Bennett 1961; Reed 2000; Rohn 1971; Shufeldt 1891; Stewart 1940), the primary difference between early cradleboards and later ones is not whether they are hard or soft. Some early cradleboards are hard, and both the early and later cradles probably were covered with thick layers of bedding (see Saunders 1973 for ethnographic illustrations of contemporary cradleboards). Rather, three physical differences distinguish early from later cradleboards: later boards lack footrests, they often are made with hoods, and in general, they required much less time to construct.

Most later cradles do not have footrests and thus are not likely to have been used to carry a child on the back. I hypothesize that footrests were eliminated because cradleboards were no longer used to carry children upright. When children were upright, their heads were unconstrained, free to move in any direction, but when children were attached to cradleboards and laid flat, propped, or hung from rafters, their heads were much more immobile. When they were awake, their attention would have been focused in the direction of activity around them. When their heads became flattened, it was almost never just in the back of the skull, but on the left or the right, depending on where they were habitually rested.

A second feature that distinguishes later from earlier cradles is the presence of hoods, probably to keep flies, dust, or sun from the child's face. Aggregated living conditions produce great amounts of waste, and flies must have been a real nuisance in Pueblo times. Hoods would have provided a frame over which a cloth could have been placed, as is often seen today in Pueblo societies. However, these bulky hoods would have been awkward to carry on a collecting trip.

Third, the frequency of expedient construction on later cradleboards may reflect a change in labor allocation. Although exceptions occur, as with the Adugegi Canyon cradleboard described by Guernsey (1931), common materials and simple construction techniques exemplify cradles from later times. Perhaps few adults had the time to construct the elaborately decorated cradleboards of Basketmaker II times. Alternatively, the sedentary farmers of Pueblo times may have focused decorative arts on other media, such as ceramics or weaving. The less stringent requirements of a cradle that does not need to be carried easily may also have allowed more variation in construction and the use of more expedient construction techniques.

Thus, I conclude that the appearance of cranial deformation at the Basketmaker III–Pueblo I transition occurred not because cradleboards were harder but because they were used in a different way. Function, not form, caused the patterning of artificial cranial deformation. Further evidence is seen in the differences in the patterning of cranial deformation among contemporary culture areas.

FURTHER IMPLICATIONS OF THE RESEARCH

During the Basketmaker to Pueblo transition, concurrent with changes in residence patterns, subsistence, artifact styles, and other cultural practices, the child-care practices for infants were altered. Babies were still placed in cradleboards but were less frequently carried on the back and were more often settled in a stationary position. This modification of previous child-raising practices appears to be a response to the need for women to spend more time working in or near the pueblo. As gathering decreased in importance, cooking techniques became more time-consuming (Crown 2000), kitchen gardens may have been intensively tended (Fish 2000), and an increasing number of children were born (Martin 2000).

The implications of these new child-rearing practices remain to be completely explored. The use of a sedentary restraining device for infants that could be placed near a nursing mother might allow men, non-nursing women, or other children to take a more active role in changing diapers, soothing and amusing the infant, feeding the child supplemental foods, and other care activities. It would even allow young children far too small to carry a cradleboard to productively participate in child care, a practice common in many societies (Whiting and Edwards 1988). D. L. Martin (2000) suggests that although the fertility rate remained high and may even have increased through time, the age at weaning may have been increasing, perhaps in an attempt to decrease child mortality rates. Higher fertility rates among agricultural populations are well documented cross-culturally (Ember 1983). A change in child-raising technique, relieving the nursing mother from carrying her child, might well be part of a strategy to allow procreation by a still-nursing mother by decreasing her caloric needs, distributing the labor of baby care, and making it possible to tend two young children simultaneously.

According to ethnographic and medical evidence, there are no detrimental developmental effects of cradleboarding.[5] Cranial sutures that close fully only in early childhood allow the infant's braincase, if squeezed, to expand in another direction, permitting normal development (Gerszten 1993:96). Ethnohistorical analyses and medical studies indicate that the Hopi, still cradleboarded in infancy, walk no later than other children (Beaglehole and Beaglehole 1935; Dennis 1940; Dennis and Dennis 1940; Leach 1974:35; Thompson and Joseph 1944). The researchers just cited, and a Navajo scholar and friend (Jennifer Denetdale, personal communication 1999), suggest that cradleboarding reproduces the security of the womb and that children often become fretful when removed from the cradle. Further research may demonstrate psychological implications of viewing the world primarily from an upright versus from a supine position, or from a mobile versus a sedentary perspective. Infants who see life head-on, as opposed to looking upward at looming figures, may grow up to relate to the world in different ways, but that is a topic for further research by others.

Although the most direct implications of my investigation of cradleboards involve aspects of child-care practices and labor allocation, insights may be gained into a much wider array of topics. These include the speed of the pithouse-to-pueblo transition, the identification of cultural affiliation, and the study of migration.

The current tendency is to view the transition from pithouse to pueblo as a gradual process (Vivian 2000), but R. H. Wilshusen and E. Blinman (1992:264) have asserted that a "fundamental error has been made in accepting a model of gradual change." Both views may be correct, depending on location and on the specific cultural change. My research indicates that cranial deformation occurred quite suddenly and provides a marker of an abrupt shift in mobility.

Parenting is learned from one's own parents and one's community. Specific child-care technique is perhaps one of the most culturally definitive markers (Lillehammer 1989:92). Because lambdoidally deformed crania occur most commonly in the Anasazi area, each type of deformation indicates a distinct style of mothering and probably marks cultural affiliations. Migration and coresidence have been discussed by some archaeologists (Cordell 1995; Haury 1958; Reid and Whittlesey 1997). Stephanie Whittlesey (Whittlesey and Reid 2001), one of the few modern archaeologists to incorporate different deformation types into research design, has suggested that the occurrence of lambdoidally deformed adult females at Grasshopper Pueblo means that Anasazi women married into the Mogollon community. In other studies, such as at Mesa Verde (Rohn 1977), where the distribution is almost half lambdoidally deformed and half occipitally deformed, the significance of variability has not been incorporated into research design.

If the deformations that occur because of variation in parenting techniques are viewed as ethnic markers, the study of different deformation types may be of particular value in examining the large-scale migrations that occurred across southern Utah and southwestern Colorado during Pueblo I times (Wilshusen and Ortman 1999:370).

ACKNOWLEDGMENTS

I thank Kelley Hays-Gilpin, chair of my thesis committee, and Kathy Kamp, editor of this volume, for mentorship, unflagging support, and enthusiasm. Dan Boone, Ron Redsteer, and Zack Huntington provided graphic expertise, and Dave Ortiz made astute comments on an early draft. Wil Grewe-Mullins of the Field Museum, Dave Wilcox of the Museum of Northern Arizona, and James Krakker of the Smithsonian Institution guided my first forays into the world of museum collections, and I thank them for sharing their knowledge. I am grateful to the anonymous reviewers who contributed thoughtful and constructive suggestions. David Lewis-Williams and Larry Loendorf helped me believe in the importance of this research topic and provided invaluable comments on early drafts. Errors and shortcomings are entirely mine.

NOTES

1. Absence of a common vocabulary to describe carriers and bedding used in prehistoric times is one of the primary difficulties in understanding the nature of child care. The term *cradle* came to be used for almost any type of children's bedding. Some descriptive terms used are *rigid type cradle, flexible grass cradle, pappoose board, toy cradle, bark cradle, problematical board, soft cradle,* and *wood plank*. All these terms perhaps have created confusion and contributed to the folk wisdom that harder cradleboards caused cranial deformation. To avoid defining an object by naming it, I use only the terms *cradle* and *cradleboard,* and I try not to distinguish differences in form or function with this terminology.

2. For a linguistic analysis of Native American names for cradleboards, see Lotrich 1941.

3. When I was growing up in Durango, this cradleboard hung inside the public reference and reading room of the public library, just to the left of a wide doorway that opened from the central vestibule. Because all the walls in that reading room were covered with bookshelves and west- and south-facing windows, the cradleboard stood out in a space of its own. One day it was removed to be photographed, and it has yet to be recovered.

4. Although I believe these transverse wooden slats to be footrests, it is possible that they provided only structural support.

5. D. Y. Holliday (1993), however, suggests that a medical condition, occipital lesions, may be caused by the pressure of a cranium on a hard surface.

4

Working for a Living

Childhood in the Prehistoric

Southwestern Pueblos

KATHRYN A. KAMP

Like archaeological reconstructions in general (Kamp 2001b), depictions of the ancestral Puebloan Southwest tend to ignore the work of children. Labor allocation, when considered, is usually dichotomized along gender lines. Children's efforts are rarely addressed or are dismissed on the grounds that working children are merely "helping" adults or "learning" the skills needed for adult life. Although Barbara Mills (2000:304–305) has noted the possible impact of children's labor on adult, specifically women's, production, the hypothesis that children's labor provided an important component of the economic strategy and that there may actually have been children's work that was just as vital to the economic system as men's work and women's work is rarely discussed.

Surveys of cross-cultural literature show that children's work is important more often than it is not. Not surprisingly, the ethnographic literature on the historic pueblos records subadults doing a variety of tasks, suggesting that the economic role of children in the prehistoric Puebloan Southwest was not an outlier in this respect and hence needs to be examined. Although a perusal of the ethnographic data is instructive and yields a strong case for the probable participation of subadults in the prehistoric labor force, archaeological evidence is ultimately required to prove it. Research on the economic roles of prehistoric children is still extremely preliminary; the actual archaeological evidence is suggestive but tenuous and sparse. Just as archaeologists have had difficulty providing concrete archaeological rationales for assigning gender identities to prehistoric activities, the relationship between age and economic roles is not easy to determine. A preliminary case study argued specifically for the prehistoric Sinagua of the Flagstaff area, but probably in many respects generalizable to much of the Puebloan Southwest, demonstrates some possibilities for assessing the contributions of prehistoric children to the economy.

CHILDREN'S LABOR CROSS-CULTURALLY

Numerous anthropologists point to the importance of children's work in a variety of cultures and contexts (e.g., C. Bradley 1993; Goddard 1985; Gulranji 1994; Mehra-Kempelman 1996; Ritchie and Ritchie 1979; Sancho-Liao 1994). The type of work performed by children varies greatly, including caring for other children, tending animals, gathering, food preparation, housework, agricultural activities, small-scale entrepreneurism, and working for wages in a variety of factory and nonfactory contexts. The differences in the amount of work expected from children are extremely situational. When children's labor can be used efficiently, it appears to be important, but when the constraints on children's usefulness reduce their productivity, children's labor contributions diminish.

Because the situational variance leading to differences in labor allocation may be fairly subtle, a case-by-case analysis is necessary. It is certainly not adequate simply to assume that one type of subsistence pattern either mandates the use of children's labor or negates its value. Thus, although the Hadza and !Kung are both hunting and gathering societies, !Kung children perform very little work (Blurton Jones et al. 1994; Draper 1976; Draper and Cashdan 1988; Shostak 1976) but Hadza children hunt, gather, and collect wood, making significant contributions to their own caloric consumption and sometimes that of others as well (Blurton Jones et al. 1994). The primary reason for the differences, which can be understood in terms of the potential efficiency of using children for gathering, relates to distribution of resources relative to the camp. The immediate surrounds of Hadza camps are relatively resource-rich, so Hadza children are able to do considerable foraging within a safe distance from camp. In contrast, !Kung children would have to venture much farther from their home base and would risk getting lost and perhaps hurt. For analogous reasons, !Kung adults do not take children with them when hunting or gathering. Since the required distances are viewed as too far for children to transverse easily, their presence on a foraging expedition is seen as decreasing rather than increasing efficiency, and they are left in camp.

High fertility rates in some cultures may be, at least in part, a reflection of the benefits of children's labor to their adult kin (Polgar 1972). The poor in India, for example, perceive that because of the potential for using child labor, "the more the children the more the economic gain of the family" (Mukherjee et al. 1987:35). A. C. Zellar (1987), using a survey of researchers working in thirteen horticultural and hunting and gathering societies, concluded that Paleolithic children would have made significant contributions to the economy and that these benefits may have, in fact, encouraged early hominid mothers to decrease the spacing of offspring, enhancing our line's evolutionary success and expansion into new territories.

The net result of the contributions of children's efforts to the group's economy varies considerably. As an infant, the child obviously does not contribute to the labor pool, but the amount of work required to care for a baby differs considerably from culture to culture, depending on local child-rearing techniques. Similarly, the age at which children begin to work and the types of work in which they engage are extremely variable. Investments in the child's upbringing, such as food, clothing, education, housing, and personal possessions, are again extremely variable. Thus, the age at which a child becomes a net economic asset to the family will also differ dramatically from culture to culture.

Children as a Drain on Resources

Despite the evidence that in many societies children represent a component of the labor force, archaeologists have tended to ignore their economic participation. That children diminish the work capability of a group is a much more common thesis. Thus, adults, particularly women, are viewed as devoting a portion of their time to child care with little or no immediate compensating labor return. This view implies that child rearing is a fairly time-intensive process, that adults are the primary caretakers for young children, and that children contribute little to the economy—all notions that apply to middle-class life today in Europe and the United States but are not generalizable through time and space. In a kind of drain/gain labor analysis, the drain of child care has generally been emphasized with little or no discussion of potential gains from the early labor of children.

Much of the discussion has revolved around the potential effect of children on women's roles. Judith Brown's (1970) work has been particularly influential. Brown argues that the degree of subsistence participation of women is directly dependent on the relative compatibility of subsistence activities with child care and proposes that this constraint limits women to tasks that can be performed near home, are repetitive, do not require much concentration, can easily be interrupted, and are safe. Obviously, restricting women's activities using these criteria would drastically limit women's potential for full societal participation. Brown describes a number of ethnographic examples of women engaging in appropriate work activities, including farming, gathering plant foods, and collecting marine resources, while caring for children. Interestingly, although in most of her examples the children being supervised are, at least to some extent, productively participating in the farming or gathering activities being described, the economic contributions of the children are not addressed; the argument merely assumes that the entire import of the children's presence in the work groups is the convenience of combining child care with necessary adult labor.

In another cross-cultural study, Carol Ember (1983) emphasizes the additional work caused by children rather than the constraints on work activities that child care imposes. In an attempt to explain the decline in women's participation as agriculture intensifies, she argues that the domestic responsibilities of women increase with intensification. Part of the reason presumably is a decrease in birth spacing and an overall increase in the number of children. Ember acknowledges some disagreement among researchers about the amount of child care shouldered by mothers but argues that "even if a mother does not directly care for her children herself, they still constitute additional household members who have to be fed and possibly clothed. Directly or indirectly, then, more children probably mean more domestic work" (1983:296). Again, however, no attempt is made to consider the possible labor contributions of the children in question. One of the reasons women are freed from some subsistence activities may be the very labor of those children. In fact, Ember (1983:296) notes that her data seem to support the idea that intensive agriculturists make "conscious attempts to increase the number of children," possibly "because they can do chores."

Both these arguments focus on the mother-child relationship and argue that children constrain women's participation in a full range of social and economic activities. Other researchers (Bolen 1992; Gero 1991:171) have argued that after the initial stages of birth and nursing, motherhood is a cultural construction and there are numerous alternative arrangements for child care, many of which do not require the active participation of the biological mother or even of women. Although these approaches avoid the unnecessary conclusion that motherhood is automatically a detriment to women, they continue to problematize childhood, implying that the net result of children is always labor loss and ignoring the possibility that within a few years of a child's birth the gain in labor resources may actually balance or outweigh the initial costs.

Reasons for Undervaluing Children's Work

Probably the tendency to belittle children's work is due to current Western perceptions of the child's value as primarily affective rather than economic (Zelizer 1985). In the late 1800s and early 1900s the issue of child labor was a controversial one in the United States and Europe. While some argued that the use of child labor was exploitative, others claimed on both practical and moral grounds that children should not be excluded from the labor market. In the twentieth century, perhaps ultimately because it became more economical and efficient to educate children than to hire them, as much as for the proclaimed philosophical reasons (Zelizer 1985:112), children were, at least in theory, removed from the workplace. Recently, this policy is being reevaluated, as experts from a variety of disciplines have begun to question the desirability of the essentially nonproductive role assumed by Western children. Nevertheless, the tendency not to view work as an appropriate child's activity may have led to underreporting of children's work in both the archaeological and ethnographic literature. Similar cultural biases have occurred as researchers have reported and interpreted women's activities (for the Southwest and Mesoamerica, see, e.g., Brown 1983; Foote and Schackel 1986; Fratt 1991; McCafferty and McCafferty 1988).

An additional problem in the discussion of children's economic contributions is the controversy over whether or not much of what children do is actually work, as distinguished from either play or learning activities. This is undoubtedly exacerbated by the aforementioned Western reluctance to class any children's activities as work. I propose a general definition of work as productive activity. Using this definition, the intent of the actor becomes unimportant; only the outcomes are measured. The child who shoots a lizard with what an archaeologist might describe as a "toy" bow and arrow, and then eats it, is unambiguously accomplishing work, whether or not from the society's or the child's perspective the activity is described as play. Similarly, children may combine work and play, watching cattle while playing a game, for instance. Like play, learning activities become less difficult to distinguish from work if analyzed using criteria of productivity. Certainly, a beginner will be less effective at any activity. In the case of very complex skills a novice may be completely unproductive. Nevertheless, as beginners attain competence and their craft products are put to use, they are accomplishing work.

A tendency to interpret children's activities in terms of modern Western models that emphasize play and learning over production may have also caused ethnographers to misinterpret the intent of some childhood activities. A common interpretation of children's hunting and foraging is that it is heavily focused on learning the knowledge and skills necessary for adulthood. A detailed analysis of shellfishing by Meriam children (Bird and Bird 2000) reveals that children learn to shellfish from other children and that children's food-acquisition patterns do not mimic those of adults. Because of size differences between children and adults, different strategies of shellfishing produce the maximum caloric yield for each group. The Meriam children appear to be using the most efficient strategy for their current status, in preference to learning adult skills. The possibility that children's efforts are geared toward production rather than skill acquisition needs to be a working hypothesis for prehistoric situations as well.

Child workers are also sometimes overlooked because they contribute to a process that is primarily controlled by adults. Crafts such as ceramics may provide a case in point. Recent ethnoarchaeological and ethnohistorical research suggests that in many (perhaps most?) societies more than a single individual is involved in the pottery-making process (Kramer 1985; Wright 1991). This should not be at all surprising when the number of steps necessary for producing a ceramic vessel is considered. In addition to shaping and finishing the vessel, clay and tempering materials need to be obtained and possibly cleaned and ground, firing materials collected, water collected, the clay and temper kneaded and processed, and so forth. A number of these steps require considerable labor but not high levels of expertise. Furthermore, some of the possible finishes applied to ceramics, such as burnishing, are very labor-intensive but relatively low-skill. Although the individual who shapes or paints the pot may receive the majority of official "credit" for the vessel, important labor is unarguably invested in other portions of the process. The use of children's labor for some of the stages in ceramic manufacture is ethnographically attested (Kramer 1997), even though the children themselves may not be considered ceramicists. This problem of unrecognized contributions when there are multiple authors of a product has been discussed primarily in considerations of the gendered division of labor (Mills 1995; Wright 1991) but is by no means unique to this realm. In fact, children may be even more frequent unrecognized contributors than adults, and their contributions may be a common factor in craft production.

A SOUTHWESTERN CASE STUDY: THE SINAGUA

The evidence is convincing that numerous opportunities for productive, efficient contributions to the economic system would have existed for prehistoric Puebloan children. Like historic Pueblo children and like children throughout the world during most of history, prehistoric Pueblo children were probably an important part of the workforce. I examine the post-eruptive Northern Sinagua of the Flagstaff area as a concrete example. Based on the specific criteria indicated by the task-differentiation analysis described below and existing archaeological evidence, likely children's jobs for the Sinagua include running errands, child care, wood and water collection, helping with fieldwork, and chasing predators from the fields during critical times for crop development. All these tasks would be suitable for the involvement of children as young as 5 or 6 or even younger. As children got a bit older, they probably also began to hunt, cook, grind corn, and produce craft items such as ceramics.

The Task-Differentiation Approach

The task-differentiation method initially proposed by Janet Spector (1983) for studying the division of labor by gender provides one possible avenue for examining the distribution of labor along the dimension of age. Using information on the historic Hidatsa for a case study, Spector tabulates the basic subsistence activities, including information about the types of individuals participating in the task, location in both time and space, and the resulting material evidence. She then looks for general patterns in the data. For the Hidatsa, women's activities appeared to be organized around a household base whereas men's activities more extensively used cross-cutting ties not necessarily based on kinship. Spector notes that the activities of males and females are distinct, making broad generalizations about cultural experience or knowledge problematic and suggesting that for important issues such as technological innovation or culture change, men's and women's roles may have been quite different. Furthermore, both men's and women's activities leave archaeological traces and are thus accessible to the researcher.

I have performed an analogous analysis for Southwestern Puebloan groups, using activities that the archaeological evidence shows have parallels in prehistoric Sinagua culture but emphasizing age rather than gender. Thus, we know that the Sinagua grew many of the same crops as their descendants. This implies the need for some similar activities. The way labor was organized for performing the requisite tasks may have been quite different, however. It is perhaps suggestive that Puebloan women made ceramic vessels, but there is no assurance that some eight hundred or more years earlier the same gender division of labor pertained.

Both personal memoirs and ethnographies of the historic Pueblos demonstrate the existence and importance of work for children. Tessie Naranjo, herself of Santa Clara, explains the vital role of work:

> One of the things that children incorporated very early into their consciousness was that work was necessary to feel good about oneself and to have others think well of you. If it was said that you were a "hard worker" you felt you were paid one of the highest compliments. . . . As children, we carried our younger brothers and sisters on our backs while we swept the plaza area, helped get clay or mixed the clay with temper. We also mixed the mud with our feet for making adobe and mortar. After the mud was mixed, we also helped carry the bricks and mortar to build the walls. Cooking was done by girls from a fairly young age. Boys were off in the fields helping with hoeing, harvesting and in the mountains hunting and fishing. (Naranjo 1992:39)

The importance of work is further emphasized by the fact that punishments were sometimes doled out if children did not satisfactorily perform their assigned duties (Dennis 1940:46).

Although the ethnographic data on Puebloan labor allocation is patchy where the participation of children is concerned, the list of economically productive activities in which children were involved is long. Ethnographies and autobiographies attest that children ran errands (Dennis 1940:40), helped adults gather food and raw materials for making basketry (Hough 1915:121), harvested crops (Dennis 1940:40; Hough 1915:121; Naranjo 1992:39), cultivated fields (Dennis 1940:41; Naranjo 1992:39), chased birds and small mammals from the fields (Dennis 1940:40; Hough 1915:56, 69, 121), carried stones for building dwellings (Hough 1915:121; Naranjo 1992:39), gathered wood (Spencer 1899:78), chopped wood (Dennis 1940:40), prepared clay for pottery (Marinsek 1958:51; Naranjo 1992:39; Spencer 1899:78) and materials for basketmaking (Spencer 1899:78), swept plazas (Naranjo 1992:39) and house floors (Dennis 1940:41), carried water (Dennis 1940:41, 83; Marinsek 1958:51; Parsons 1925; Spencer 1899:78; Whitman 1947:42), ground grain (Dennis 1940:41; Hough 1915:63; Marinsek 1958:51), cleaned (Dennis 1940), shelled corn (Dennis 1940:41), cooked (Dennis 1940:41; Naranjo 1992:39), hunted and fished (Naranjo 1992:39), and cared for other children (Dennis 1940:41, 85; Eickemeyer and Eickemeyer 1895:85; Hough 1915:56; Naranjo 1992:39; Spencer 1899:78; Wyaco 1998:12). In addition, ceremonial activities in which children sometimes participated (Parsons 1936a:126) should emically be considered work. Perhaps even more activities would be included had ethnographers paid more attention to children's work.

Both the gender and the age of children were important determinants of the specific jobs allocated to them (Dennis 1940:40–41; Hough 1915:56–69; Marinsek 1958:51; Naranjo 1992:39–40). Wayne Dennis (1940), in perhaps the most complete study of Hopi children, notes that boys were fairly free until about age 6. They then started helping their fathers, gradually increasing the amount of time spent working and the range of their tasks as they matured. Analogously, he reports that "the girl's work is a miniature of the tasks done by her mother" (Dennis 1940:41). By age 8 girls were grinding corn, and by 12 they were expected to stay at home much of the time, which further increased their domestic contribution. In general, as children got older, the amount of time devoted to work appears to have increased, as did the skill levels required for some of the tasks. Cross-cultural studies of children's work show that an early division of labor along gender lines, as observed in recent Puebloan cultures, is the norm (C. Bradley 1987, 1993). When children's work crosses gender lines, it is most frequently boys doing jobs normally associated with women rather than girls participating in men's activities. This is particularly true for young children and may be because in many cultures the young are more frequently in the company of women than men, making it easier for women to control the children's labor (C. Bradley 1993).

An analysis of the patterns of work in historic pueblos (Table 4.1) shows that, not surprisingly, the tasks done most frequently by younger children tend to be easier jobs and ones that need to be performed daily, such as carrying water and caring for children. This pattern reduces the amount of time spent learning, as opposed to doing. Many children's tasks also appear to be time-extensive, that is, they require long periods of involvement but not intense concentration. Examples of such tasks are guarding fields and looking after smaller children. Allocation of this type of work to children allows adults to accomplish jobs for which the children lack the necessary strength or expertise. Because the jobs are daily or in some cases seasonal but daily during the relevant time period, the

TABLE 4.1. TASKS IN HISTORIC PUEBLOS, BY LOCATION AND
FREQUENCY.

Daily	Sporadic	Seasonal
	Dwelling	
Cleaning	House construction	Preparing crops for storage
Chopping wood	Wall plastering	
Grinding corn	Weaving	
Cooking	Sewing	
Sweeping	*Making pottery*	
	Making baskets	
	Making tools	
	Spinning	
	Fields	
	Field maintenance	Planting crops
		Hoeing/Weeding
		Guarding fields
		Harvesting
	Outside the Settlement	
Getting water	Acquiring raw materials	
Bringing firewood	Making trading trips	
	Gathering	
	Hunting and trapping	
	Waging war	
	No Fixed Locale	
Running errands		
Child care		

Notes: Tasks in italics are described as done by children in at least one Pueblo ethnography.
Tasks in bold are done by very young children.

amount of work obtained from the child relative to the period of learning
is maximized. If ethnographic parallels hold, it is also highly likely that
children learned many of their tasks from other children rather than
adults, further reducing the drain on adult energies (Bird and Bird 2000).
Often the work done by children also involves temporal and spatial conflicts with adult work, making the use of children's labor the efficient solution. Thus, bringing water or running errands might require an adult to
leave activities ongoing in the dwelling or in the fields. Guarding a field
necessitates a constant presence, which may not be possible for a single individual if a number of dispersed fields are to be both guarded and cultivated while cooking and other daily, nonseasonal activities continue.

Obviously, tasks given to children cannot surpass their physical or mental capabilities. As children mature, the tasks allotted to them begin to in-

crease in variety and in the strength and expertise required, until they fully mimic adult responsibilities. Thus, by the time children are 8 or 10, they can grind or do fieldwork requiring some strength and are capable of beginning skilled craft production.

Running Errands and Collecting Fuel and Water

For some possible types of children's work, there are either no direct archaeological traces or it is hard to demonstrate that children, rather than another age group, were the laborers. There is no concrete evidence that Sinagua children were used to run errands, collect wood or water, chase small predators from the fields, or care for younger children. Nevertheless, given the criterion of economic productivity in the particular prehistoric circumstances, and coherence with the task-differentiation patterns observed in the nearest ethnographic analogue, it seems likely that these were children's tasks. When possible, methods for archaeologically testing the proposition are suggested below.

Probably few would deny the utility of using children as errand runners, especially when adult work areas were dispersed. For example, at New Caves Pueblo, where we have been excavating recently, the living areas are located a steep 150 to 200 meters from the nearest fields at the base of the cinder cone. For us this means a walk of at least 10 to 15 minutes. Though many of the local inhabitants may have been more adept hikers, the time saving for adults in using children to deliver messages or transfer objects is undeniable, and surely they served this function.

Cross-culturally, gathering fuel is the most common task for children less than 6 years of age (C. Bradley 1993:93). In one-fourth of the societies Candice Bradley sampled, children under 6 gathered fuel. Children in the 6- to 10-year age range collected fuel in 88 percent of the cultures. The vegetation used in fires at Northern Sinagua sites such as Lizard Man Village is primarily piñon and juniper (Hunter et al. 1999), which may well have been gathered as relatively small wood from areas fairly proximate to living sites. Thus, wood gathering for daily use would probably have been physically possible even for very young children.

Cross-culturally, water carrying is another common child's task. For children 6 to 10, 97 percent of Bradley's sample engaged in water carrying, although only 13 percent in the under-6 category did so. In the historic southwestern pueblos, bringing water was one of the first tasks with which children assisted. According to Dennis (1940:83), by the time they were 4, Hopi children were making trips to obtain water, albeit using much smaller containers than their older relatives. Little is known about how the Sinagua acquired their water supplies. Standing and running water is widely dispersed, and most occupation sites are not located immediately adjacent to water. During at least certain seasons of the year each household probably would have needed to make multiple trips to obtain water every day. Given distances from water of up to a couple of miles, this task would have been quite time-consuming and a good use for younger workers. During time periods when metal pails, rather than ceramics, were the method of carrying water, ethnographers noted Hopis providing their young children with appropriately sized containers so that they could help carry water. William Longacre (1981:64) reports that among the Kalinga, "most commonly pots are broken by children, usually on the paths to or from the spring or at the spring as they are cleaning them." Perhaps an analysis of the distribution in the size of water jars found as pot busts in the vicinity of prehistoric water sources or on possible trails leading to them could be used to determine whether children were likely to have been carrying water.

The usefulness of children for the three tasks discussed above clearly depends on the distances the children needed to transverse and/or the culturally perceived appropriateness of the children being unescorted far from home. Clearly, there are some errands that could be done close to home and others that would have necessitated more mobility. For wood and water, the situation is more complex. Wood may have been locally available, but it is also possible that at some sites or in some time periods the immediate surround became somewhat deforested, requiring longer wood-collecting forays. As mentioned earlier, for most sites, accessibility of water resources was always a problem. The ability to use children's labor for more far-flung tasks would presumably depend in part on the safety with which they could venture far from home.

An interesting hypothesis is that this situation may have changed through time for the Sinagua. During the early occupation of the piñon-juniper (ca. A.D. 1050–1250) the political situation appears to have been fairly peaceful. Furthermore, there were many small settlements, none very far apart. Perhaps under these circumstances the surround was viewed as a relatively safe place and children were allowed to have considerable mobility. By the time New Caves was inhabited (ca. A.D. 1250–1300), the population had agglomerated into fewer centers, each much farther apart, and the Sinagua region may have been experiencing the unsettled times characteristic of many other areas of the Southwest (LeBlanc 1999). It is not unlikely that tasks that took children, especially younger ones, far

from home would have been seen as less safe at this time and may have
been removed from children's repertoire.

Crop Protection

Ethnographically, one of the important tasks of southwestern Pueblo children was guarding crops from predators. This is consistent with cross-
cultural data. In C. Bradley's (1993:76, 93) cross-cultural sample, the participation of the very young children (less than 6 years old) in agricultural
activities was not great, but the most common activity, reported in 16 percent of the cultures in her sample, was tending crops, which usually consisted of weeding and/or chasing away birds. The dispersion of fields in
both historic (Beaglehole 1937:15) and prehistoric (Kamp and Whittaker
1999:186–187) times provided an ecological buffer against comprehensive
crop failures. Ancient Puebloan farmers must have spent considerable effort protecting crops from birds and other predators. The necessity of providing almost constant surveillance of fields undoubtedly led to conflicts
with necessary adult activities. One solution would be using children.
Albert Yava, a Tewa born in 1888, recalled that when he was a child, it
was the responsibility of boys to keep "field rats" and crows from the
crops (Yava 1978:6). Similarly, Dennis (1940:40) notes that one of the first
tasks for small boys was guarding the fields from birds and prairie dogs.

Providing almost constant protection during vulnerable periods in the
growing cycle is particularly difficult when fields are dispersed. Frank
Hamilton Cushing (1920) describes temporary structures, often called
field houses, that were constructed by the Zuni near their fields to increase
the convenience of working in areas far from the main pueblo. The prehistoric Sinagua had a similar solution to the dilemma of dispersed fields.
Sinagua field houses are quite numerous, comprising perhaps one-third of
Northern Sinagua sites (Pilles 1976:128). Although field houses appear as
early as the Rio de Flag phase, they do not become abundant until the
post-eruptive expansion of settlement in the piñon-juniper zone. Here
arable land is located both along major drainage systems and in scattered
pockets. A family would have needed to exploit more than a single soil
pocket, which presumably led to population dispersion and the need for
temporary habitation near scattered field sites. The abundance of field-
house sites would be further explained if soil depletion of relatively shallow deposits mandated the periodic abandonment of field areas.

Peter Pilles (1976) compared 31 sites excavated by the Museum of
Northern Arizona as part of the Interstate 40 mitigation procedures (20

field-house sites and 11 habitation sites). He defined field-house sites as small sites (one to four rooms) with relatively unsubstantial architecture, defined as masonry walls of a meter or less, presumably capped by jacal or brush superstructures. Artifact assemblages from field houses, relative to those from habitation sites, were both sparse and limited, possibly with an emphasis on grinding activities; rooms were small, and burials were rare. Generally, hearths were lacking. The Interstate 40 data may not provide the best source for detailed artifact analysis, however, since according to the museum's files, many of the sites had to be excavated very rapidly with no screening. Often small sites were excavated in a single day, which may account for the preponderance of grinding stones relative to smaller artifact categories. More analysis needs to be done to examine the possibility that the remains from field houses represent not just limited activity areas but a limited segment of the workforce, perhaps primarily children and older individuals.

Child Care

Cross-culturally, the care of young children above infant age is almost universally accomplished by other children. In 97 percent of the 91 cultures analyzed by C. Bradley (1993:93), children between the ages of 6 and 10 participated in child care. In some settings even much younger children took charge, usually of younger siblings and other relatives. B. B. Whiting and C. P. Edwards (1988) postulate that children in the 6- to 10-year age range have a particular affinity for the occupation of looking after younger children, which may account for the cross-cultural prevalence of young babysitters. For the historically known Pueblos, numerous ethnographic accounts assign the task of child care to children only slightly older than their charges. Babies were generally entrusted to the care of an older child when they were but a few months old (Dennis 1940:35), and by the age of 5, girls were caring for younger children (Dennis 1940:84). Although babies were generally entrusted to girls, younger children, especially boys, were often looked after by boys as well. Virgil Wyaco (1998:12), a Zuni, recalls:

> In old Zuni, brothers and sisters looked after the younger ones. Mothers were mostly concerned with babies who were still nursing and with food preparation. . . . It was my job to look after my little brother, Lee. Lee went with me everywhere. In winter, up until the time I started school, it didn't matter, because I never went anyplace. In the summertime, though, I was forever having

to wait for him to catch up. My friends all had little brothers, too, so I never felt unfairly burdened.

Although it is impossible to demonstrate archaeologically, it is highly likely that, just as in more recent times, a significant portion of the care of very young children was left to slightly older ones.

Grinding Corn

Grinding corn, hunting, and manufacturing may have also been in the realm of children's work. Because they require more skill or strength than the tasks described above, these tasks may not have been usually allocated to the youngest children. Craft production, specifically ceramic manufacture, is discussed in more detail below, since it is one activity for which I have fairly definitive evidence of the economic productivity of older children. For grinding, the analysis of skeletal remains may provide evidence of girls' participation; for the moment, however, I leave it to someone more clever than I to figure out how to determine the gender of hunters and the age at which they began hunting.

Historically, Pueblo women spent several hours each day grinding corn, since the average family, at least at Hopi, consumed about a quart of cornmeal a day (Bartlett 1933). The amount of time needed for grinding would undoubtedly have made this an attractive chore to share. Walter Hough (1915:63) noted, "Little girls are taught early to grind, and they are often prevailed upon to display their accomplishment before visitors." As mentioned earlier, Dennis (1940:41) put the age at which Hopi girls learn to grind corn at about 8. On the surface, grinding appears to be a daily, repetitive, fairly simple task and thus suited to even earlier learning, but a degree of physical strength and stamina is required for the activity to be effective. It seems unlikely that much efficient grinding could be accomplished by extremely young children, which suggests that historically girls were probably incorporated in this task at as young an age as possible. By puberty girls were expected to be competent grinders, and grinding corn was a component of puberty ceremonies (Dennis 1940:79).

Bone modifications diagnosed as the result of activity patterns such as horseback riding and atlatl use have been identified in a number of archaeological populations (Larsen 1997). Because hours spent grinding corn puts stress on particular bones and muscles, it may be possible to discern archaeologically the involvement of women in grinding by analyzing stress patterns and muscle attachments. In particular, degenerative disease of the elbow has been associated with mano and metate use (Miller 1985; Nagy and Hawkey 1993, cited in Spielmann 1995:96). To some extent these identifications should be considered tentative at present, since despite a considerable literature on the effect of occupational and sports-related traumas, the failure of some researchers to take into account confounding variables such as genetics, weight, age, prior injuries, and bone density casts some doubt on the reliability of much of the research (Jurmain 1999). This problem, plus the fact that a number of possible behavior patterns can yield similar osteological results, makes secure archaeological interpretations complex. Of particular interest to the study of children's labor is some evidence that the young may be at particular risk of damage from repetitive stress on joints (Jurmain 1999). Further research on the sequence and rate of development of osteological indications of stress in conjunction with the analysis of prehistoric populations may yield more information about the youthful assumption of grinding as a household chore.

Craft Production: Ceramic Manufacture

Though an examination of more recent Puebloan societies and cross-cultural data can provide hypotheses about possible labor allocations, the archaeological data are the ultimate referent. The most concrete evidence I have for the economic contributions of children is in ceramic manufacture. Previously, I have argued that it is possible to discern the approximate age of the individuals who formed ceramic vessels based on measurements of the ridges of fingerprints impressed in the damp clays during manufacture (Kamp et al. 1999).

Since fingerprint patterns remain the same while finger size increases during growth, the breadth of the ridges found in fingerprints can be used as a rough index of age. Archaeologically, ridge breadth is a particularly convenient attribute because a complete fingerprint is not required for its measurement. Although there is some variability in ridge breadths among fingers on the same individual and on average between both adult males and females and adults of different ethnic backgrounds, the greatest variation is due to the increases in body size that occur with maturation.

Measurements taken on fingerprints left on small experimentally produced clay quadrupeds produced an equation for predicting age using ridge breadth. Using this equation with a correction factor for clay shrinkage (see Kamp et al. 1999 for details), one can predict the average age of a group of ceramic manufacturers at a 95 percent level of confidence with a margin of error of less than a year. For the prediction of individual ages, the margin of error for a comparable level of confidence is, of course, much higher—about 4.5 years.

A comparative study of the fingerprints on a group of Sinagua figurines and corrugated vessels indicates the potential usefulness of this technique. The figurines examined are small, often poorly formed, and generally of quadrupeds. (Although the Sinagua did produce some human figurines as well, they were not examined.) Fingerprints on figurines from our own excavations (Kamp and Whittaker 1999) and from collections at the Museum of Northern Arizona that showed clear prints were measured. Only 26 specimens showed prints clear enough to include in the sample. For comparison, the prints found in the corrugations of 31 full-sized, locally made Sunset and Elden Corrugated vessels were measured. The average ridge breadth of the fingerprints found on the figurines was 0.37 mm, suggesting an average age of 12. The smallest prints would have been made by someone about 4 (plus or minus 4.5 years) and the largest by an adult. The fingerprints on the ceramic vessels predicted an average age of "adult" with an age range of 10 (plus or minus 4.5 years) to adult.

Thus, the evidence suggests an age dichotomy between the producers of the figurines and those of the full-sized ceramics. The fingerprints from both artifact types suggest some variability, however. Some figurines seem to have been made by adults or at least older teens whose finger ridges were indistinguishable from those of adults. The smallest prints on the corrugated vessels suggest an age of about 10 years. Perhaps not unexpectedly, some of the less expertly made ceramics are within this group. Of the six vessels that I noted were somewhat sloppily made, four had child-sized finger-ridge breadth measurements. Even these vessels are beyond the scope of a very novice potter, however, and are clearly usable ceramics.

I have argued elsewhere (Kamp 2001a) that children begin learning basic ceramic strategies by producing clay figurines and miniature vessels to be used as toys; they progress to small but usable ceramic forms; and then finally, while still in childhood, they make larger, full-sized ceramics such as these corrugated vessels. Similarly, Patricia Crown (1999 and this volume) and Elizabeth Bagwell (this volume), both of whom analyze ceramic production in light of cross-cultural patterns known from child psychology, see children as active in ceramic vessel manufacture. Crown studies primarily the painted designs on ceramics whereas Bagwell concentrates on more plastic elements. All three of us cite ethnographic data supporting the possibility of the involvement of children in ceramic production, but our approaches to the archaeological data are quite different. Nevertheless, the conclusions are strikingly similar that prehistoric Pueblo children made ceramics. In all these instances the children's production appears to be functional, and in some cases the vessels show clear evidence of use wear.

The concrete evidence of children's contribution to southwestern ceramic manufacture is limited to the actual shaping and painting of vessels, but it is likely that juveniles also contributed to other aspects of the manufacturing process: collecting firewood, burnishing, and so forth. Since many of these tasks are easier to learn than the shaping and painting of vessels, the contribution of younger children to these facets is even more likely, and indeed, several ethnographic accounts record juveniles assisting with craft production (Marinsek 1958:51; Naranjo 1992:39–40; Mills 1995; Spencer 1899:78). The issue of the multiple authorship of craft products has been discussed in more detail above.

The reasons for the early incorporation of children into ceramic production can certainly be disputed. On the one hand, involvement in craft production might have been merely a necessary part of the educational process, preparing a child for adult activities. On the other hand, there might have been an actual advantage to incorporating supplementary labor into the production process as rapidly as possible. J. A. Brown (1989) asserts that in the northern Southwest the manufacture of ceramics was more time efficient than making textile or basketry containers because of the labor savings possible with batch production and the fact that the labor required for pottery production was easily incorporated into existing task structures. Crown and Wills (1995a and b), however, argue that the labor required for ceramic manufacture was in fact quite costly. This was less because of the actual labor required to produce a finished ceramic than because of scheduling conflicts with agricultural activities. The cold temperatures of winter in these regions made firing pottery more risky, and therefore ceramic manufacture occurred in the warmer months, precisely the time when labor was needed for agriculture. It could be added that for cultures such as the Sinagua that continued to rely on considerable consumption of wild plants to supplement cultigens, a similar conflict occurred for gathering activities. If in fact scheduling was a problem, the addition of children to the workforce would have both provided more potential person-hours of labor and added flexibility to the organization of the tasks that needed to be completed.

CONCLUSIONS

Archaeologists have tended to underestimate the potential role of children as components of the prehistoric labor force and their ability to accomplish real work. In a study of migrant laborers Robert Coles (1971:63) notes that children "take care of one another, pick crops fast, go fetch water and food at the age or two or three." Similarly, during the industrial revolution children began working in factories at ages as young as 3 or 4 years. Historic Pueblo children had similarly important roles, and children were viewed as an economic asset rather than a liability (Whitman 1947:93).

My examination of the archaeological evidence shows that Sinagua children were definitely producing usable ceramics at an early age. This conclusion corroborates the findings of Crown (1999, this volume) and Bagwell (this volume) and suggests a verifiable economic role for at least some subadults. The participation of children in other jobs, such as child care, running errands, collecting water, guarding agricultural fields from small predators, and grinding, is suggested ethnographically as well as by a task-differentiation analysis à la Spector. As with discerning gender divisions of labor, it may not always be possible to assign ages to specific tasks. Research in this area is, if one can excuse a small pun, just in its infancy, but if we merely allot subadults the role of economic dependent, we are probably misreading the past.

ACKNOWLEDGMENTS

I would like to thank John Whittaker, Michele Hegmon, and an anonymous reviewer for their comments on a previous version of this chapter. A number of students, including Nikki Timmerman, Jules Graybill, and Ian Natowsky, helped with the experiments on finger ridges. The Museum of Northern Arizona, thanks to Tracy Murphy and David Wilcox, provided a hospitable research environment for investigating prehistoric figurines. Obviously, all errors of fact or interpretation remain my own.

5

Ceramic Form and Skill

Attempting to Identify
Child Producers at
Pecos Pueblo, New Mexico

ELIZABETH A. BAGWELL

In the past the products of child ceramic producers have often been identified by their "small" size and "poor" craftsmanship. In this chapter I introduce a technique that quantifies these qualities. This technique measures motor skill gained both through regular practice and through the brain development that comes with age, as it is demonstrated in the production of ceramic forms.

Two sets of literature help establish the basic expectations of this study and provide guidance for measuring the varying abilities of children as they learn to form ceramic vessels. First, archaeological studies of craft production suggest that experience and practice reduce product variability (Blackman et al. 1993; Costin and Hagstrum 1995; Stark 1995). Therefore, as children gain more experience forming vessels, these vessels should be increasingly uniform in shape. Second, psychological studies of cognitive development and motor skills demonstrate that children, as their brains and bodies grow, pass through defined developmental levels (Brown 1975; Crown 1998; Golomb 1993; Harris 1963; Smilansky et al. 1988). At each level, children are developmentally capable of only certain parts of the vessel-forming process, allowing a determination of the minimum age at which a child could have plausibly made that vessel. Attributes found to be sensitive to changes in both experience and developmental level include vessel forming (e.g., pinching vs. coiling, symmetry of vessel form), vessel finishing (e.g., smoothing cracks), and the production of identifiable forms (e.g., bowls vs. jars, Santa Fe Black-on-white). This chapter uses these attributes to compare a sample of miniature and crudely made vessels from Pecos Pueblo, New Mexico, which others (e.g., Kidder 1932) have argued were produced by children, with a set of bowls probably made by adults from the same site. Results of the analysis of these 78 vessels have two broad implications. First, it appears that both children and adults made the Pecos vessels originally identified as the products of children. Second, some attributes of form appear to be more sensitive indicators of age and experience than others.

SKILL AND FORM

One of the ways archaeologists evaluate the skill of a craftperson is to determine the amount of standardization in the products, which is believed to be the result of "the craftperson's experience, proficiency, and talent" (Costin and Hagstrum 1995:623). Standardization is argued to be the reduction of variability (Blackman et al. 1993) or an increase in the uniformity of the product (Stark 1995). If a person spends part of every day making ceramic vessels, his or her skill is expected to increase along with experience. Therefore, when trying to identify levels of skill archaeologically, researchers generally associate higher skill with lower variability, and lower skill with higher variability.

Ethnographic studies of ceramic producers suggest that some of the variables particularly sensitive to increases in skill are related to forming technique (Costin and Hagstrum 1995). These variables include construction and finishing techniques, vessel symmetry and form, rim angles, and vessel wall thickness. Although archaeologists generally accept that forming techniques reflect skill, the measurement of the attribute of skill as it relates to form has rarely been addressed archaeologically, even by authorities on ceramics analysis such as Anna Shepard (1956) and Prudence Rice (1987). The standardization studies mentioned above, however, imply that children and adults new to ceramic production will produce pots that have more variable, irregular forms resulting from a lack of experience. In this study I identify probable child ceramic producers by incorporating the attributes associated with standardization and skill listed above with attributes related to cognitive development and motor skills described below.

AGE AND FORM

Several techniques have been used to determine the relationship between age and skill in prehistoric ceramic producers. Generally, these techniques involve measuring variables that reveal the small size of children's bodies (Kamp et al. 1999), the level of a child's physical development or motor skills, and the level of a child's cognitive development (Crown 1998, 1999, this volume). Cross-cultural studies of motor skills and cognitive development are especially useful sources of attributes that can be used in archaeological studies. In particular, the Harris-Goodenough "Draw-a-Man" cognitive development test (Harris 1963), which has been applied widely to children all over the world, has resulted in a well-known set of stages based on the motor skills and cognitive development through which most children progress. For the most part, these developmental stages have demonstrated cross-cultural validity, are applicable to prehistoric populations, and have been used in archaeological analyses with success. For example, Patricia Crown has applied these general guidelines to the study of poorly decorated prehistoric vessels from three southwestern cultures, where she found that age of introduction to pottery painting varied by region (1998, 1999, this volume).

In light of the extremely successful results of the Harris-Goodenough Test using the two-dimensional medium of drawing, it seems logical that child psychologists and educators would experiment with 3–D mediums such as clay to determine if children's 2–D and 3–D abilities progress at similar rates. Unfortunately, little research of this type has been done, and the few studies that focus on clay and child development adapt the Harris-Goodenough Test to a 3–D medium rather than create new tests (Brown 1975; Golomb 1993; Smilansky et al. 1988).

E. V. Brown (1975) and S. Smilansky et al. (1988), for example, base their research directly on the "Draw-a-Man" test. In Brown's study, whose purpose was to determine at what age children are capable of making certain clay formations, a group of 450 children aged 3 through 11 were asked to form a human shape out of clay. Brown found that at age 3, children rarely made recognizable figures or heads, but they did "push, pull, pat, pound, squeeze, and make holes in the clay with the sharpened dowels or their fingers" (1975:51). At age 4, children were able to make "snakes," balls, and "mud-pies." At age 5, children showed a noticeable increase in their ability to create recognizable human figures. Between ages 9 and 11, children made increasingly realistic human figures. Brown argues that these oldest children are capable of much more than the simple pinch pots and ashtrays they were frequently asked to make. When compared with drawings of men made by the same children, the clay figures were found to be distinctly less sophisticated. Nevertheless, Brown argues convincingly that this disparity reflects a lack of exposure to 3–D media at an early age.

The results of these studies are promising for archaeologists interested in identifying the age of child ceramic producers. There are two problems with applying the results of the "Draw-a-Man" type of test to archaeological studies of form and skill, however. First, this test is based on a scale of realism in depiction (Smilansky et al. 1988, the "Cognitive Clay Test"). Realism in the depiction of human figures is a skill that is valued in Western industrialized societies, but that is not necessarily the case in other cultures (Golomb 1993:3); thus, archaeological models based on this test must take cross-cultural variability into account (Crown 1999). One way to avoid this difficulty is to deemphasize the importance of human figures, which may often be represented symbolically rather than realistically. Further, the identification of *any* recognizable form successfully measures the skill of "realism of depiction," even if the form is a human with a bird's head and a snake's tail.

Second, most "stage" theories "stress the young child's cognitive limitations and base their interpretation on so-called childlike characteristics of drawing, for example, mixed views, the flatness of figures, the juxtaposition of sides, transparencies, and lack of three-dimensional skill in the portrayal of a scene" (Golomb 1993:3). Claire Golomb argues that some of the primitive qualities in drawings that have been interpreted as cognitive immaturity may in fact represent the child's struggle to represent three-dimensional objects in a two-dimensional medium, a skill that many adults never master. In addition, she maintains that conceptualizing three-dimensionally is a cognitive ability that develops as early as the ability to conceptualize one- or two-dimensionally. For example, her study of 109 children aged 4 to 13 found that all the children were capable of producing the three-dimensional qualities of a cup, although the younger children's models were cruder.

The point here is that we cannot take it for granted that increasing skill in clay modeling has the same developmental progression as in drawing. Therefore, age estimates based on the "Draw-a-Man" test, or variations of it, may not be as reliable for estimating the age of 3–D producers as it appears to be for estimating the age of prehistoric 2–D producers. Nevertheless, I believe that some of the child development literature specifically devoted to clay, especially Brown's 1975 work, has enough information to allow us to create preliminary archaeological models. Based on Brown 1975 and Crown 1999, I argue that children are unlikely to begin making pots before the age of 4. At this point they are capable of making pinch pots, which are clearly three-dimensional but may not be symmetrical. Children are capable of making recognizable forms by age 5 but are more secure in this ability by age 9. From this perspective, I expect that by age 9 children should be capable of making recognizable "forms" of pots (Table 5.1).

THE ANALYTIC TECHNIQUE

I propose a technique that combines Crown's (1999) and Brown's (1975) adaptations of 2–D cognitive development tests with archaeological studies of standardization in craft production, as described above. This technique measures key attributes that reflect the skill and associated age of the producer, using forming techniques, symmetry, and the reproduction of known shapes (Brown 1975; Costin and Hagstrum 1995; Crown 1999; see Kamp 2001a for a similar analysis). Specifically, the attributes are construction technique, symmetry of the maximum dimension, evenness of the rim, consistent wall angle, how well the base holds the vessel flat and even, presence of cracking, consistent rim thickness, and recognizable forms. Decorative attributes—in particular, polish, slip, paint, and glaze—are not part of this technique since there is a possibility that the person who formed the vessel and the person who decorated the vessel were different individuals with different skill levels (Golomb 1993). Following Crown (1999), each attribute is assigned two to four levels representing various levels of skill that are assumed to correspond to increasing levels of both experience and age. Lower numbers represent a lower level of

TABLE 5.1. TWO- AND THREE-DIMENSIONAL ABILITIES, BY AGE (AFTER CROWN 1999).

Age (years)	Two Dimensions (drawing)	Three Dimensions (Forming Techniques)
<2	Materials used but nothing really made (scribbling)	Materials used but nothing really made (push, pound, squeeze, make holes)
4	Hold tools in adult manner, make symmetrical designs	Snakes, balls, mud pies; symmetry possible
5–7	Basic geometric shapes possible	Recognizable forms common
8–13	Culturally specific styles; realistic drawings; perspective and proportion	Increasing realism; secure in recognizable forms; near adult forming techniques

skill, and higher numbers represent a higher level of skill (Table 5.2). By adding the value of each attribute for each pot, a total "skill score" between 8 and 21 is calculated.

This technique employs attributes related to construction techniques, symmetry, and standardization into recognizable types. In the case of *construction techniques*, pinched pots are considered easier to make than coiled pots. Pinched pots are one of the earliest forms that children are capable of making, perhaps as young as the age of 4 (Golomb 1993). At what age children are able to construct coiled pots is unclear, although at the age of 4 they can form coils, or "snakes." It is likely that there is a relationship between age and the size of coil a child is able to make. Small, very long coils, such as those used in ceramic production, are probably

TABLE 5.2. SCORES OF ATTRIBUTES USED TO CALCULATE LEVEL OF SKILL.

1. Construction technique
    1—pinched
    2—coiled
2. Cracking
    1—cracks related to forming or drying and not smoothed before firing
    2—no cracks of this type
3. Symmetry—maximum dimension (viewed from above)
    1—very irregular
    2—irregular
    3—oval or egg-shaped (firing related?)
    4—nearly round
4. Evenness of rim
    1—very irregular
    2—irregular
    3—even/smooth
5. Consistent rim thickness
    1—range greater than 4 mm
    2—range between 2 and 4 mm
    3—range less than 2 mm
6. Consistent wall angle (viewed from the side)
    1—no
    2—yes
7. Base holds vessel flat and even
    1—no
    2—yes
8. Form identifiable to a specific glaze or b/w period
    1—no
    2—identification slightly ambiguous but can be narrowed to a few types
    3—yes

more difficult to make, but this topic needs more study. In addition, skilled potters usually smooth away cracks resulting from the forming or drying of a vessel. If the cracks cannot be smoothed away, these vessels are usually discarded before firing (Rye 1981). The presence of cracks, therefore, suggests that the producer has less skill.

The *symmetry* of a ceramic vessel can be determined by examining its shape from above, the profile of its walls and rim, and the shape of its base. In the case of the symmetry of a vessel's maximum dimension, perfectly round, highly standardized shapes or standardized irregular shapes (e.g., Navajo wedding vessels) are considered the most difficult to make and irregular shapes are considered the least difficult (Costin and Hagstrum 1995; Blackman et al. 1993; Hagstrum 1985; Stark 1995). Large vessels made by skilled adult potters have even rims often trimmed or smoothed with a tool. Even rims with less variation represent more skill, and bumpy rims with more variation less skill (Costin and Hagstrum 1995; Blackman et al. 1993; Hagstrum 1985; Stark 1995). In the case of rim thickness, I assume that less variability in a range of four measurements per vessel indicates a higher level of skill (Blackman et al. 1993; Costin and Hagstrum 1995; Hagstrum 1985; Stark 1995). Keeping the wall angle (the shape of the profile) of a bowl at a consistent, standard angle requires more skill than allowing it to vary (Blackman et al. 1993; Costin and Hagstrum 1995; Hagstrum 1985; Stark 1995). Finally, determining if a vessel base holds it flat and even is essentially a measure of consistent wall height as well as stability. Since many prehistoric bowls have rounded bottoms, they cannot be expected to be perfectly stable. Nevertheless, a bowl should not tip so severely when placed on a flat surface that the contents spill out. The construction of a bowl that does not tip severely and a lack of variation in wall height require more skill (Blackman et al. 1993; Costin and Hagstrum 1985; Hagstrum 1995; Stark 1995).

Brown (1975) and Crown (1998) argue that all children reach a point where they are able to make recognizable and culturally appropriate forms. This stage appears to occur around the age of 9. Therefore, in this technique I assume that vessels that can be assigned to a specific archaeological type require more skill to make than those that cannot be assigned to a specific type. In the case of the Pecos classification, vessels are primarily distinguished by vessel form, particularly that of the rim, and broad decorative attributes. For example, the lead glaze paint used on these vessels becomes increasingly runny over time, indicating higher and higher lead content. Paste composition, in contrast, is primarily geographically rather than temporally sensitive (Shepard 1956).

Because of a lack of experimental data from psychologists, educators, and archaeologists, "skill scores" calculated using this 3–D technique are difficult to associate with actual ages. The highest scores most likely represent an adult producer age 16 or older, and the lowest scores likely represent a very young child producer no younger than 4 years old (Brown 1975; Crown 1999). Unfortunately, there are a variety of reasons why a pot might appear "poorly made" to an archaeologist. An adult may not choose to put a large amount of effort into the project; he or she may be developmentally limited as a result of injury, disease, or extreme old age; or an individual may adopt ceramic production as an adult (also discussed by Crown, this volume). This study therefore produces a minimum estimate of age. Still, the advanced motor skills of a normal adult make it unlikely that vessels produced by inexperienced or inattentive adults would receive an extremely low skill score.

Finally, the presence or absence of use wear (Schiffer and Skibo 1989) is recorded in the hopes of finding differential wear patterns on different sized and poorly made vessels. In her study of poorly painted southwestern ceramics, Crown (1998, 1999) found that many of these vessels exhibited high use wear, implying that they were considered acceptable for daily use. If poorly made vessels functioned as children's practice pieces, a high level of use wear might imply a similar kind of acceptance. Since most ceramic vessels functioned as containers (Braun 1983), miniatures and poorly made vessels that were practice pieces or toys are expected to show wear consistent with their use as containers. Such wear includes interior marks that suggest stirring and worn spots on the bottom of the vessel where it was regularly set on a rough surface during use. As use wear is not related to producer skill, the presence or absence of use wear is not included as part of the evaluation of skill level.

THE SAMPLE

Miniature and Poorly Made Vessels in the American Southwest

Scholars who study ceramic vessels of the Prehispanic American Southwest often attribute miniature and poorly made vessels to child producers, for two main reasons. First, it is proposed that these vessels were made by children to be used as toys, and second, it is suggested that they were made as practice pieces by children learning to become potters. Children are assumed to be less skilled at pottery making than adults—one possible explanation of the crude forms of some miniatures. Ethnographic studies have found that in some cultures children make miniature objects to use as toys, findings supported by archaeological evidence (Kamp et al. 1999;

Kamp 2001a). Other studies suggest that children make vessels to practice or imitate adults while being socialized as craft specialists or learning the domestic tasks necessary to run a household (Crown 1998, 1999, this volume). These two approaches are by no means mutually exclusive, as play activities may enhance the learning process for very young children (Kamp 2001a).

Other scholars have argued that miniature and poorly made vessels were made by adults for ritual purposes. Vessels with ritual functions have been noted by the art historian S. G. Kenagy (1986). She points out that population movements and settlement aggregation in the Southwest between A.D. 1300 and 1600 are associated with an increase in Pueblo miniature ceramic forms found in ritually suggestive contexts. Alfred Kidder (1932) also noted these vessels and suggested that caches of them were part of the fulfillment of a ritual or part of the paraphernalia of an esoteric society. Ethnographic accounts support these interpretations. For example, Katherine Bartlett (1934) notes that Hopi potters occasionally leave small, poorly made vessels as offerings at clay sources. In some Tewa villages, miniature vessels are described as holding water from each of the cardinal directions, with a seventh holding water from all directions mixed together. Other accounts describe the vessels as filled with water, hung from a large image of the water serpent, and carried through town (Kenagy 1986). Clearly, distinguishing between adult and child producers will have the additional advantage of clarifying the function of some vessels.

The Pecos Collection

In order to distinguish between child and adult producers, I applied the "skill score" method described above to a sample of 78 bowls—large and small, poorly made and well made—from the site of Pecos, New Mexico. Pecos was a large farming village that was occupied between A.D. 1300 and 1838 by an estimated maximum of 1,000 inhabitants. The Spanish established a large mission there around A.D. 1620. The site is on a high flat ridge about a mile west of where the Pecos River emerges from the Sangre de Cristo Mountains. Kidder excavated this site between 1915 and 1929. Much of his excavation was focused on trenching the extremely deep middens at the site, although he also excavated many rooms, kivas, and part of the plaza (Kidder 1924). Kidder's excavations resulted in the collection of nearly 2,000 human skeletons and a large number of artifacts. Unfortunately, the artifact collection is biased toward whole and unusual specimens and so cannot be considered a representative sample. In addition,

Figure 5.1. Miniature bowls from Pecos, natural size. Kidder 1932:134, Figure 111. Courtesy of Yale University Press.

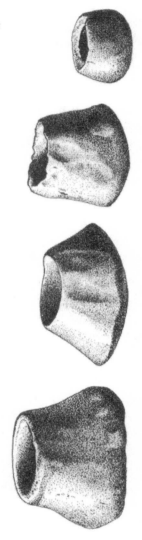

Figure 5.2. Miniature pot-shaped vessels from Pecos, natural size. Kidder 1932:135, Figure 112. Courtesy of Yale University Press.

only artifacts associated with burials have specific proveniences. Other artifacts are referred to the kiva, room, or trench in which they were discovered, but no other provenience is provided.

The ceramics from this excavation were compiled into the well-known Rio Grande Glaze Sequence (Kidder and Shepard 1936), in which types were distinguished primarily by rim form. This sequence, designated A–F or I–VI, places Rio Grande Glaze Ware bowls into six overlapping phases between A.D. 1315 and 1700. Petrographic analyses of vessels from Pecos have determined that although many were produced at the site, a large number were made in other parts of the Rio Grande region, particularly the Galisteo Basin. Since its formulation, this temporal sequence has been used by archaeologists to date archaeological sites in the northern Rio Grande area (Lange et al. 1989).

An unusual aspect of the Pecos ceramic collection is the large number of miniature vessels, perhaps the largest collection from a single site in the entire Southwest. Kidder identifies 81 bowls, 201 jars, 34 ladles, and 8 unusual shapes—324 vessels in all (see Figures 5.1 and 5.2). He defines these vessels by three attributes: a maximum diameter of less than 3 inches (7.5 cm), "crude" manufacture, and a lack of slip, paint, or polish. Kidder's functional explanations of these unusual vessels are explicit in their assumptions about the relationship between children and these vessels: "The natural supposition that they were toys is strengthened by their battered condition. Their contemporaneity with the effigies and bells, and their similarity in material and workmanship to those possibly ceremonial objects, makes it appear that with them they constituted a complex of small clay cult objects, which, perhaps, were turned over to the children after they had fulfilled their primary function" (1932:137). In other words, Kidder argues that these vessels were *made* by adults for ritual purposes and then *used* by children at some later time, perhaps in a pattern similar to that noticed by Bartlett (1934) among the Hopi. At other sites in the Southwest, however, extremely similar vessels have been argued to be the products of children (Crown 1998, 1999, this volume; Kamp et al. 1999). The technique proposed here provides a way of testing the assumptions of Kidder and others about the relationship between children and miniature and poorly made vessels.

To perform this test, I selected a sample of 78 bowls from the Pecos collection. The sample was limited to bowls for several reasons. First, bowls are the most abundant miniature vessel type in the Pecos collection; the sample was large enough that I was able to use a single site for the analysis rather than combine vessels from several sites. Second, the Pecos collection contains a large sample of intact larger vessels, presumably made by adult producers, that could reasonably serve as a comparative set. Kidder and Shepard (1936) note several patterns in these vessels. Glaze I and II bowls can be divided into two distinct size classes: large, or 10.5–13.5 inches (26.25–33.75 cm), and small, or 6–9 inches (15–22.5 cm). In Glazes III through V, however, vessel size forms an even gradation increasing through time: Glaze III, 6–13 inches (15–32.5 cm); Glaze IV, 8.25–13.5 inches (20.6–33.75 cm); and Glaze V, 9–16.25 inches (22.5–40.6 cm). My sample of 78 vessels was chosen to form an even gradation between 2.9 and 34.6 cm, including 34 vessels Kidder defines as miniatures (< 7.5 cm), 28 he defines as full-size vessels (15–40.6 cm), and 16 intermediate vessels (> 7.5 and < 15 cm) that do not fit into either classification. In addition, the full range of vessel quality was represented in each of these size classes. Third, the identification of the vessel form to a specific type is based on the Rio Grande Glaze Sequence, which is most reliable for bowls. In this case the temporal aspect of the sequence is not important, only that the vessels can be grouped into recognizable forms. Finally, since symmetry of the maximum dimension was one of the key variables related to both brain development and experience, I further limited my analysis to bowls whose the maximum dimension could easily be measured.

RESULTS

The 3–D skill-score technique was applied to the sample described above, and the results have implications for the success of this method in measuring levels of cognitive development and for the function of these vessels. After examining each vessel and recording the eight variables related to skill—construction technique, symmetry, evenness of rim, consistent wall angle, base holds vessel flat and even, cracking, consistent rim thickness, and identifiable form (Table 5.2)—I calculated an overall "skill score" for each vessel. This score can range from 8, representing the least skill, to 21, representing the most skill. In the Pecos sample I found that the distribution of skill level is tri-modal (Figure 5.3). There is a cluster of 53 vessels with a skill level in the high range, between 18 and 21. The second cluster, 13 vessels, has middle-level skill scores, between 15 and 17. The lower scores cluster between 12 and 14, with a total of 12 vessels. These clusters may represent cognitive developmental stages of the people who formed the vessels.

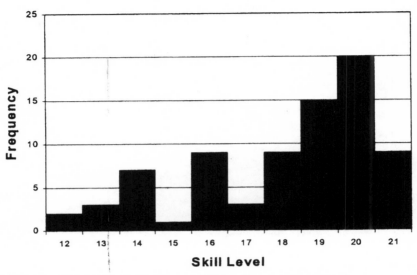

Figure 5.3. Tri-modal distribution of skill level in ceramic production.

Age, Skill, and Ceramic Production

Some of the data fits with what we know about child development and form, and some of it does not (Table 5.3). Vessels in the low-skill group were likely made by children who could make pinch pots (100 percent) but had not yet become very skilled at it, so their pots often cracked (50 percent) during forming and drying. Some of these children were capable of making recognizable forms (8 percent), but most were not. Few of these individuals (8–17 percent) were capable of forming even rims, consistent wall angles, or flat and even vessel bases. They were distinctly more successful in creating a symmetrical maximum dimension (42 percent). Based on Brown (1975) and Crown (1998, 1999), these data suggest that the children who made these vessels were between the ages of 4 and 9.

Vessels in the medium-skill group also have some characteristics that fit with what is known about cognitive development and some that do not. There appears to have been an increase in skill between the low- and medium-skill groups (Table 5.3). This increase implies changes in cognitive development, but these results are not as conclusive as results from

TABLE 5.3. KEY ATTRIBUTES AND THEIR RELATIONSHIP TO SKILL LEVEL (IN PERCENT).

Attribute	Skill Level		
	Low Skill (score of 12–14; n = 12)	Medium Skill (score of 15–17; n = 13)	High Skill (score of 18–21; n = 53)
Coiled construction	0	23	75
No cracking	50	31	92
Symmetrical maximum dimension	42	92	100
Even rim	8	94	94
Consistent rim thickness	91	92	94
Consistent wall angle	8	69	94
Flat and even base	17	15	96
Form identifiable	8	23	62
			68

drawing-related studies such as Crown's (1998, 1999). If this "medium" level represents a cognitive stage, it is at this stage that children become capable of making coiled pots (23 percent) and more skilled at representing recognizable forms (23 percent). Brown (1975) has noted that children become increasingly skilled at making realistic figures between the ages of 9 and 11, but there is no research available that can tell us when children are capable of performing any of the other tasks mentioned above using the clay medium. Some aspects of the ability to create symmetrical forms go through dramatic changes at this stage. Few of these individuals are able to make vessels with flat and even bases (15 percent). Other abilities, however, increase: creating a symmetrical maximum dimension increases from 42 to 92 percent, making even rims from 8 to 92 percent, and forming consistent wall angles from 8 to 69 percent. The first two attributes reach full adult status at the medium skill level, but the third does not, suggesting that forming consistent wall angles may be a more difficult task and thus a key attribute for future studies.

Vessels in the high-skill category appear to represent a cognitive level of development associated with adults (Table 5.3). These individuals appear to have mastered some of the more difficult skills involved in forming a ceramic vessel: using the coiling technique (75 percent), making a recognizable form (68 percent) (Figure 5.4), preventing a vessel from cracking while forming it (92 percent), and forming a symmetrical vessel in most aspects (62–100 percent). For example, Figure 5.4 shows the profile of a large and a miniature bowl, both of which can be identified as Glaze 5

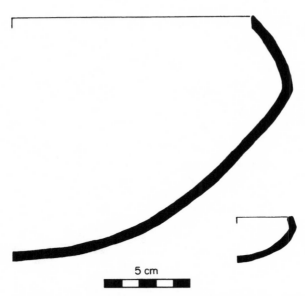

Figure 5.4. Pecos Collection Glaze 5 shouldered bowls 65054 and 72993. Drawing by the author.

shouldered bowls in the Rio Grande Glaze Sequence. Forming a flat and even base continues to be either a difficult skill to master or one that was not considered particularly important for the successful functioning of the vessel. Clearly, the people who made these pots were both skilled and experienced. Unfortunately, the order in which young potters are capable of learning to form pots that are symmetrical, coiled, uncracked, and have identifiable forms is not known. Further experiments specifically oriented toward archaeological interests are needed to help refine our ability to identify additional age groups.

The Function of Miniature and Poorly Made Vessels

The assumptions regarding function underlying our definitions of southwestern miniature and poorly made pots can be formulated as the following hypotheses: (1) large, normal-sized vessels were made by skilled adults and will show evidence of use as a container (use wear); (2) small vessels functioning as toys or as practice pieces will show a low level of skill and were made by children; and (3) small vessels designed to function in ritual contexts were made by adults and will show a high level of skill. In order

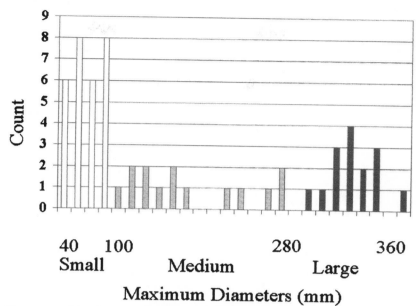

Figure 5.5. Distribution of maximum diameters for small, medium, and large vessels.

to evaluate the relationships between skill score and vessel size, between skill score and context of vessel recovery, and between vessel size and use wear, I divided the sample of 78 bowls from Pecos into three size classes based on maximum diameter. Three size classes different from those defined by Kidder are apparent: the 42 "small" pots are those with a maximum diameter between 3.5 cm and 9.5 cm, the 21 "medium" pots are those with maximum diameters between 9.6 cm and 28.5 cm, and the 15 "large" pots are those with maximum diameters between 28.6 cm and 36.5 cm (Figure 5.5). I then calculated the average skill score for each size class. Large vessels had an average skill score of 20.07, well within the high or adult skill level group shown in Table 5.4. Eighty-six percent of the vessels in the large size class also show evidence of use wear, suggesting that they were used regularly as containers. The first hypothesis is thus confirmed by the data in this study. Medium vessels had an average skill score of 19.43, which is also well within the high or adult skill level group. In addition, 86 percent of these vessels had use wear. Overall, these results suggest that vessels in the medium-size class should be grouped with vessels in the large-size class, since all of them appear to have been made by adults and used in a similar manner.

TABLE 5.4. RELATIONSHIP BETWEEN VESSEL SIZE AND SKILL LEVEL.

Vessel Size	Average Skill Level	Standard Deviation	Corrected CV
Small	16.70	2.36	14.19
Medium	19.43	1.98	9.25
Large	20.07	0.92	4.64

The results of the analysis of the small-size class are more complicated. The average skill score for this size class is 16.7, clearly in the medium skill level, which ranges between 15 and 17 points (Figure 5.5). These results suggest the producers of these small vessels were considerably less skilled than the producers of the medium and large vessels. Further, since only 24 percent of the small vessels show any evidence of use wear, these vessels clearly had a different function from that of the medium and large vessels. In order to get a better understanding of the small vessels' functional role, I performed a corrected coefficient of variation test exploring the relationship between size and skill level. I found that the medium and large vessels had relatively low amounts of variation (Table 5.4). This test confirms the results of the other tests I performed on these size classes. All of them suggest that all these vessels were made by people with a high level of skill. Variation among the small vessels, however, was relatively large. This result suggests that some of the small vessels were made by highly skilled producers, and others were made by producers with less skill. This is exactly the pattern one would expect if the second and third hypotheses above are correct. Small vessels made by adults for ritual purposes should have high skill scores whereas small vessels made by children should have low skill scores. Therefore, it appears that all the hypotheses have been confirmed. In the specific case of Pecos, however, Kidder's argument that the miniature and crudely made vessels were made by adults for ritual purposes has been only partially supported. Some of the vessels in the sample indeed seem to have served that function. The others, I argue, show clear evidence of being formed by children.

CONCLUSIONS

The technique I have presented for identifying the age of a ceramic producer by examining attributes related to experience and cognitive development was partially successful, in that distinct changes were noted. The attributes relating to the ability to create identifiable forms, use coiled construction, and form a consistent wall angle co-vary, suggesting a progression through low, medium, and high skill levels. Attributes relating to the ability to prevent vessel cracking, form a symmetrical maximum dimension, form an even rim, and create a flat and even base appear to be less sensitive indicators, differentiating only between low and high skill. The attribute of consistent rim thickness was consistent at all skill levels and therefore may not be useful for this sort of analysis. This method has a great deal of potential, but it needs to be supported by more knowledge about how children learn to work with clay. Cross-cultural tests that focus on archaeological questions rather than psychological ones need to be developed and implemented. Finally, the results suggest that contrary to Kidder's original assumption, miniature vessels at Pecos Pueblo were made by both children and adults and probably served as toys and practice pieces as well as ritual objects. This finding suggests that archaeologists need to take a closer look at miniature and poorly made vessels before assuming their function is known. Future discussions of these vessels would be greatly improved by the availability of a set of terms to describe their large amount of variation. In particular, since vessel form is so dependent on terms implying perfect symmetry, terms and techniques that can describe and measure asymmetry would be especially helpful.

ACKNOWLEDGMENTS

I would like to thank the Robert S. Peabody Museum of Archaeology and the Pecos National Historical Park for permission to study the vessels used in this study. In particular, the assistance of Bill Crutz, Judy Reid, and Malinda Blustain was invaluable. I would also like to thank Kathryn Kamp for inviting me to participate in this volume and Patricia Crown for providing inspiration and guidance. Finally, the comments of Shawn Penman, Ana Steffen, Debra Murray, Christine VanPool, Todd VanPool, Michelle Hegmon, and an anonymous reviewer for the University of Utah Press greatly improved this chapter.

6

Learning and Teaching
in the Prehispanic
American Southwest

PATRICIA L. CROWN

Maintenance of cultural traditions requires transmission of knowledge from one generation to the next. Much learning begins in childhood, as children seek and are taught the knowledge they need to become competent adults. Yet the specific means by which knowledge is transmitted to children differ among cultures. Some of the differences are the ages at which children begin learning adult tasks, the traditional learning frameworks, and the degrees to which adults are involved in teaching. These issues are pivotal in understanding how children are incorporated into the craft production process, the importance of child labor in the production of crafts, how individuals become fully functioning members of a community of craftspeople, the potential for error or innovation in creating crafts, and how adult potters allocate time.

Studies of middle-range and complex societies reveal that children often perform crucial aspects of craft production, particularly during periods of peak demand (Arnold 1999; Lackey 1982; London 1986; Mills 1997). In the production of ceramics among full-time craft specialists, children are often brought into pottery production at an early age, performing whatever tasks they can and gradually learning to become skilled potters (Lave and Wenger 1991). The labor of children has economic value for such potters (C. Bradley 1993). Potters who produce ceramics in a domestic context for their own use may not require as much help in the production process, but in these less complex, middle-range societies, children must learn to manufacture pottery along with other domestic chores to prepare to run their own households (e.g., DeBoer 1990; Sillar 1994).

Learning frameworks include observation and imitation, verbal instruction, hands-on demonstration, and self-teaching (Schiffer and Skibo 1987:597; Whiting and Edwards 1988:16–17). In middle-range societies, observational learning and imitation of skilled adults is a common form of transmitting knowledge (Bunzel 1972; Crown 1999; DeBoer 1990; Fortes 1938; Goody 1989; Lave and Wenger 1991; Pettit 1946; Roe 1995:51; although see Gosselain 1998:94 and Wallaert-Pêtre 2001). An analysis of 100 middle-range societies documented in the Human Relations Area Files reveals that among the 25 pottery-making groups for which observations were available, in 48 percent children learned pottery production by observation/imitation alone, in 24 percent they received some verbal instruction from adults in domestic contexts, and in 28 percent they learned through more formal apprenticeships.

Ethnographic accounts from the American Southwest corroborate these cross-cultural data. Historically, Pueblo girls learned to make pottery in domestic contexts largely by observation and imitation of their mothers, aunts, grandmothers, or other adult females (Bunzel 1972; Lewis et al. 1990; Fowler 1977; Hill 1982:139; John-Steiner 1975; Stanislawski and Stanislawski 1978; Wyckoff 1985). Girls decided when they were interested in learning to make pottery, although they were expected to have mastered all the tasks associated with running a household by the marriageable age of 15. Formal direct instruction was rare, although adults sometimes corrected children who were imitating them and gave brief instructions or critiqued their finished products (Fowler 1977:29; Hill 1982:139). Questioning was discouraged, and if brief instructions were given, they were offered only once. Adults are quoted as stating that children understood the process more thoroughly when they learned through trial and error (Lewis et al. 1990). Learning apparently followed a sequence that mirrored the production process, with forming of vessels at the youngest age, followed by decoration and finally firing, with the progression largely driven by the child's interest and skill level. There is no mention of children aiding adults in making or decorating pots.

In this chapter I examine Prehispanic southwestern learning frameworks and adult involvement in the learning process using a large sample of ceramic vessels (see also Crown 1999, 2001). The interaction between child and skilled potter necessary for learning the craft varied in cultures throughout the Prehispanic Southwest, with children receiving varied input and adults allocating varied effort to the task of teaching. Adults had greater involvement than is documented in the ethnographic record. Furthermore, in some areas and some time periods unskilled children learned partly through working collaboratively with skilled adults in pottery production rather than simply observing and imitating as described in historic accounts. Finally, I found that children were potential sources of labor in finishing vessel designs.

DATA AND METHODS

Virtually all sedentary populations living in the American Southwest after A.D. 500 regularly used pottery with painted decorations. Studies indicate that nonspecialist potters produced most southwestern pottery for household use, although part-time specialized production of pottery occurred at specific times and places (see chapters in Mills and Crown, eds. 1995). Females were probably responsible for forming and firing the vessels and in most areas for decorating them as well. Researchers draw these inferences using cross-cultural analogy, historical data on southwestern groups, and the incidence of potter's kits in Prehispanic mortuary contexts (Mills and Crown 1995). Some scholars argue that men painted the representational imagery on Mimbres pottery, based on the subject matter (Brody 1977:116; Hegmon and Trevathan 1996; Jett and Moyle 1986:716–717). Among the historic Pueblos, men often painted vessels made by women.

Since 1996 I have examined whole vessels in collections throughout the United States in order to understand how children learned to become competent craftspeople in the middle-range societies of the American Southwest. The study makes a number of assumptions. First, I assume that there were children in the Prehispanic Southwest, and that, like children worldwide in all time periods, these children were expected to learn the skills required in adult life. The production of ceramics was only one of many skills required of adults. I assume that, like other activities, children learning to make ceramics left residues in the archaeological record. These residues can be recognized by using methods and theory for distinguishing the work of learners from the work of knowledgeable potters.

There is a vast literature in educational psychology, with a strong cross-cultural framework, on how children learn to draw and gain knowledge of culturally appropriate techniques and styles. Children worldwide acquire skill in drawing in regular patterns of development, which are based on burgeoning cognitive maturity, improving motor skills, and practice (defined here as repeated action). Although these skills are tied to the relative age of the child, the exact chronological age at which a child acquires specific skills varies, depending on a number of factors, including access to materials and amount of practice (Crown 1999:31, 2001). This research provides an appropriate theory that can be extended into the past through a uniformitarian argument. That is, if the children throughout the world in the last century acquired drawing skills in the same sequence, children in the past did as well. Although children in the American Southwest did not have pencils and paper, they had paintbrushes and pigments, and with these materials they progressed through the same stages of learning their own artistic styles as children do today. Studies in educational psychology also provide a strong methodology for assessing this learning process among Prehispanic southwestern children. Drawing tests used for educational and psychological evaluation of children examine specific attributes of the drawings that provide a measure of relative age and cognitive maturity of the artist (see particularly Goodnow 1977; John-Steiner 1975). Similarly, researchers find that children working with clay progress through developmental sequences similar to those with drawing materials, with greater motor control over the finished product and greater ability to produce a symmetrical, stable form (Brown 1975; Golomb 1993; Smilanksy et al. 1988; see also Bagwell, this volume).

Thus, I assume that just as the work of modern child artists and artisans is distinguishable from the work of adult artists and artisans on the basis of certain features (see also DeBoer 1990), so the work of ancient child artisans is distinguishable from the work of their contemporary adult artisans (Bernbeck 1999). Learning a craft entails moving toward competence in completing a task, including efficiency in executing gestures and replicability in achieving a desired finished product. Experienced craftspeople make objects that exhibit skill in technology and design. Their work reflects motor coordination and cognitive maturity. Their designs fit within culturally appropriate parameters, which are recognizable on the basis of large samples of vessels with similar designs, symmetries, layouts, and execution. They execute even intricate designs with efficient, minimal gestures, for instance, painting a spiral as a single, graceful line. In contrast, inexperienced learners make objects that lack skill in technology and design and that reflect their lesser motor coordination and cognitive maturity. Their designs have errors, poor execution, faulty layout, and unintentional asymmetry. Tellingly, learners are not efficient in completing tasks and paint lopsided spirals as series of short, choppy lines. Because of these differences in ability, when a type of pottery requires a high level of skill, including intricate designs, some vessels in an assemblage stand out as lacking the technology, form, or design qualities characteristic of the products of skilled potters (Bernbeck 1999). Such vessels are largely the products of child learners.

After a pilot study (Crown 1999) I examined collections of whole vessels from the Arizona State Museum, Field Museum of Natural History, Museum of Northern Arizona, Museum of New Mexico, Peabody Museum at Harvard University, Smithsonian Institution/Museum Support Center, and Weisman Art Museum in Minneapolis, searching for vessels with the attributes distinctive of unskilled learners. At each of these museums I inspected all Prehispanic decorated vessels, focusing particularly on bichrome and polychrome wares made after about A.D. 700 in the Chaco, Hohokam, Hopi, Mimbres, Reserve, Salado, and northern Chihuahua areas. These wares were selected because previous research provides information on production locales and the organization of production for each and because the technology and designs on the vessels are generally of a high quality. The fact that the great majority of vessels are well made and well painted makes it easier to distinguish the small sample of poorly made and poorly painted vessels of these wares. From each ware I selected vessels for further analysis that exhibited attributes characteristic of unskilled learners. I also selected a small sample of vessels characteristic of highly skilled artisans for comparative purposes. I ultimately selected 845 vessels from the collections for further analysis, a sample that represents less than 5 percent of the total vessels examined.

In comparison with the "standard" vessels in the assemblages, the designs, forms, or technology of the sample vessels reflected poor motor coordination and less cognitive maturity in understanding traditional pottery making and decorating sequences. There are various possible explanations for the poor quality of these vessels, most related to the lower motor skills and cognitive maturity of the artisans. The most likely possibilities are that the artisans were mentally or physically impaired adults or were children. On strictly logical grounds, it seems most probable that children were involved in making these vessels because the incidence of children in villages is certain whereas the incidence of mentally or physically impaired individuals is speculative. Two art educators viewed the designs on the vessels used in the pilot study and confirmed that children likely painted them, although they could not rule out adults with the motor skills or cognitive ability of children (Haine Crown [art therapist] and Caroline Wix [associate professor of art therapy, University of New Mexico], personal communications 1996). Research shows that children with intellectual impairment of some kind draw at the level of children with a similar mental age rather than chronological age (Cox 1997:59).

Most alternative explanations for these vessels were considered and rejected for the following reasons. First, regarding the possibility that elderly potters painted them: children lack both motor coordination and cognitive maturity, so that their pots are clumsily executed and reflect a poor to nonexistent grasp of the culturally appropriate design rules. Elderly potters may paint a shaky line, but they know how to lay out a design and what a design should look like. Many elderly Pueblo potters continued to produce superb designs until their deaths; their vessels would never be mistaken for the work of children. Other aging potters stopped making pottery when they could no longer produce it with their characteristic quality (Blair and Blair 1999:179–180). The art therapists consulted indicated that truly senile artisans (with, for instance, Alzheimer's disease) would likely not make, decorate, and fire pots. Furthermore, mortuary studies in the Southwest indicate that people rarely lived to the age where they might have been senile; the number of children in any population would greatly outnumber the number of senile adults. Second, regarding the possibility that the pots were made by artisans under the influence of drugs or alcohol: there is no evidence in historical documents or the archaeological record that artisans made or painted pottery under the influence of drugs or alcohol (drugs and alcohol, if consumed, were associated with ritual activities and not everyday life); furthermore, the modern art work of individuals using drugs or alcohol is not generally characterized by the same distinctive traits as the art work of children.

There is an additional possible explanation for some of the vessels. Peter Roe (1995:49) discusses "realms of protected deviation," which are specific domains or audiences for nontraditional works. For instance, among the Cashinahua, adult potters make crude ceramic toys for their daughters in unusual shapes that would not meet with approval in full-scale versions (Kensinger 1975:64). The southwestern vessels used in this study lack the innovative qualities inherent in Roe's discussion; on the contrary, these vessels suggest attempts at imitating rather than deviating from skilled versions. The ethnographic record for the American Southwest indicates, however, that during the historic period skilled potters in the Hopi area made small crude vessels as offerings for clay sources (Bartlett 1934) or as offerings for the fire to ensure a good outcome for the rest of the vessels in a firing (Blair and Blair 1999:159). This practice suggests that firing and clay source offerings were "realms of protected deviation," in this case specific domains in which crudely made vessels were acceptable. The vessels are described as made by pinching and cursorily painted with slaps of a paintbrush. These offerings were purposefully crude and are apparently visually similar to the work of unskilled child potters (Mark Tahbo, Hopi potter, personal communication 2000). If this tradition has an ancient basis, it would probably not be possible to distinguish such purposefully crude offerings from the work of unskilled learner-potters. There are a few vessels in my sample that match the descriptions of these offerings as small pinched bowls with slapdash designs, and they are all Ancestral Hopi wares. Indeed, these few vessels were so crudely made and decorated that they appeared to be made by the youngest of children. I cannot eliminate the possibility that such pots were indeed made by skilled potters as offerings, although none was found in or near firing pits or in clay sources. The vast majority of my sample does not match this description. I acknowledge this possible alternative explanation for a few of the pots, but in the absence of any method of determining the actual source for these few vessels, I continue to include them in this study. I did not see evidence for such purposefully crude vessels in other wares, in which the pots indicate attempts to replicate, albeit unsuccessfully, the work of skilled potters.

I am not the first archaeologist to suggest that children made such poor-quality southwestern vessels. Frank Hamilton Cushing interpreted some vessels from his excavations in the Hohokam area as the work of children, as indicated on original catalog cards at the Peabody Museum at Harvard University; Neil Judd (1954:199) interpreted some small, crudely made vessels from Pueblo Bonito as the work of children. Unfortunately, because the vessels are all decorated and most are slipped, no fingerprints were available for the type of analysis performed by Kathy Kamp (described in this volume) for Sinagua pottery.

For each vessel, I recorded a variety of attributes, including standard aspects of form, technology, and decoration. I also recorded attributes derived from studies of children's drawings by educational psychologists and art educators (Crown 1999). As indicated above, there is a vast literature in these fields on how children learn to draw and how drawings reflect both cognitive maturity and motor skill development (Biber 1962; Cox 1993, 1997; Deregowski 1980; Goodnow 1977; Krampen 1991; Thomas 1995). Studies based on cross-cultural data indicate regularities in the ages at which children are able to draw certain forms and in their ability to render them in an accurate manner (Dennis 1940, 1942:347; Fortes 1940; Havighurst et al. 1946; Paget 1932; Russell 1943; Wilson and Ligtvoet 1992; Wilson and Wilson 1984). Ultimately, I recorded 44 attributes for each vessel. In addition, my research assistant and I photographed, videotaped, and drew each vessel.

LEARNING AND TEACHING

Because the ethnographic record for southwestern potters indicates that girls learned through observation and imitation of adults and that they made, decorated, and fired their own vessels, part of this research involved exploring whether this was the case with the Prehispanic material as well. The results indicate greater direct involvement by skilled potters in teaching pottery production and suggest that learning in the past involved more than observation and imitation of largely silent adults. To understand adult involvement in the learning process, I focus here on two attributes: the skill level of the individual who made the vessel and the skill level of the individual who painted the vessel. Each of these attributes was assessed as the final attributes for each vessel; they represent a qualitative judgment of the skill levels of maker and painter based on thorough examination of each vessel. In assessing these final attributes, I asked two questions: first, was the individual who made the pot a skilled potter? And second, does the skill level of the decoration on the pot suggest that the same individual was capable of both making and painting the pot? I assume that a skilled potter made vessels that were symmetrical in shape (except the few unusual forms, such as effigies), exhibited standard forming techniques, had relatively even wall thicknesses, and reflected quality of materials and firing technology. Unskilled learners made vessels that were lumpy, asymmetrical in form, made of poor materials, often used nontraditional forming techniques, and fired poorly (often soft and marred by fireclouds). Similarly, skilled potters carefully executed designs with standard-sized paintbrushes, traditional motifs, typical symmetry patterns, and efficient application of paint, whereas unskilled learners lifted and replaced brushes often in painting lines, could not make lines meet squarely, produced shaky lines, and had difficulty executing complex design elements such as the scroll. In some instances designs on single vessels showed the imprint of two painters, one skilled and one unskilled. I recorded these as decorated by "two hands."

Within the entire sample there are five combinations reflecting varied degrees of involvement by children and adults in producing these vessels. Unskilled children made and painted 68 percent of the vessels (Figure 6.1a). For an additional 4 percent, children made the vessel and a skilled potter painted it (Figure 6.1b). Three percent of the vessels were made by children and then painted by a child and adult working cooperatively (Figure 6.1d). Fifteen percent of the vessels were made by skilled potters and painted by children (Figure 6.1c). The final 10 percent of the vessels

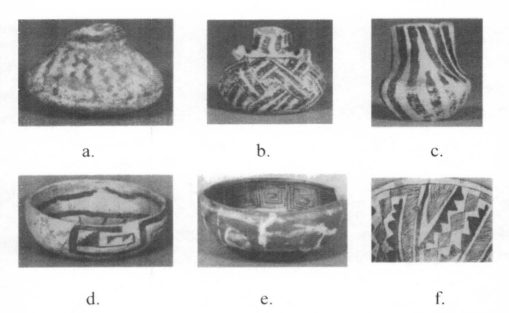

a.   b.   c.

d.   e.   f.

Figure 6.1. Examples of vessels used in a study of child potters in the American Southwest. All photographs taken by Marianne Tyndall. *a*. Miniature Hohokam red-on-buff jar made and painted by a child. Design is laid out improperly so some extra lines were added to fill space. Vessel is 44 mm high. GP 47,816 (ASM). *b*. Miniature Tularosa Black-on-white jar made by a child and painted by an adult. Note that the vessel is lumpy and asymmetrical but the design is quite complex with fine linework. Vessel is 51 mm high. GP 2496 (ASM). *c*. Miniature Cibola Whiteware jar made by an adult and painted by a child. The jar is nicely made with a symmetrical form and slight shoulder; the design is poorly laid out so some lines were crowded in. The jar is 67 mm high. GP 38,675 (ASM). *d*. Hopi Black-on-yellow bowl made by a child and decorated jointly by an adult and a child. The vessel is asymmetrical and lumpy, indicating that a child formed it. The interior design is poorly laid out and executed. It is not a traditional Hopi design. The exterior design is carefully executed with straight lines and traditional motifs. Vessel is 72 mm high. Catalog no. A157770, Department of Anthropology, Smithsonian Institution. *e*. St. Johns Polychrome bowl made by an adult and painted jointly by a child and adult. The interior design, although sloppy, is symmetrical and evenly laid out. The lines meet perfectly with few brush liftings. Such a complex design is indicative of a skilled potter. In contrast, the exterior design appears to have been applied by finger painting and has no clear pattern. This exterior design was painted by an unskilled child potter. The bowl is 83 mm high. GP 1975 (ASM). *f*. Close-up of a Tularosa Black-on-white bowl made by an adult and painted jointly by a child and adult. The careful rendering indicates that an adult laid out and executed most of the design, allowing a less skilled potter to complete some of the hatching. Note particularly the difference in quality between the hatching in the squares and the hatching in the triangle. The lines in the triangle are not parallel, have brush liftings in midline, and run over the outlines in places. The bowl is 109 mm high. Catalog no. 258538, the Field Museum.

were made by skilled potters and decorated by an adult and a child working together (Figure 6.1e–f).

These varied products suggest varied learning environments. The children who made and painted vessels by themselves probably learned through observation and imitation of adults, matching the ethnographic descriptions of learning frameworks in the American Southwest. But the vessels completed jointly by an adult and child do not match ethnographic descriptions of how southwestern Native American children learned to become potters. Instead, they suggest greater adult involvement in the learning process and, in some cases, alternative forms of learning and teaching in the past.

The vessels made by children but painted by more skilled potters are poorly formed; these pots could well have been the earliest efforts of children too young to begin painting their own vessels. These vessels suggest indulgent adults who were willing to decorate the early creations of young potters. Although such designs may have offered a template for the budding potters to follow at a later time, they did not provide the children with practice in executing designs and so represent demonstration more than skill enhancement.

Vessels crafted by adults and painted by unskilled children reveal even greater adult effort in the finished product. Nevertheless, such vessels do not necessarily require adult instruction of the child. Quite young children, who probably lacked the motor skills to form a normal-sized vessel, apparently decorated some of these vessels made by adults. The finished pieces were not enhanced by the child's contribution. Indeed, the degree of adult effort on these vessels suggests indulgence of young children or attempts to keep them occupied rather than instruction (Whiting and Edwards 1988; Whiting and Whiting 1975).

In contrast, the vessels made by children or adults and then painted cooperatively suggest more direct interaction in the instruction process. The vessels made by children and painted cooperatively are of considerably poorer quality than those made by adults and painted cooperatively. Adults and children worked together on these vessels in three distinct ways (Table 6.1). On some vessels an adult completed one field of decoration, and then a child decorated the other field. For instance, adults often decorated jar bodies and bowl interiors, and children decorated jar necks and bowl exteriors (Figure 6.1e). Such vessels could have been painted without much actual guidance from adult to child because the designs are spatially separate and artistically unrelated (that is, the unskilled design does not employ the motifs of the skilled design or copy it in any other fashion). As

Table 6.1 indicates, the majority of the vessels formed by children and painted by two hands were decorated in this way. On a small number of vessels children laid out the design and completed at least some of the motifs, having skilled potters complete the final detail work, such as hatching. On the remaining vessels adults laid out the design, providing the framework for the symmetry and motifs. The adults then completed at least one of the motifs, leaving the remaining motifs or other detail work to a much less skilled child potter. For instance, children completed the hatching of some motifs (Figure 6.1f). The majority of the vessels formed by adults and painted by two hands were completed jointly in this way (Table 6.1). Completion of these vessels almost certainly necessitated some instructional guidance from the adult to the child as the adult explained what the child needed to do to finish the vessel and provided the template in the completed portions of the design.

These vessels authored by two hands reveal much about adult effort in training children in correct painting techniques. They are indicative of a way of teaching and learning that is not documented in the ethnographic record for the Southwest. Furthermore, such pottery suggests that for some of the vessels made by adults and painted cooperatively, child labor had potential economic value in helping adults complete the most tedious, least risky tasks associated with pottery production (London 1986). Adults may have used child labor to increase their productivity.

For more detailed understanding of how children learned and adults taught pottery production, it is necessary to examine the results from different parts of the Southwest. As noted earlier, the majority of vessels examined represent eight areas or major wares in the Southwest. Because the same analytic methods and standards were applied to all wares, differences among wares in degree of adult involvement suggest differences in

TABLE 6.1. VESSELS DECORATED IN COLLABORATION BETWEEN AN UNSKILLED CHILD AND SKILLED ADULT POTTER.

Vessels jointly decorated by child and adult	Vessel formed by unskilled child (%)	Vessel formed by skilled adult (%)
Adult and child each decorate different field of design	56	39
Child lays out and completes most of design and adult fills some details	19	6
Adult lays out and completes most of design and child fills some details	26	56

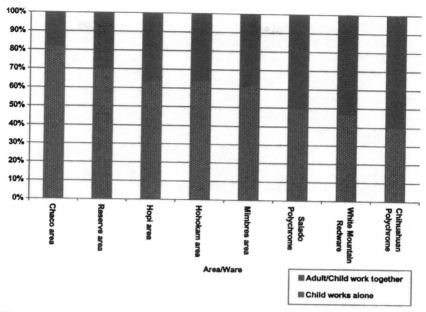

Figure 6.2. Degree of adult involvement in ceramic production, by area/ware.

teaching methods relating to technology, intended vessel use, or the organization of production in these areas. Table 6.2 and Figure 6.2 show the counts and relative frequencies, respectively, of vessels formed and decorated by children alone versus vessels made cooperatively by an adult and child: for most areas and most wares, children made and painted their own vessels with little direct adult involvement. But some wares, particularly the late polychromes, reveal higher levels of adult involvement. These same wares also have small sample sizes, not because I examined fewer vessels of these wares but because fewer of the vessels exhibited attributes indicative of the work of child potters.

The type of adult involvement differed among the various areas and wares. As Table 6.3 reveals, adults worked on vessels with children in different ways, only some of which likely involved instruction that deviated from the traditional observation and imitation. Figure 6.3 shows the percentage of vessels of each area/ware made by children or adults and then decorated by two hands. Several patterns emerge. First, none of the Salado polychrome vessels was decorated cooperatively, although adults often made vessels that they allowed children to paint. Second, adults and children were more likely to paint vessels jointly if the vessels were formed by the skilled adult potter than if the vessels were formed by the unskilled

TABLE 6.2. COUNTS OF VESSELS MADE BY CHILDREN VERSUS VESSELS
MADE COOPERATIVELY BY CHILDREN AND ADULTS.

Ware/Area	Child Alone	Adult/Child Work Together	Together
Chaco	70	15	85
Reserve	178	75	253
Hopi	106	59	165
Salado PC	10	10	20
Mimbres	56	35	91
Hohokam	54	30	84
Chihuahuan PC	6	9	15
White Mountain Redware	14	16	30
Total	494	249	743

child potter. Finally, the White Mountain Redware and Chihuahuan
Polychrome samples stand out as having the highest proportion of vessels
made by adults and painted cooperatively by an adult and a child. These
results suggest that in different culture areas within the Southwest, children learned and adults taught pottery making in distinct ways.

A comparison of the black-on-white vessels from the Reserve area with
the polychrome White Mountain Redware vessels reveals that learning

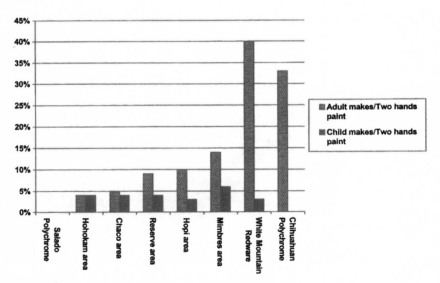

Figure 6.3. Percentage of vessels painted by two hands.

TABLE 6.3. MAKER/PAINTER RELATIONSHIPS FOR WHOLE SOUTHWESTERN VESSELS.

Ware/Area	Child make/Child paint	Child make/Adult paint	Child make/Two hands paint	Adult make/Child paint	Adult make/Two hands paint
Chaco area	X	X	X	X	X
Reserve area	X	X	X	X	X
Hopi area	X	X	X	X	X
Mimbres area	X	X	X	X	X
Hohokam area	X	X	X	X	X
Salado PC	X			X	
Chihuahuan PC	X	X		X	X
White Mountain Redware	X	X	X	X	X

frameworks changed through time as well. The Reserve area here refers to a portion of east-central Arizona and west-central New Mexico where potters produced both Cibola White Ware black-on-white vessels (Cibola White Ware vessels from Chacoan sites are specifically excluded from this discussion) and the White Mountain Redware polychrome vessels. These two wares are characterized by distinct paste and slip but essentially identical decorative styles. Within the Reserve area, black-on-white vessels made by children are relatively common whereas polychromes made by children are rare. Furthermore, adult involvement is proportionally much higher for the polychromes than for the black-on-white types, particularly for the vessels formed by adults and then painted with the help of children. Though we could conclude that polychrome technology was associated with different teaching and learning methods, the patterning becomes more complex when changes over time are taken into account. Figure 6.4 reveals that the proportion of vessels formed by adults and then painted cooperatively by adults and children changed dramatically for both wares after A.D. 1100, when skilled potters increased their involvement in training unskilled children how to become competent potters. Such training included greater direct guidance in providing design templates for children to follow as they worked cooperatively on some vessels. Interestingly, the much greater frequency of black-on-white vessels made or decorated by children during this time period indicates that children likely learned the technology to make black-on-white vessels first. Once they had attained some competency on the simpler bichrome pottery, they were introduced to the greater complexity of making polychrome vessels. Such a scenario suggests that in this area, children learned pottery production initially

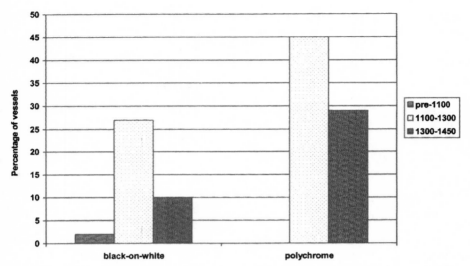

Figure 6.4. Percentage of Cibola White Ware and White Mountain Redware vessels formed by an adult and painted cooperatively by an adult and a child.

through observation and imitation but were given more direct instruction once they had gained the competency to help complete vessels made by adults. At the same time, it appears that adult potters did not often allow children free access to the materials necessary to make polychrome vessels, instead bringing the children into this technology under more controlled conditions.

CONCLUSIONS

Most learning frameworks in the Prehispanic Southwest involved observation and imitation. When adults were involved in the process, they most often provided unfinished vessels for children to paint or painted unfinished vessels made by children. Such adult effort in the learning process is not recorded in the ethnographic record for the Prehispanic Southwest, but it does not necessarily indicate deviation from the traditional observation/imitation learning framework.

In some areas adults apparently began teaching children pottery production by another method as well. Particularly after A.D. 1100 in northern Chihuahua and the Reserve area, adults sometimes formed vessels and worked cooperatively with children on finishing the vessels. Completing such vessels almost certainly required close guidance of the learner, because the skilled adults provided the template for unskilled children to finish the designs. This interaction gave children more direct training in vessel decoration and practice in motor coordination at the same time as it provided adults with labor to complete tedious tasks associated with vessel design.

Ethnographic studies reveal several possible reasons for children to perform adult tasks (C. Bradley 1993; Kamp, this volume; Whiting and Edwards 1988; Whiting and Whiting 1975). First, the work occupies children and keeps them out from underfoot. Second, children's work may increase adult productivity. Third, such tasks provide opportunities for children to learn in the context of doing (Lave and Wenger 1991). Vessels made by adults and given to children to decorate may reflect adults' attempts to occupy children. The vessels made by adults and decorated jointly by adults and children suggest that children were being used to increase adult productivity. In both contexts children learned from the experiences. But the joint completion of designs offered an opportunity for verbal interaction and close guidance that other learning contexts probably did not. In a series of experiments in learning among potters in Africa, Hélène Wallaert-Pêtre (2001) found that learning frameworks that involve verbal communication as well as visual observation produce greater long-term memory than frameworks based on observation and imitation alone. Study of learning frameworks may thus aid in understanding rates of change in pottery technology and design (Crown 2001).

Although rich in information, the ethnographic record for the American Southwest does not describe the types of adult involvement in the teaching of pottery production that are revealed in the Prehispanic vessels from this area. It is possible that this discrepancy is due to a lack of detail in ethnographies and biographies; ethnographers may have missed these less common forms of adult/child interaction, or adult potters may have forgotten the adult help they received as children. Since the archaeological record indicates that learning frameworks varied over time and space in the Southwest, however, it is possible that the adult involvement so apparent in the Prehispanic record disappeared as circumstances changed after A.D. 1540. Indeed, Figure 6.4 indicates that the percentage of vessels painted cooperatively by adults and children began to dwindle in the Reserve area after A.D. 1300 for both black-on-white and polychrome ceramics, suggesting yet another shift in learning frameworks.

The research raises additional questions concerning the transfer of technology and access to knowledge. These issues are particularly important, given the secrecy common among potters. For instance, unskilled learners appear to have had variable access to information about pottery technology in the Reserve area, learning the technology and designs of black-on-white pottery before beginning to make and decorate polychrome pottery. Skilled potters may have controlled such access based on the ability of children to complete specific tasks; because of secrecy associated with material sources, techniques, or symbols; or because of taboos associated with gender, age, or social status. Such control might also relate to the specific uses of the finished ceramics (ritual versus mundane) or the organization of production (specialists versus nonspecialists). Teasing out the specific causes in this instance is beyond the scope of this chapter.

Ultimately, an understanding of why the learning frameworks of the Prehispanic Southwest varied through time and across space has great potential to inform a variety of important issues. But this understanding will require careful attention to a complex variety of factors and openness to possibilities beyond the ethnographic record.

ACKNOWLEDGMENTS

An earlier version of this chapter was presented at the 65th Annual Meeting of the Society for American Archaeology in Philadelphia in April 2000. Kathy Kamp did a wonderful job of organizing and chairing this session. Discussants Nan Rothschild and Alice Kehoe and two anonymous reviewers provided critical comments of great value. This research was funded by grants from the National Endowment for the Humanities, an independent federal agency (RZ-20362–98), and from the Wenner-Gren Foundation for Anthropological Research (Small Grant 6318). Completion of the manuscript was aided by a Sabbatical Fellowship from the American Philosophical Society. I gratefully acknowledge this support. Thanks to the administrators and staff of the Arizona State Museum, Field Museum of Natural History, Museum of New Mexico, Museum of Northern Arizona, Peabody Museum at Harvard University, Smithsonian Institution, and Weisman Art Museum for allowing me to use their collections in this study. My research assistant, Marianne Tyndall, aided in many aspects of data collection and analysis and did so with great good humor under often trying conditions.

7

Children's Health in
the Prehistoric Southwest

Kristin D. Sobolik

A number of researchers have examined children's health in the prehis-toric Southwest, mostly from a local, site-specific perspective. Here I synthesize data from previously analyzed human skeletal remains in differ-ent cultural contexts (Anasazi, Mogollon, Hohokam, and Sinagua), site sizes (small and large), and time periods (A.D. 1–Protohistoric) to address the issue of children's health from a broader, southwestern perspective. My intent is review and discuss the main health indicators observable on human skeletal material and to ascertain patterns of children's health through time and across cultural boundaries in the prehistoric Southwest.

Southwestern archaeologists have long speculated on the human bio-logical consequences of the adoption of corn agriculture in such a poten-tially marginal environment. There is strong evidence that the climate in the Southwest was almost always marginal for subsistence on corn agri-culture. A. M. Palkovich notes that human diet and health would have suf-fered in that context, going from bad to worse as the agricultural subsistence base increased in importance and use through time, inducing "endemic nutritional inadequacy" (1984:436) for southwestern popula-tions. A. L. W. Stodder (1990) also indicates that health problems in-creased through time and at larger sites as populations became more sedentary and reliance on corn agriculture became more pervasive, in-creasing the rate of infectious disease transfer. Population aggregation and the subsequent growth in site size associated with reliance on corn agriculture has also been cited by P. L. Walker (1985) as probable cause for an increase in health problems such as anemia.

As the health of prehistoric southwestern populations decreased through time under these conditions, the health of children declined drastically and infant mortality rates increased. In this chapter I synthesize the analysis of human skeletal remains from a large number and variety of archaeological sites in the Southwest to discern potential differences in health status, especially as they affect children's health.

METHODS

To obtain information on children's health throughout the Southwest, I searched the literature for reports on analyzed human skeletal remains. In particular, I was interested in reports of subadult burials, stature estimates, and pathology relating to health. This search revealed a large number of research projects, many of which are described in Master's theses and Ph.D. dissertations. Reports on human remains were not included if relevant information, such as number of subadult burials and pathological analyses, was not provided.

A total of 9,703 human remains from the Southwest were reported (Table 7.1). I categorized these individuals by the site from which they were excavated, the site size as recorded by the analyst, cultural affiliation, and time period. Anasazi (also known as Ancestral Puebloan) human remains were the most frequently recovered and reported, and an analysis of differences in children's health by site size and time period was conducted with this large sample using chi-squared analysis. Because of small sample sizes for Mogollon, Hohokam, and Sinagua burials, analysis of significant differences as they relate to site size and time period could not be conducted.

HEALTH INDICATORS

A number of pieces of information directly relating to an individual's health can be obtained from a human skeletal sample. Health patterns revealed on adult skeletons are, in many cases, the result of that individual's health as a child. Therefore, analysis of children's health involves an analysis of all individuals in the population and of the population's health in general. The health indicators I use here are childhood mortality rates, adult stature, evidence of anemia through porotic hyperostosis and cribra orbitalia, growth arrest indicators through linear enamel hypoplasias and Harris lines, and evidence of infection (periostitis).

TABLE 7.1. HUMAN SKELETAL INFORMATION USED IN THE ANALYSIS.

Site	Site Size[a]	Cultural Affiliation	Time period	No. of Individuals[b]	Reference
Black Mesa	Small	Anasazi	BMII (200 B.C.–A.D. 200)	7	Martin et al. 1985; Martin et al. 1991
Puerco Valley, AZ	Small	Anasazi	BMIII (A.D. 750–850)	17	Wade 1970
Mesa Verde region	Small	Anasazi	BMIII–early PII (A.D. 600–975)	168	Stodder 1984
Yellowjacket sites	Small	Anasazi	BMIII–PIII	52	Swedlund 1969
Puerco Valley, AZ	Small	Anasazi	PI–earlyPII (A.D. 850–1000)	19	Wade1970
Black Mesa	Small	Anasazi	A.D. 800–1050	49	Martin, Piacentini, and Armelagos 1985; Martin et al. 1991
Glen Canyon sites	Small	Anasazi	PII (A.D. 1000–1150)	40	Ryan 1977
Mancos Canyon sites	Small	Anasazi	PII–III (A.D. 900–1275)	53	Robinson 1976
Mesa Verde region	Small	Anasazi	late PII–late PIII (A.D. 975–1300)	276	Stodder 1984
Puerco Valley, AZ	Small	Anasazi	Late PII–early PIII (A.D. 1000–1150)	96	Wade 1970
Black Mesa	Small	Anasazi	A.D. 1050–1150	111	Martin, Piacentini, and Armelagos 1985; Martin et al. 1991
Chaco Canyon (Bc59)	Small	Anasazi	PII–III (A.D. 900–1156)	32	El-Najjar et al. 1976
Chaco Canyon (Bc51, 53, 59, Kin Neole)[c]	Small	Anasazi	A.D. 1050–1130	218	Palkovich 1982
Sundown	Small	Anasazi	A.D. 1100–1200	26	Merbs and Vestergaard 1985
Glen Canyon sites	Small	Anasazi	PIII (A.D. 1150–1250)	35	Ryan 1977
Carter Ranch Pueblo	Small	Anasazi	PIII (A.D. 1100–1225)	34	Danforth et al. 1994
Puerco Valley, AZ	Small	Anasazi	PIII (A.D. 1150–1250)	39	Wade 1970
Mesa Verde	Small	Anasazi	A.D. 750–1300	179	Miles 1966
Chaco Canyon[c]	Small	Anasazi	Wide age range	135	Akins 1986

TABLE 7.1. HUMAN SKELETAL INFORMATION USED IN THE ANALYSIS. (cont.)

Site	Site Size[a]	Cultural Affiliation	Time period	No. of Individuals[b]	Reference
Canyon de Chelly	Large	Anasazi	BMII–III (A.D. 400–700)	136	El-Najjar et al. 1976
Mesa Verde	Large	Anasazi	BMIII–PIII (A.D. 450–1350)	202	Bennett 1975
Navajo Reservoir	Large	Anasazi	PI–II (A.D. 700–1100)	92	El-Najjar et al. 1976
Canyon de Chelly	Large	Anasazi	PI–PIII (A.D. 700–1300)	78	El-Najjar et al. 1976
Pueblo Bonito	Large	Anasazi	A.D. 1020–1120	112	Akins 1986; Palkovich 1982, 1984
Mesa Verde, Site 34	Large	Anasazi	PIII	27	Reed 1965
Cochiti sites	Large	Anasazi	approx. A.D. 1225–1550+	174	Heglar 1974
Inscription House	Large	Anasazi	PIII (A.D. 1250–1300)	24[d]	El-Najjar et al. 1976
Glen Canyon sites	Large	Anasazi	late PIII (A.D. 1250–1300)	103[d]	Ryan 1977
Zuni Pueblo de los Muertos	Large	Anasazi	A.D. 1280–1320	26	Wheeler 1985
Gran Quivira	Large	Anasazi	PIV–V (A.D. 1315–1673)	361	El-Najjar et al. 1976; Reed 1981
Arroyo Hondo Pueblo	Large	Anasazi	A.D. 1300–1425	120	Palkovich 1980
Tijeras Pueblo	Large	Anasazi	A.D. 1300–1425	64	Ferguson 1980
Kechipawan Site	Large	Anasazi	A.D. 1300–1600	54	Lahr and Bowman 1992
Paa-ko	Large	Anasazi	A.D. 1300–1600s	57	Ferguson 1980
San Antonio	Large	Anasazi	A.D. 1300–1600s	28	Ferguson 1980
Old Walpi	Large	Anasazi	after A.D. 1300–1620	137	Ryan 1977
Pecos Pueblo	Large	Anasazi	A.D. 1300–1846	1,254	Hooton 1930
Hawikku	Large	Anasazi	A.D. 1400–1680	188	Stodder 1990
San Cristobel Pueblo	Large	Anasazi	A.D. 1400–1680	268	Stodder 1990
Total Anasazi large-site individuals		3,505			
Dolores Project sites	Variable	Anasazi	A.D. 600–1250	64	Wiener 1984; Stodder 1987
Total Anasazi individuals	5,155				

TABLE 7.1. HUMAN SKELETAL INFORMATION USED IN THE ANALYSIS. (cont.)

Site	Site Size[a]	Cultural Affiliation	Time period	No. of Individuals[b]	Reference
La Ciudad	Large	Hohokam	Preclassic	183	McGuire 1992
La Ciudad	Large	Hohokam	Preclassic	24	Fink and Merbs 1991
Grand Canal Ruins	Large	Hohokam	Classic (A.D. 1100–1450)	72	Fink and Merbs 1991
Las Colinas	Large	Hohokam	Classic (A.D. 1100–1450)	16	Harrington 1981
Casa Buena	Large	Hohokam	Classic (A.D. 1100–1450)	43	Fink and Merbs 1991
Total Hohokam individuals 338					
Point of Pines	Large	Mogollon	pre A.D. 400–1000	19	Bennett 1973
NAN Ranch	Large	Mimbres Mogollon	A.D. 700–1125	209	Patrick 1988; Marek 1990
Galaz Ruin	Large	Mimbres Mogollon	approx. A.D. 900–1150	934	Provinzano 1968
Point of Pines	Large	Mogollon	A.D. 1000–1285	282	Bennett 1973
Grasshopper Pueblo	Large	Mogollon	A.D. 1275–1400	674	Kelley 1980; Hinkes 1983; Berry 1985[a]
Point of Pines	Large	Mogollon	A.D. 1285–1450	207	Bennett 1973
Total Mogollon individuals 2,325					
Early Salado phase	Varied	Salado	A.D. 1200–1300	129	Hohmann 1992
Besh-Ba-Gowah Pueblo	Large	Salado	A.D. 1225–1450	282	Hohmann 1992
Late Salado phase	Varied	Salado	A.D. 1300–1450	421	Hohmann 1992
Total Salado individuals 832					
Angell-Winona Phase sites	Varied	Sinagua	A.D. 1050–1100	96	Hohmann 1992
Padre Phase sites	Varied	Sinagua	A.D. 1100–1125	141	Hohmann 1992
Early Elden Phase sites	Varied	Sinagua	A.D. 1125–1150	41[c]	Hohmann 1992
Late Elden Phase sites	Varied	Sinagua	A.D. 1150–1200	167	Hohmann 1992
Oak Creek Pueblo	Small	Sinagua	approx. A.D. 1000–1300	7	Taylor 1985

TABLE 7.1. HUMAN SKELETAL INFORMATION USED IN THE ANALYSIS. (cont.)

Site	Site Size[a]	Cultural Affiliation	Time period	No. of Individuals[b]	Reference
Lizard Man Village	Small	Sinagua	A.D. 1050–1300	15	Whittaker et al. 1999
Tuzigoot	Large	Sinagua	A.D. 1000–late A.D. 1300s	429	Caywood and Spicer 1935; Forsberg 1935
Nuvakwewtaqa (Chavez Pass Ruin)	Large	Sinagua	A.D.1200–1450	157	Iwaniec 1989
Total Sinagua individuals	1,053				
Total Prehistoric Southwest individuals	9,703				

[a]Site size designation as listed in reference.

[b]Largest number of analyzed individuals from that reference set.

[c]It is unknown what overlap, if any, there is between these data sets.

[d]Data potentially include individuals reported from Inscription House by El-Najjar et al. 1976.

[e]Excludes data from Lizard Man Village as originally reported in reference.

Childhood Mortality Rates

Childhood mortality rates are a direct reflection of the health of children in a population, assuming that the recovered human remains are a direct representation of the living population. Nevertheless, there are a number of biases in the use of subadult burial rates to estimate childhood mortality rates for a population (Moore et al. 1975). In archaeological contexts, burials of children and infants tend not to be as well preserved as burials of adults because infants' and children's bones are smaller and less dense, making preservation problematic in a potentially destructive environment. Burials of infants and children also contain many more smaller bones than those of adults, and early archaeological techniques, which focused on recovery of larger, showy remains usually with the aid of shovels, was not conducive to the recovery of such burials. Even when these remains were recovered, early archaeologists did not tend to be interested in their study or curation, and many times they were discarded or not excavated at all. Some of the largest sample sizes used here are from early excavations. Therefore, the number of recorded and analyzed subadults from southwestern sites is clearly an underrepresentation of the number of subadults that actually died and were buried from a particular population.

Childhood mortality rates, as reflected in the number of subadult burials, are very high (Table 7.2). High rates are also observed by Stephanie Whittlesey (this volume) at Grasshopper Pueblo and by Cynthia Bradley (this volume) at Sand Canyon. The proportion of subadult to adult burials for the entire Southwest is 42 percent. In modern times such a high childhood mortality rate is approached only by populations experiencing severe malnutrition and stress (Gordon et al. 1967; Puffer and Serrano 1973; Stini 1985; Wills and Waterloo 1958). Frequencies of subadult to adult burials in southwestern populations vary from 25 percent for Hohokam sites to 51 percent for Mogollon sites.

Anasazi small sites have a 44 percent subadult/adult burial proportion, and Anasazi large sites have a 35 percent subadult/adult burial proportion (Table 7.3). This significant difference contradicts perceptions that as site size increases, childhood mortality rates increase as well.

In addition, significant temporal differences are noted between ratios of subadult/adult burials in early versus later time periods at Anasazi sites (Table 7.4). Childhood mortality rates are actually higher at earlier time periods than at later time periods, again contrary to beliefs that children's health decreases through time. Pueblo Bonito samples are both included and removed from this analysis because of their atypical age distribution

TABLE 7.2. SUBADULT BURIALS.

Sites	Time Period[a]	Ratio of Subadults to Adults and Percentage of Subadults[b]	Reference
Small Anasazi sites			
Black Mesa	E BMII (200 B.C.–A.D. 200)	4/7 (57%)	Martin et al. 1991
Mesa Verde region	I BMIII–early PII (A.D. 600–975)	53/150 (35%)	Stodder 1984
Yellowjacket sites	E BMIII–PIII	24/46 (52%)	Swedlund 1969
Puerco Valley, AZ	I BM III (A.D. 750–850)	9/17 (53%)	Wade 1970
Puerco Valley, AZ	I PI–early PII (A.D. 850–1000)	11/19 (58%)	Wade 1970
Black Mesa	I A.D. 800–1050	24/49 (49%)	Martin et al. 1991
Glen Canyon sites	II PII (A.D. 1000–1150)	14/40 (35%)	Ryan 1977
Puerco Valley, AZ	II late PII–early PIII (A.D. 1000–1150)	52/96 (54%)	Wade 1970
Black Mesa	II A.D. 1050–1150	55/11 (50%)	Martin et al. 1991
Chaco Canyon (Bc51, 53, 59, Kin Neole)	II A.D. 1050–1130	92/218 (42%)	Palkovich 1982
Sundown	II A.D. 1100–1200	16/26 (62%)	Merbs and Vestergaard 1985
Mesa Verde region	II/III late PII–late PIII (A.D. 975–1300)	76/178 (43%)	Stodder 1984
Glen Canyon sites	III early, middle PIII (A.D. 1150–1250)	14/35 (40%)	Ryan 1977
Carter Ranch Pueblo	III PIII (A.D. 1100–1225)	9/34 (26%)	Danforth et al. 1994
Puerco Valley, AZ	III PIII (A.D. 1150–1250)	23/39 (59%)	Wade 1970
Mesa Verde	E A.D. 750–1300	86/179 (48%)	Miles 1966
Mancos Canyon sites	E PII–III (A.D. 900–1275)	24/53 (45%)	Robinson 1976
Chaco Canyon	E wide age range	50/135 (37%)	Akins 1986
Total Anasazi small-site subadults 636/1432 (44%)			
Large Anasazi sites			
Mesa Verde	E BMIII–PIII (A.D. 450–1350)	81/202 (40%)	Bennett 1975
Pueblo Bonito	II A.D. 1020–1120	27/112 (24%)	Palkovich 1982
Mesa Verde, Site 34	III PIII	11/27 (41%)	Reed 1965

TABLE 7.2. Subadult Burials. (cont.)

Sites	Time Period[a]	Ratio of Subadults to Adults and percentage of Subadults[b]	Reference
Glen Canyon sites	III PIII (A.D. 1250–1300)	49/103 (48%)	Ryan 1977
Zuni Pueblo de los Muertos	III A.D. 1280–1320	11/26 (42%)	Wheeler 1985
Cochiti sites	III/IV A.D. 1225–1550+	58/174 (33%)	Heglar 1974
Gran Quivira	IV PIV–V (A.D. 1315–1673)	212/361 (59%)	Reed 1981
Arroyo Hondo Pueblo	IV A.D. 1300–1425	67/120 (56%)	Palkovich 1980
Tijeras Pueblo	IV A.D. 1300–1425	22/64 (34%)	Ferguson 1980
Paa-ko	IV A.D. 1300–1600s	29/57 (51%)	Ferguson 1980
San Antonio	IV A.D. 1300–1600s	8/28((29%)	Ferguson 1980
Pecos Pueblo	IV A.D. 1300–1846	270/1254 (22%)	Hooton 1930
Hawikku	IV A.D. 1400–1680	85/188 (45%)	Stodder 1990
San Cristobal Pueblo	IV A.D. 1400–1680	120/268 (45%)	Stodder 1990
Total Anasazi large-site subadults 1050/2984 (35%)			
Dolores Project sites	E A.D. 600–1250	11/64 (17%)	Stodder 1987
Total Anasazi subadults 1,697/4,480 (38%)			
Hohokam sites			
La Cuidad	Preclassic	50/183 (27%)	McGuire 1992
La Ciudad	Preclassic	8/24 (33%)	Fink and Merbs 1991
Grand Canal Ruins	Classic (A.D. 1100–1450)	10/79 (13%)	Fink and Merbs 1991
Las Colinas	Classic (A.D. 1100–1450)	4/16 (25%)	Harrington 1981
Casa Buena	Classic (A.D. 1100–1450)	15/49 (31%)	Fink and Merbs 1991
Total Hohokam subadults 87/351 (25%)			
Mogollon sites			
Point of Pines	pre A.D. 400–1000	3/19 (16%)	Bennett 1973
NAN Ranch	A.D. 700–1125	113/209 (54%)	Marek 1990

TABLE 7.2. SUBADULT BURIALS. (cont.)

Sites	Time Period[a]	Ratio of Subadults to Adults and percentage of Subadults[b]	Reference
Galaz Ruin	approx. A.D. 900–1150	449/934 (48%; original excavation) 38/98 (39%; Provinzano study)	Provinzano 1968
Point of Pines	A.D. 1000–1285	109/282 (39%)	Bennett 1973
Grasshopper Pueblo	A.D. 1275–1400	456/674 (68%)	Hinkes 1983
Point of Pines	A.D. 1285–1450	63/207 (30%)	Bennett 1973
Total Mogollan subadults 1,193/2,325 (51%; original Galaz excavation); 782/1,489 (53%; Provinzano Galaz study)			
Salado sites			
Early Salado sites	A.D. 1200–1300	42/129 (33%)	Hohmann 1992
Besh-Ba-Gowah Pueblo	A.D. 1225–1450	113/282 (40%)	Hohmann 1992
Late Salado sites	A.D. 1300–1450	152/421 (36%)	Hohmann 1992
Total Salado subadults 307/832 (37%)			
Sinagua sites			
Angell-Winona phase sites	A.D. 1050–1100	32/96 (33%)	Hohmann 1992
Padre phase sites	A.D. 1100–1125	51/141 (36%)	Hohmann 1992
Early Elden phase sites	A.D. 1125–1150	21/41 (51%)*[3]	Hohmann 1992
Oak Creek Pueblo	approx. A.D. 1000–1300	6/7 (86%)	Taylor 1985
Lizard Man Village	A.D. 1050–1300	7/15 (47%)	Whittaker et al. 1999
Late Elden phase sites	A.D. 1150–1200	59/167 (35%)	Hohmann 1992
Tuzigoot	A.D. 1000–late A.D. 1300s	268/429 (62%)	Caywood and Spicer 1935
Total Sinagua subadults 444/896 (50%)			
Total subadults 3,728/8,884 (42%)			

[a]Time period determination: I = A.D. 750–1000, II = A.D. 1000–1150, III = A.D. 1150–1300, A.D. = A.D. 1300 +, E = Excluded from temporal study.

[b]Subadults determined at different ages by researchers; most frequent determination is less than 18 years or less than 15 years.

[c]Excludes samples from Lizard Man Village as presented in reference.

TABLE 7.3. CULTURAL AFFILIATION AND SITE-SIZE DIFFERENCES IN SUBADULTS.

Cultural Affiliation	Ratio of Subadults to Adults	% of Subadults
Anasazi small sites	636/1,432	44
Anasazi large sites	1,050/2,984	35
Anasazi total sites[a]	1,697/4,480	38
Hohokam sites	87/351	25
Mogollon sites[b]	1,193/2,325	51
Salado sites	307/832	37
Sinagua sites	444/896	50

[a]Data include Dolores Project sites; see Table 7.2.
[b]Using data from original Galaz excavation; see Table 7.2.

TABLE 7.4. TEMPORAL DIFFERENCES IN ANASAZI SUBADULTS.

Time Period[a]	Ratio of Subadults to Adults	% of Subadults
I A.D. 750–1000	97/235	41
II A.D. 1000–1150 (without Pueblo Bonito samples)	229/491	47
II A.D. 1000–1150 (with Pueblo Bonito samples)	256/603	42
I/II combined (without Pueblo Bonito samples)	326/726	45
I/II combined (with Pueblo Bonito samples)	353/838	42
III A.D. 1150–1300	117/264	44
IV A.D. 1300+	813/2,340	35
III/IV combined[b]	925/2,640	35

[a]Data used from sites listed in Table 7.2.
[b]Including data from Cochiti sites; see Table 7.2.

and their supposed high-ranking status (Palkovich 1982). Removal of Pueblo Bonito samples does not affect the significant differences noted with chi-squared analysis. It is unfortunate that there are no large human skeletal samples from hunter-gatherer time periods in the Southwest so that comparisons can be made between populations living on a varied subsistence base versus populations more dependent on agriculture.

Stature Estimation

Adult stature is used by modern human biologists as a measure of overall health and is a good measure of cumulative stress throughout childhood (Falkner and Tanner 1986; Huss-Ashmore et al. 1982). Stature has a number of causative agents, including genetics, environmental stress, nutritional intake, disease rates, and psychological stress. Southwestern stature estimations are made using measurements of long bones, mainly the femur and tibia, and usually follow formulae devised by Santiago Genoves (1967) with Mesoamerican populations.

Stature seems to be very similar throughout prehistoric populations in the Southwest, although some trends are apparent. The mean stature for prehistoric populations ranges from 147.7 cm for Anasazi Carter Ranch Pueblo females to 169.3 cm for Pueblo Bonito males (Tables 7.5 and 7.6). Pueblo Bonito males and females have the highest stature range for southwestern samples, another potential indicator of their high-ranking status. The Sinagua tend to have the lowest stature range. Anasazi male stature in small sites seems to be slightly higher than for males in larger sites (if Pueblo Bonito samples are excluded), and Sinagua females seem to be slightly shorter, on average, than females from other southwestern areas. Unfortunately, these trends cannot be statistically compared because the number of individuals used to determine mean stature in each population was not provided by all researchers. Therefore, stature ranges can only be quantified and overall trends observed.

Porotic Hyperostosis

The etiology of porotic hyperostosis has been discussed by a number of researchers (El-Najjar et al. 1976; Martin et al. 1985; Mensforth et al. 1978; Walker 1985). Porotic hyperostosis is exhibited by expansion of the diploe and cranial lesions and pitting on the surface of frontal, parietal, and occipital bones (Figure 7.1) as well as in the eye orbits (called *cribra orbitalia*; Figure 7.2). The etiology of cribra orbitalia and porotic hyperostosis is the same, so some researchers do not record these pathologies as separate entities, although cribra orbitalia seems to be an early expression of anemia and porotic hyperostosis a more severe reflection (Lallo et al. 1977).

The etiology of porotic hyperostosis is a synergistic reaction revolving around dietary insufficiency and malnutrition. Diets dependent on corn agriculture are deficient in a number of essential amino acids, as well as

TABLE 7.5. STATURE ESTIMATION.

Site	Stature Estimation (cm)[a]		Reference
	Male	Female	
Anasazi small sites			
Black Mesa A.D. 800–1050	167.0	156.5	Martin et al. 1991
Yellowjacket sites	158.75	160.52[b]	Swedlund 1969
Black Mesa A.D. 1050–1150	163.1	152.5	Martin et al. 1991
Sundown	166.0	155.0	Merbs and Vestergaard 1985
Mancos Canyon sites	168.5	157.5	Robinson 1976
Carter Ranch Pueblo	162.2	147.7	Danforth et al. 1994
Chaco Canyon	164.7(U)	157.4(U)	Akins 1986
Anasazi large sites			
Mesa Verde	162.0	152.0	Bennett 1975
Pueblo Bonito	169.3 (U)	162.0 (U)	Akins 1986
Mesa Verde, Site 34	161.3 (U)	148.6 (U)	Reed 1965
Gran Quivira	166.7 (TG)	153.6 (TG)	Scott 1981
Arroyo Hondo Pueblo A.D. 1300–1370	163.87	156.24	Palkovich 1980
Arroyo Hondo Pueblo A.D. 1370–1425	165.64	153.47	Palkovich 1980
Tijeras Pueblo	160.13	150.35	Ferguson 1980
Paa-ko	164.44	151.61	Ferguson 1980
San Antonio	162.63	153.00	Ferguson 1980
Cochiti sites	164.41 (U) 163.86 (TG)	154.64 (U)	Heglar 1974
Pecos Pueblo	161.7	150.1	Hooton 1930
Dolores Project sites	162.31	155.95	Stodder 1987
Hohokam sites			
La Ciudad	164.1	155.6	Fink and Merbs 1991
Grand Canal Ruins	165.3	160.2	Fink and Merbs 1991
Casa Buena	163	153	Fink and Merbs 1991
Mogollon sites			
NAN Ranch	162.2	154.9	Patrick 1988
Galaz Ruin	166.88	156.57	Provinzano 1968
Point of Pines	161.3	152.85	Bennett 1973
Point of Pines	162.1	153.7	Bennett 1973
Sinagua sites			
Lizard Man Village	160.5	152.0	Whittaker et al. 1999
Tuzigoot	166.4	154.6	Caywood and Spicer 1935; Forsberg 1935
Nuvakwewtaqa (Chavez Pass Ruin)	147.3–172.1 Mean = 158.2		Iwaniec 1989

[a]Stature estimation using formula developed by Genoves (1967) unless otherwise indicated; TG = Trotter and Gleser 1958; U = unknown formula.

[b]One tall individual has increased female stature estimation.

TABLE 7.6. STATURE ESTIMATE RANGES.

Sites	Male (cm)	Female (cm)
Anasazi small sites	158.75–168.5	147.7–160.52
Anasazi large sites	160.13–169.3 (Pueblo Bonito)	148.6–162.0 (Pueblo Bonito)
	160.13–166.7	148.66–156.24
Anasazi combined	158.75–169.3 (Pueblo Bonito)	147.7–162.0 (Pueblo Bonito)
	158.75–167.0	147.7–157.4
Hohokam	163.0–165.3	153.0–160.2
Mogollon	161.3–166.88	152.85–156.57
Sinagua	160.5–166.4	152.0–154.6

iron. With the increased dependence on corn agriculture, particularly in a marginal environment such as the Southwest, iron-deficiency anemia can develop in individuals who are relying heavily on corn to the detriment of other food items and who thus are not getting diverse nutrient intake. With fluctuating climatic conditions and environmental changes such as periods of drought, reliance on corn as a dietary staple increases iron-deficiency anemia.

Other causative agents in this synergistic cycle include the prevalence of

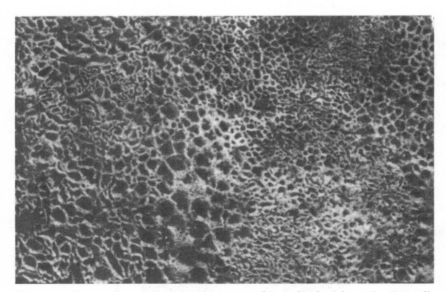

Figure 7.1. Porotic hyperostosis on the crania of an individual from the Grinnell Site in southwest Colorado. Photo by Stephen Bicknell.

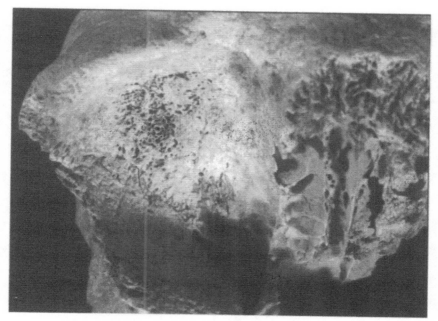

Figure 7.2. Cribra orbitalia on the crania of an individual from the Grinnell Site in southwest Colorado. Photo by Stephen Bicknell.

disease and parasites. Disease tends to be spread in larger, more sedentary populations with a lack of waste-disposal practices. Disease also tends to increase in populations that are malnourished, in essence proliferating anemia in individuals already malnourished. Additionally, it has been observed that prehistoric southwestern populations were infested with a number of potentially debilitating parasites (Reinhard 1985). Parasite infestation robs the body of much-needed nutrients and may block the absorption of iron, again participating in the proliferation of iron-deficiency anemia.

Severe porotic hyperostosis tends to be found more frequently in infants and children because their bones are thinner and not fully mineralized whereas adult bone is more resistant. In addition, by six months of age children have depleted the accumulated iron stores obtained from their mother in utero and must triple their blood supply (hematopoietic activity), thus requiring more iron (El-Najjar et al. 1976). The increased need for iron confounded by malnutrition and the lack of iron in the diet produces severe iron-deficiency anemia. If a child with porotic hyperostosis survives into adulthood, the lesions and pitting remain, eventually healing and becoming remodeled and less evident on the bone (El-Najjar et al. 1976).

Evidence of porotic hyperostosis in prehistoric Southwest populations is difficult to quantify because researchers record their results differently (Table 7.7). Some researchers record only the percentage of affected individuals without providing the number of individuals; some combine the percentage of porotic hyperostosis and cribra orbitalia into one number, making it impossible to separate the two for comparative purposes; and others record only the frequency of porotic hyperostosis present in infants and children.

Overall, however, it appears that a large segment of each population was affected with iron-deficiency anemia as exhibited by porotic hyperostosis. Rates of porotic hyperostosis at Anasazi sites in which researchers recorded number of infected individuals indicate that frequencies of anemia were very high. Populations at smaller sites had significantly greater frequencies of anemia than those at larger sites (Table 7.8), and populations in earlier time periods had significantly greater rates of anemia than those in later time periods (Table 7.9). This is the case even when E. A. Hooton's data from Pecos Pueblo are removed from the calculations. Hooton did not understand the etiology of porotic hyperostosis, which he termed "symmetrical osteoporosis" and a "mysterious disease" (Hooton 1930:316), so it is unknown whether he correctly identified porotic hyperostosis in all cases. Porotic hyperostosis rates at other cultural sites were not statistically compared because of small sample sizes.

Much of the data used for comparing porotic hyperostosis and therefore anemia rates comes from El-Najjar et al. 1976. This study looked at anemia rates at a variety of southwestern sites and concluded that the rates were higher at sites in canyon regions, in which the population was more dependent on agriculture, than at sites in sage plain regions, where there was better access to iron-rich animal products. Nevertheless, the data for this study indicate that site size and time period of occupation are important: larger sites and later times have lower rates of anemia.

Linear Enamel Hypoplasias

Linear enamel hypoplasias (LEH) are developmental growth disturbances that appear as linear depressions in the surface of tooth enamel (Figure 7.3). These depressions represent temporary cessation of enamel formation owing to nutritional stress or infectious disease. The location of LEH determines how old the individual was when tooth enamel was forming

TABLE 7.7. EVIDENCE OF POROTIC HYPEROSTOSIS AND CRIBRA ORBITALIA.

Site	Time Period[a]	Porotic Hyperostosis	Cribra Orbitalia	Reference
Anasazi small sites				
Black Mesa	I/II	79.8%	54.3%	Martin et al. 1991
Mesa Verde region	I	—	52/72 (72%)	Stodder 1984
Yellowjacket sites	E	4/12 young (33%)		Swedlund 1969
Mancos Canyon sites	E	5/27 (19%)[b]	4/24 (17%)	Robinson 1976
Puerco Valley, AZ	E	42/113 (37%)[b]	43/105 (41%)	Wade 1970
Chaco Canyon (Bc59)	I/II*[3]	23/32 (72%)[b]	—	El Najjar et al. 1976
Glen Canyon sites	II*[3]	5/28 (18%)[b]	—	Ryan 1977
Sundown	II*[3]	9/13 (69%)[b]	—	Merbs and Vestergaard 1985
Mesa Verde region	II/III	—	68/93 (73%)	Stodder 1984
Glen Canyon sites	III*[3]	3/31 (10%)[b]	—	Ryan 1977
Carter Ranch Pueblo	III	2/5 before 2 yrs. (40%)	4/5 before 2 yrs. (80%)	Danforth et al. 1994
Mesa Verde	E	6 infants	—	Miles 1966
Chaco Canyon	E	22/36 (61%)[b]	24/31 (77%)	Akins 1986
		109/280 (39%)[b]		
Anasazi large sites				
Canyon de Chelly	pre I[c]	67/136 (49%)[b]	—	El-Najjar et al. 1976
Navajo Reservoir	I/II[c]	12/92 (13%)[b]	—	El-Najjar et al. 1976
Canyon de Chelly	I/III	43/78 (55%)[b]	—	El-Najjar et al. 1976
Mesa Verde, Site 34	III	—	1 sm. child with severe case	Reed 1965
Glen Canyon sites[d]	III[c]	10/79 (13%)[b]	—	Ryan 1977
Inscription House	III[c]	13/24 (54%)[b]	—	El-Najjar et al. 1976
Zuni Pueblo de los Muertos	III/IV	7/7 children (100%)	—	Wheeler 1985
Gran Quivira	IV[c]	27/177 (15%)[b]	—	El-Najjar et al. 1976

TABLE 7.7. EVIDENCE OF POROTIC HYPEROSTOSIS AND CRIBRA ORBITALIA. (cont.)

Site	Time Period[a]	Porotic Hyperostosis	Cribra Orbitalia	Reference
Arroyo Hondo Pueblo	IV[c]	14/120 (12%)[b] all children	9/120 (8%) 8 children	Palkovich 1980
Tijeras Pueblo	IV	3/19 infants (16%)	—	Ferguson 1980
Kechipawan Site	IV	57.4 % both combined		Lahr and Bowman 1992
Paa-ko	IV	14/18 infants (78%)	5/11 children (46%)	Ferguson 1980
San Antonio	IV	4/7 infants (57%)	1/1 child 100%	Ferguson 1980
Old Walpi	IV[c]	5/133 (4%)[b]	—	Ryan 1977
Pecos Pueblo	IV[c]	19/581 (3%)[b] 9 children	—	Hooton 1930
Hawikku	IV	127/151 (84%) both combined		Stodder 1990
San Cristobal Pueblo	IV	188/209 (90%) both combined		Stodder 1990
Dolores Project	E	2/21 (10%)	27/33 (82%)	Stodder 1987
		210/1,420 (15%) with Hooton 1930[c]		
		176/627 (23%) without Hooton 1930[c]		
Hohokam sites				
La Ciudad		7/13 (54%)	—	Fink and Merbs 1991
Grand Canal Ruins		26/61 (43%)	—	Fink and Merbs 1991
Casa Buena		12/24 (50%)	—	Fink and Merbs 1991
Mogollon site				
Grasshopper Pueblo		15/375 (4%)	54/386 (14%)	Hinkes 1983
Grasshopper Pueblo		30/369 (8%)	27/369 (7%)	Kelley 1980

TABLE 7.7. EVIDENCE OF POROTIC HYPEROSTOSIS AND CRIBRA ORBITALIA. (cont.)

Site	Time Period[a]	Porotic Hyperostosis	Cribra Orbitalia	Reference
Sinagua sites				
Oak Creek Pueblo		7/7 (100%)	—	Taylor 1985
Lizard Man Village		3/12 (25%)	3/12 (25%)	Kamp and Whittaker 1999
Nuvakwewtaqa (Chavez Pass Ruin)		41/44 (93%) both combined		Iwaniec 1989

[a]Time period determination: I = A.D. 750–1000, II = A.D. 1000–1150, III = A.D. 1150–1300, IV = A.D. 1300+, E = Excluded from temporal study.

[b]Porotic hyperostosis data used in comparative analyses in Table 7.8.

[c]Porotic hyperostosis data used in comparative analyses in Table 7.9.

[d]Data potentially include individuals reported from Inscription House by El-Najjar et al. 1976.

TABLE 7.8. FREQUENCIES OF ANASAZI POROTIC HYPEROSTOSIS.

Cultural Affiliation	Porotic Hyperostosis	%
Anasazi small sites	109/280	39
Anasazi large sites (excluding Hooton 1930)	191/839	23
Anasazi large sites (with Hooton 1930)	210/1,420	15

and stress occurred (Goodman and Rose 1990), although LEH may be lost on teeth that have severe wear (Stodder 1990). Severe tooth wear is ubiquitous in southwestern populations. Most researchers analyze the buccal surface of incisors and canines for evidence of LEH. The presence of more than one LEH per individual indicates that the individual underwent multiple stresses.

The problem of comparing LEH in southwestern populations is that, again, researchers are not consistent in how they record pathology (Table 7.10). Some researchers provide only the percentage of individuals with LEH and do not provide the number of individuals actually affected; other researchers record the percentage of teeth that are affected and do not provide the number of individuals these teeth represent; and other people record both deciduous and permanent teeth that are affected, again with no indication of the number of individuals represented by each sample. Therefore, statistical comparisons of LEH across cultural boundaries and through time in the Southwest cannot be made.

LEH and the nutritional and disease-related problems causing it usually show up in high frequencies in human skeletal samples that have been analyzed for that particular pathology (Table 7.10). The presence of LEH

TABLE 7.9. TEMPORAL FREQUENCIES OF ANASAZI POROTIC HYPEROSTOSIS.

Time Period[a]	Porotic Hyperostosis	%
pre I/II	116/301	39
III/IV (excluding Hooton 1930)	72/564	13
III/IV (with Hooton 1930)	91/1145	8

[a]Temporal affiliations listed in Table 7.7.

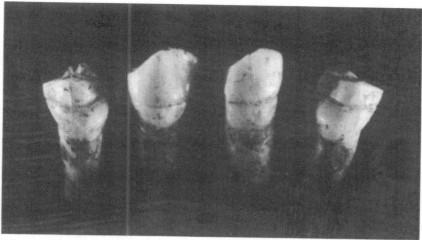

Figure 7.3. Enamel hypoplasia on the lower incisors of an individual from the Lower Pecos region of southwest Texas. Photo by Stephen Bicknell.

ranges from a high of 94 percent of permanent teeth at Hawikku to a low of 7 percent in the individuals of Arroyo Hondo Pueblo. This low figure is unusual in light of the very high childhood mortality rate at Arroyo Hondo (56 percent; Table 7.2); LEH represents a temporary cessation of growth and development, however, not a permanent condition. The children at Arroyo Hondo may not have had the chance to resume growth after a serious stress event.

Harris Lines

Harris lines, like LEH, are growth arrest lines that occur on long-bone shafts. Harris lines are actually lattice-like plates of bone that form in the metaphyses of long bones after growth resumes following an acute disruption. There is great debate, however, on the cause of Harris lines, although severe nutritional stress and disease most likely played a significant role. Some researchers estimate that the process of growth arrest and resumption may take place in as little as one week (Goodman et al. 1984; Steinbock 1976). Harris lines are visible on a-p radiographs and therefore are not determined in many skeletal analyses.

Only a few researchers analyzed human skeletal material for Harris lines (Table 7.10). Adults from Carter Ranch Pueblo exhibited an 80 percent rate of Harris lines whereas Grasshopper Pueblo exhibited a 20 percent rate. Other researchers recorded the average number of Harris lines

TABLE 7.10. EVIDENCE OF LINEAR ENAMEL HYPOPLASIAS, PERIOSTEAL INFECTIONS, AND HARRIS LINES.

Site	Linear Enamel Hypoplasias	Periosteal Infections	Harris Lines	Reference
Anasazi small sites				
Black Mesa A.D. 800–1050	—	100% of 1 yr. olds 57% of adults	—	Martin et al. 1991
Yellowjacket sites	—	2 individuals	—	Swedlund 1969
Mancos Canyon sites	—	1 individual	7.18 lines/indiv. in immature sample	Robinson 1976
Glen Canyon sites PII	0/38 decid. teeth 40/241 perm. teeth	0%	—	Ryan 1977
Black Mesa A.D. 1050–1150	4/25 (16%)	80% of 1 yr. olds 46% of adults	—	Martin et al. 1991
Mesa Verde region BMIII	6/35 (17%) teeth	—	—	Stodder 1984
Mesa Verde region PI	48/112 (43%) teeth	—	—	Stodder 1984
Mesa Verde region A.D. 600–975	—	—	23/31 (74%)	Stodder 1984
Puerco Valley, AZ	—	8 observations	—	Wade 1970
Mesa Verde region PII	39/103 (38%) teeth	—	—	Stodder 1984
Mesa Verde region PIII	74/241 (31%) teeth	—	—	Stodder 1984
Mesa Verde region A.D. 975–1300	—	—	16/30 (53%)	Stodder 1984
Glen Canyon sites PIII early, middle	0/98 decid. teeth 24/275 perm. teeth	0%	—	Ryan 1977
Carter Ranch Pueblo	70% of adults	13/24 (54%)	80% of adults	Danforth et al. 1994
Mesa Verde	2 observations	—	—	Miles 1966
Chaco Canyon	19/22 (86%)	1 observation	—	Akins 1986

TABLE 7.10. EVIDENCE OF LINEAR ENAMEL HYPOPLASIAS, PERIOSTEAL INFECTIONS, AND HARRIS LINES. (cont.)

Site	Linear Enamel Hypoplasias	Periosteal Infections	Harris Lines	Reference
Anasazi large sites				
Glen Canyon sites PIII late	0/267 decid. teeth 139/653 perm teeth	3 individuals	—	Ryan 1977
Arroyo Hondo Pueblo	8/120 (7%) all children		—	Palkovich 1980
Old Walpi	0/7 decid. teeth 122/851 perm. teeth	1 individual	—	Ryan 1977
Pecos Pueblo	—	13/503 (3%)		Hooton 1930
Hawikku	7/23 (30%) deciduous 104/111 (94%) permanent	29/57 (51%) subadults	n = 38, 158 lines, 4.16 lines/tibia	Stodder 1990
San Cristobal Pueblo	3/52 (6%) deciduous 124/146 (85%) permanent	15/67 (22%) subadults	n = 42, 154 lines, 3.66 lines/tibia	Stodder 1990
Dolores Project	20/64 (31%)	3/64 (5%)	11/24 (46%)	Stodder 1987
Hohokam sites				
La Ciudad	7/17 (41%)	—	—	Fink and Merbs 1991
Grand Canal Ruins	16/72 (22%)	—	—	Fink and Merbs 1991
Casa Buena	9/43 (21%)	—	—	Fink and Merbs 1991
Mogollon site				
Grasshopper Pueblo	28/248 (11%)	34/369 (9%)	53/267 (20%), 7.4 lines/individual	Hinkes 1983
Sinagua site				
Nuvakwewtaqa (Chavez Pass Ruin)	14%	21/157 (13%)	—	Iwaniec 1989

per individual; Grasshopper Pueblo individuals had an average of 7.4 Harris lines whereas those at Hawikku exhibited 4.16 lines and San Cristobal Pueblo individuals exhibited 3.66 lines. Since relatively few researchers analyzed long bones for the presence of Harris lines, a comparison of southwestern samples cannot be made.

Periosteal Infection

Periosteal lesions are nonspecific infections seen on the outer surface of bone, and osteomyelitis and osteitis are infections involving the inner cortex and marrow cavity of bone. Periosteal lesions are usually caused by treponematosis and treponemal disease, such as pinta, yaws, syphilis, and endemic syphilis, but can also be caused by tuberculosis and leprosy. Researchers do not agree on the actual cause of most periosteal lesions, but a diagnosis of infection and infectious disease can be made.

Only a few researchers recorded the presence of periosteal infections (Table 7.10), and these, of course, were recorded in different ways. Periosteal infection seems to have been a prevalent problem for prehistoric populations. M. A. Kelley (1980) states that infectious disease was the main causative factor in the death of infants and children in the Southwest. W. D. Wade states that in Puerco Valley "certainly the major cause of death in infants can be attributed to disease" (1970:172). Finding the actual source and cause of periosteal infections and therefore infectious disease is the problem. The effects of infectious disease would have been intensified by underlying morbid conditions of dietary deficiency, malnutrition, and parasitism (Hinkes 1983), conditions prevalent in the prehistoric Southwest.

Some researchers have indicated that children's mortality could have been swift in prehistoric populations because of virulent gastrointestinal and upper respiratory infections (Hinkes 1983). Such swift deaths would not have allowed pathological evidence, such as porotic hyperostosis, enamel hypoplasias, Harris lines, and periosteal infections, to manifest itself on bone and teeth. This may be the reason these pathological markers are less frequent in populations from larger sites and from later time periods.

Other Potentially Problematic Pathologies

Although not identified or recorded in great quantities by researchers, a few other potential health indicators could have been deleterious for children's health. These include tuberculosis, ear infections as evidenced through mastoid infections, and infections resulting from cranial deformation through the use of cradleboards and as evidenced through occipital lesions.

Tuberculosis is caused by infection with *Mycobacterium tuberculosis* and is observed on skeletal material mainly on the spine but also in other areas such as the ribs, sternum, and knee (El-Najjar 1979). It was once believed that tuberculosis originated in the Old World and spread to the New World after contact by Columbus et al. (Buikstra 1981). It is now believed that tuberculosis was present in the New World before A.D. 1492, as demonstrated by increasing evidence of tubercular lesions on prehistoric skeletons. In the Southwest, tubercular lesions have been observed on a growing number of samples (see Hinkes 1983:Table 6.8 for a list), although researchers argue whether a specific infection can be attributed to tuberculosis or is a reflection of other infectious diseases (Fink 1985). Even if a small number of individuals from a population are observed to be infected with tuberculosis, the infection rate for the population would be much higher, as it has been observed that only 5 to 7 percent of all tubercular cases are manifested on bone (Steinbock 1976). Therefore, the small prevalence of observed tuberculosis on skeletal samples from the Southwest could indicate that a large portion of the population was infected, potentially indicating high infection rates for infants and children and a high incidence of childhood mortality.

Mastoiditis, mastoid infection of the cranium indicating ear infection, is not commonly reported for prehistoric southwestern populations. L. L. Titche et al. (1981) analyzed 742 skulls from various Mogollon sites in an attempt to understand patterns of high otitis media (ear infection) in modern Indian populations. Seventeen percent of the prehistoric individuals exhibited evidence of ear infection. Titche et al. considered this rate to be low in comparison with infection rates in modern populations. D. L. Martin et al. (1991) indicated the presence of mastoid infections in up to 16.6 percent of the prehistoric population from Black Mesa. Only in rare and very severe cases would ear infections cause death, but chronic ear infections can lead to serious hearing loss in an individual.

Cranial modeling through the use of cradleboards in newborns and infants was a prevalent cultural practice in prehistoric and protohistoric southwestern populations. It is unknown whether cranial modeling occurs intentionally or unintentionally as a result of infant transport in cradleboards. The results are differing degrees of occipital flattening that can be observed in subadult and adult crania. Researchers are starting to realize the potential deleterious effects of cranial modeling and their probable association with occipital infections and supra-inion depression, which may result in newborn and infant death (Derrick 1994; Holliday 1993; Stewart 1976). D. Y. Holliday states that "the pressure and friction of an infant's head against a cradleboard may have (1) produced ischemic ulcers, (2) produced the conditions favorable for bacterial infections such as impetigo or carbuncles, or (3) complicated the treatment of other infections appearing on the back of the scalp" (Holliday 1993:283). S. McCormick Derrick (1994) analyzed healed supra-inion lesions in adults and one active lesion in a cranially modeled infant from prehistoric populations from Texas and Arkansas, indicating that the infant may have died as a result of cranial infection exacerbated and/or caused by cradleboarding. Researchers in the Southwest rarely report occipital lesions as a possible result of cranial modeling. It is unknown whether this absence indicates little to no infection from this source or whether researchers are not looking for this particular pathology.

CONCLUSIONS

Children's health in the southwestern United States after the introduction of agriculture illustrates a pervasive pattern of high infant mortality, malnutrition, and disease infestation. This pattern is present from the earliest well-preserved skeletal samples at the turn of the first century through the Protohistoric period. Children's malnutrition and ill health does not seem necessarily to increase through time; in fact, evidence indicates that the initial onset of agricultural practices and sedentism led to the most frequently and highly observed rates of infant mortality, anemia, and infection. In conjunction, children at small sites seemed to suffer more ill-health effects than children at larger sites. These findings do not mean, however, that children's health greatly improved through time and at larger sites. It seems that children at *all* sites and at *all* times after the advent of agriculture suffered pervasive ill health, chronic malnutrition, and high infectious disease rates that seemed to function in a synergistic interaction. Whittlesey (this volume) states that although maternal care of children was high, the interaction of adverse environmental and subsistence conditions predestined the high death rate of children. Even children of supposedly high-ranking lineages were not immune to the pervasive pattern of ill health. Children found in Pueblo Bonito burial rooms experienced dietary inadequacy, shown by high frequencies of anemia and infections (Palkovich 1982). In addition, Bradley (this volume) has observed that the supposedly better-nourished children at the ritual center of Sand Canyon exhibited perimortem cranial trauma, possibly indicating that they did not die from natural causes such as poor health and nutritional deprivation.

In effect, children's pervasive ill health in the prehistoric Southwest was influenced by a variety of factors surrounding the advent of agriculture in a marginal environment: malnutrition stemming from the adoption of a nutritionally inadequate subsistence base developed in a frequently unstable environment, the growth and spread of infectious disease through an increasingly susceptible population weakened by malnutrition, and an increase in anemia owing to malnutrition, infectious disease, and parasitic infections prevalent in a more sedentary, aggregated population. Children would have been particularly susceptible to these factors because of their increased nutritional needs for growth and development and the seemingly adverse effects of weaning at a critical juncture developmentally in this population. Children's health in the prehistoric Southwest is a contradiction in terms.

ACKNOWLEDGMENTS

I want to thank Grinnell College for providing me with an academic home and extensive resources to use during my sabbatical year, when I wrote this chapter. Grinnell's interlibrary loan department was extremely helpful. Kathy Kamp provided the idea and the impetus behind this research, and Stephen Bicknell took the photographs.

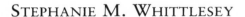

8

The Cradle of Death

Mortuary Practices,

Bioarchaeology, and the

Children of Grasshopper Pueblo

STEPHANIE M. WHITTLESEY

In the treatment, circumstances, and education of children, we can often glimpse the keys to a society's long-term success, for the future of any human group lies with its children. How best to study children among prehistoric populations? My position is similar to what I have proposed regarding gender studies in prehistory (Whittlesey 1999). Inferring the presence of children solely from material culture in archaeological contexts is complicated and prone to error; alternative explanations are difficult to rule out. For example, some sloppily painted ceramic vessels may have been children's work, but others could just have easily been painted by older adults with poor eyesight. Little pinch pots such as those often attributed to children's manufacture appear on ceremonial room floors at Grasshopper Pueblo (Reid and Whittlesey 1999), suggesting an adult and ritual function. I maintain that there is no better place to seek children than where children can unquestionably be seen—in bioarchaeological and mortuary data.

Building on this conviction, this chapter explores the lives of the children of Grasshopper Pueblo, a Pueblo IV–period Mogollon Pueblo settlement in east-central Arizona, as reconstructed from the circumstances of their deaths. I use mortuary and bioarchaeological data to discuss the health, treatment, and status of Grasshopper's children and contrast their circumstances with those of other social groups. Extremely high subadult mortality rates (see Sobolik, this volume) were coupled with relatively good health among older children, suggesting that Grasshopper's children were valued and cared for (see Bradley, this volume, for a similar argument) but that inadequate maternal nutrition and resulting poor health affected them greatly. Mortuary practices indicate clear parallels between women and children that support an inferred social organization based largely on age and gender and stressing the importance of ceremonial memberships and ritual knowledge. The bioarchaeological and mortuary data also support the inference that Grasshopper Pueblo was occupied by at least two different ethnic groups (Reid and Whittlesey 1999). In the children of Grasshopper Pueblo we also have a window on women's issues and behavior related to gender. Comparing Grasshopper with contemporaneous sites indicates differences in mortuary treatment and health that may have been culturally constituted.

GRASSHOPPER PUEBLO, BIOARCHAEOLOGICAL DATA, AND MORTUARY DATA

The Grasshopper region is a mountain plateau in the heart of east-central Arizona north of the Salt River. This rugged region was occupied prehistorically by the Mogollon and today is home to the White Mountain Tribe of the Western Apache. Grasshopper Pueblo was the largest settlement in the region and one of the most intensively studied prehistoric sites in North America (Reid and Whittlesey 1999). Research by the University of Arizona Archaeological Field School began at Grasshopper in 1963 and continued until 1992. Three decades of study have resulted in one of the largest, best-provenienced, and best-documented collections of human remains and associated burial goods from a single population in the world (Longacre and Reid 1974:9). Studies of the 674 individuals distributed among 655 assigned burial numbers and thousands of associated artifacts have resulted in a wealth of knowledge about prehistoric demography, subsistence, migration, cultural affiliation, and social organization (Berry 1983, 1985a, 1985b; Birkby 1973, 1982; Clark 1967; Ezzo 1991, 1993, 1997; Fenton 1998; Fulginiti 1993; Griffin 1967, 1969; Hinkes 1983; Reid and Whittlesey 1999; Shipman 1982; Whittlesey 1978, 1989, 1999). A similar collection is unlikely to be obtained ever again, in light of today's political, academic, and economic climate.

Grasshopper Pueblo consists of more than 500 masonry rooms distributed among three room blocks with three associated plazas, which together form the main pueblo, and a number of smaller, outlying room blocks. It represents a classic case of aggregation and coresidence by multiple ethnic groups. Grasshopper was established around A.D. 1300 by settlers from three earlier pueblos, including some people of probable Anasazi (also known as Ancestral Pueblo) affiliation. Growth peaked in the A.D. 1330s when one of the plazas was converted into a great kiva. Dispersion into adjacent settlements had begun by A.D. 1350, and by 1400 the pueblo was abandoned (Reid and Whittlesey 1999). Several lines of evidence, including cranial deformation, bone-chemistry analyses (Ezzo 1991, 1993), architectural data (Riggs 1999), and ceramic evidence (Triadan 1997; Van Keuren 1999), indicate that Grasshopper was a multiethnic community consisting of indigenous Mogollon, coresident Anasazi, and possibly other groups (Reid and Whittlesey 1999).

Bioarchaeological data of many kinds have been collected on the Grasshopper burial collection over the years. It is important to note that when J. Jefferson Reid assumed directorship of the field school in 1979, a growing awareness of the concerns of the White Mountain Apache Tribe prompted him to establish a policy of nonexcavation of human remains. No burials were excavated from Grasshopper or other sites investigated by the field school after that date.

This chapter relies on Madeleine Hinkes's (1983) bioarchaeological data recorded for the subadult population of Grasshopper, supplemented with baseline age, sex, and cranial deformation data collected by Walter Birkby of the Arizona State Museum, University of Arizona. Discussion of mortuary ritual is based on a sample of 411 complete, relatively undisturbed interments, as revised from my dissertation research (Whittlesey 1978). The remaining individuals (263, or 39.0 percent) represent disturbed and disarticulated interments resulting from the practice of burying the dead within rooms. The typical practice at Grasshopper Pueblo, as discussed below, was to bury the deceased, primarily children, in abandoned rooms, or even occasionally in occupied rooms in the case of the youngest children. Apparently, there was no method of marking graves, for as rooms continued to be used for interment, graves of later interments commonly encountered earlier burials. The skeletal remains and associated goods of the earlier interments were moved and redeposited, evidently close to the original location. Although many of these cases can be used in bioarchaeological research (e.g., Hinkes 1983), they do not constitute strong cases for describing mortuary practices or inferring social organization and ritual (see Whittlesey 1978).

The nature and representativeness of the complete burial sample have been discussed previously (Ezzo 1993; Hinkes 1983). The sample is skewed toward subadults and, among adults, toward females. J. A. Ezzo (1993:29) concluded that "the evidence suggests that the burial series may be treated as a viable sample of the inhabitants of the site in terms of age ranges, social/ethnic affiliations, and probably in status positions." The same claim is made for the sample of complete, undisturbed interments.

Demography and Mortality

Sadly, life was short for the children of Grasshopper Pueblo. Of the 674 individuals, only 231 are aged 15 years or older—a striking 65.7 percent subadults. Hinkes (1983) noted that this percentage is extremely high compared with other prehistoric southwestern sites. Archaeological recovery procedures contributed somewhat to the high percentage of subadults. Excavation focused on rooms, from which 90 percent of subadults were recovered (Hinkes 1983:19). Extramural areas, particularly plazas, in which proportionately more adults were buried, were excavated less intensively, contributing to the relatively low proportion of adults.

Subadult mortality was undeniably great, however. The mortality curve for the Grasshopper skeletal series (Hinkes 1983:Table 1) corresponds to curves seen among undeveloped countries (e.g., Weiss 1973). The pattern is one of extremely high infant mortality, high but declining mortality from ages 1 to 5, and a steadily decreasing rate until the ages of 10 to 15, the time of lowest mortality. Fetuses and infants less than 1 year in age represent more than 40 percent of subadults (Table 8.1). Hinkes (1983:86) noted fetal immaturity at Grasshopper and attributed it to nutritional stress in the mother.

Hinkes (1983:148) suggests, based on the absence of bony evidence to the contrary, that common infectious diseases of the respiratory and gastrointestinal systems were the primary killers of the children of Grasshopper Pueblo. Weaning between 2 and 3 years of age was a particularly critical time. Because the diet may have been less than optimal, susceptibility to infectious diseases was even greater at this age. Children who endured this ordeal successfully were likely to live to adulthood.

Health and Nutrition

At least some of Grasshopper's children experienced poor health and retarded growth, probably because of dietary deficiencies and poor maternal nutrition. Hinkes (1983) recorded a number of stress markers among the

TABLE 8.1. AGE AND SEX DISTRIBUTION OF GRASSHOPPER BURIALS.

Age Class and Sex (Years)	Number	% Total Burials	% Burial Class
Fetal	40	6.6	10.6
Birth–1	116	19.1	30.8
1–3.9	106	17.4	28.1
4–11.9	109	17.9	28.9
12–14.9	6	1.0	1.6
(Male)	(3)		
(Female)	(3)		
Subtotal subadults	377	62.0	100.0
(Male)	(3)		(50.0)
(Female)	(3)		(50.0)
15–19.9	30	4.9	
(Male)	(13)		
(Female)	(17)		
20–29.9	57	9.4	
(Male)	(20)		
(Female)	(37)		
30–39.9	58	9.5	
(Male)	(24)		
(Female)	(34)		
>40	86	14.1	
(Male)	(34)		
(Female)	(52)		
Subtotal adults	231	38.0	
(Male)	91		(39.4)
(Female)	140		(60.6)
Total	608	100.0	
(Male)	94		(39.7)
(Female)	143		(60.3)

Note: Based on age and sex information provided by Hinkes (1983: Table 1); excludes 66 unanalyzable subadult burials. (Note that some of Hinkes's age categories differ; e.g., Hinkes classified the 12–19.9 classes as 12–14 and 14–20.)

Grasshopper subadults, including cortical bone loss, cribra orbitalia, porotic hyperostosis, femoral growth retardation, linear enamel hypoplasia, and Harris lines. The incidence of most of these stress markers was relatively low. Porotic hyperostosis affected few children and only very young children (birth to 6 months). Hinkes (1983) noted that this was perhaps the lowest documented frequency in a prehistoric skeletal collection of such size. Cribra orbitalia was the most common stress marker, yet it affected only 14 percent of subadults. The greatest incidence occurred between 12 and 18 months, possibly owing to nutritional deficiencies during weaning. There was little occurrence of growth retardation as measured by femoral length. Harris lines were the second most commonly observed stress marker, yet lines were not generally frequent or patterned. Lines were found most often in children aged 6 to 8 years at death. Prenatal dental defects were particularly high among fetal, neonatal, and perinatal infants (Hinkes 1983:146).

Multiple stress markers were relatively rare and occurred most often in children less than 3 years of age. The precipitating stresses appeared to Hinkes (1983:143) to be systemic, and some were prenatal in origin. Together these data suggested to Hinkes the possibility of differential access to food.

When Hinkes (1983) stratified the subadult sample into spatial and temporal groups, differences emerged. The incidence of stress markers differed among the three room blocks in the main pueblo, with the highest incidence found in Room Block 1 and the lowest in Room Block 3. Nutritional stress apparently increased through time. Children buried in the latest-occupied portions of the pueblo were younger and exhibited more stress markers than those found in the earlier portions (Hinkes 1983:168, 177). The highest incidence in Grasshopper Pueblo as a whole occurred in burials found in the outliers, a group of rooms built and abandoned late in the pueblo's history (Reid 1973). Hinkes suggested that we may be seeing the effects of resource depletion, food shortages, or an increase in infectious diseases over time.

It would be tempting to explain Hinkes's findings by positing differential maize consumption and dependence. Maize is a notoriously poor foodstuff, and maize-dependent diets are likely to result in increased iron-deficiency anemia due to the phytic acid content of maize hulls, particularly if the corn is not treated with lime (El-Najjar et al. 1976; Ivanhoe 1985; Snow 1990; Walker 1985). At first glance, Hinkes's results suggest that the occupants of Room Block 1 were more maize dependent than those of Room Block 3.

This interpretation is not supported by bone-chemistry analyses carried out by Ezzo (1991, 1993), whose results were the complete opposite of Hinkes's findings. He found that dietary variability existed among the room blocks. The diets of Room Block 1 residents "indicate greater utilization of wild plant resources" whereas "Room Block 3 diets were oriented more toward consumption of agricultural products than Room Block 2" (Ezzo 1993:83). The two studies are only partly comparable, however. Ezzo analyzed only adult burials, for example.

The interpretation that diets decreased in nutritional value through time is supported by both studies. Ezzo (1993) interpreted spatial variability as reflecting differential access to farmland and resources. The bone-chemistry data indicated that consumption of wild resources decreased and use of maize increased through time. This would correlate well with the high incidence of stress markers among the latest-buried children.

Mortuary Practices

Turning to mortuary practices, we find that in death the children of Grasshopper Pueblo were treated differently from adults. Among the Grasshopper burials, children displayed the most variability in aspects of grave type and body positioning and the least variability in artifactual accompaniments. Standardization in the former and variation in the latter increased with increasing age at death.

Subadults were more likely than adults to be buried within rooms. The youngest infants and fetal burials often were placed in pits immediately below the floors of occupied rooms. Subfloor burial has been explained with reference to ethnographically documented Pueblo practices (Bunzel 1932:482; Eggan 1950:47; Parsons 1939:71; Voth 1912:103; White 1942:164). Certain types of graves were used more frequently for subadults, including slab-covered pits and stone-lined cists. The majority of slab-covered and stone-lined grave pits occurred with children less than 4 years of age. The high-energy-expenditure types of graves, such as log-crib-covered pits, were seldom used. Although burial in trash without benefit of a formal pit was not common at Grasshopper, about 90 percent of these few interments represented subadults, and many were fetal burials. Children were seldom wrapped in reed matting or other types of body cover.

Children also were variable in body positioning. About three-fourths of the few flexed and semiflexed burials recovered were subadults. There was greater variation in placement of the limbs and extremities as well. The majority of the burials that were oriented with the head to a direction other than east were subadults.

By contrast, there was little variability in the artifacts that accompanied children; the type and the number of accompaniments were limited. Children tended to be buried with ceramic vessels and personal ornaments of particular types. The ornaments that signified membership in sodalities (Reid and Whittlesey 1982, 1999) and the utilitarian and ceremonial items that accompanied adults were not found among subadults. Subadults always were accompanied by fewer grave goods (mean = 2.03 artifacts) than adults (mean = 6.03 artifacts), regardless of burial provenience.

The number of associated artifacts increased along with the age of the child at death, and types of accompaniments varied with age. Younger children were buried less frequently with painted vessels. No vessels were found with fetal burials; roughly one-third of the burial vessels interred with subadults aged birth to 4 years were painted, and 50–60 percent of the vessels buried with individuals aged 4 years and older were painted.

The location of burials inside rooms and the variability in aspects of grave preparation and body positioning suggest that it was most likely the deceased child's immediate family and other close kin who prepared the body for burial and that the burial of children was not a public event. This also implies that whereas it may have been necessary to treat adults in highly normative ways to prepare them for the afterlife, such preparation was not needed for children. The limited number and type of grave goods indicates that children did not participate in the wider circle of social and ceremonial obligations that were criteria of adult status.

At least two transitions in the life cycle of children apparently existed and were recognized socially. The first was birth. Fetal burials differed from those of full-term infants in location of interment (room floors, trash) and associated grave goods (typically none). This suggests that membership in the natal kinship unit was bestowed on a full-term infant at birth, and premature and stillborn infants were not regarded in the same way (Whittlesey 1989). There is ethnographic support for this notion as reported by Frank Hamilton Cushing for Zuni (Green 1979:205).

A second transition took place at about 1 year of age, when the number of ceramic vessels accompanying children increased dramatically. More than two-thirds of children aged less than 1 year at death lacked ceramic vessels, contrasted with only one-third of children aged 1 to 4 years at death. This difference may indicate a transition in status, perhaps marking membership in a kinship group, initiation into a pueblo ceremonial group, or a formal naming ceremony. Mischa Titiev (1944) reported that at Oraibi a child who died before its katsina cult initiation was given a distinctive type of burial. Alternatively, the pattern may indicate simply that children less than 1 year of age were not yet weaned and therefore did not require food and water in the afterlife (Whittlesey 1989).

SUMMARY AND COMPARISONS

The children of Grasshopper Pueblo evidently were cherished and cared for as well as their parents' circumstances allowed. The high infant mortality, presence of stress markers primarily among the youngest children, and increasingly good health after weaning indicate that it was insufficient maternal nutrition and resulting health status that contributed largely to the poor health and high mortality of Grasshopper's children. These patterns are echoed in the mortality rates of women. The striking majority of females (60 percent of sexed burials) at Grasshopper (see Table 8.1) has been noted as unusual among burial samples from contemporaneous populations (Berry 1985a). Archaeological recovery techniques probably were not responsible for this disparity, as burial locales were not separated by sex. The predominance of females does not seem puzzling given the conditions of life at Grasshopper Pueblo. Women no doubt also experienced complications of pregnancy and labor, and the lack of medical care must have resulted in many deaths.

Ezzo (1993:54–55) presented evidence derived from bone-chemistry data that diets of men and women differed, at least during the earlier portions of the pueblo's history when men evidently subsisted more heavily on meat than women. Late in Grasshopper's occupation the amount of meat and wild plant foods in everyone's diets declined as maize became the dietary mainstay. The lesser amount of protein in women's diets combined with the nutritional deficiencies that result from subsisting almost completely on maize (Cravioto et al. 1945; El-Najjar et al. 1976; Ivanhoe 1985; Snow 1990; Walker 1985) may have created impoverished nutrition and poor health, particularly during pregnancy and lactation. L. S. Cummings noted that pregnant women are more susceptible to folate-deficiency-induced megaloblastic anemia because the body's need for folate doubles during pregnancy: "If the diet was composed largely of corn, megaloblastic anemia undoubtedly increased the death rate among pregnant women and nursing mothers" (1995:344).

The increase in both infant mortality and incidence of stress markers late in Grasshopper's history supports Ezzo's observations of dietary change through time and suggests that as women's nutritional status declined, so did the health of their unborn and newly born children. As Hinkes (1983:146) notes, "Sickly or very young mothers produce babies less likely to survive and thrive. Those term infants surviving the birth trauma may have succumbed to hypoxic or other stress due to immature organ systems and lack of medical intervention. . . . Infants who might have survived for a few months simply did not have enough time to register any stress on the skeleton and may have died from a single severe attack of diarrhea or upper respiratory infection."

The mortuary information supports bioarchaeological data suggesting that Grasshopper's children were treated with care, regardless of their health and vigor. Although there is worldwide ethnographic data to support infanticide, neither the bioarchaeological data nor the mortuary ritual indicates that this took place at Grasshopper. Indeed, in a population whose incredibly high infant mortality rate must have threatened demographic replacement, infanticide would have made little sense. There is also no skeletal evidence for child abuse. Because there is no skeletal evidence, however, these interpretations must remain only a logical supposition.

The interesting correlation between the treatments accorded women and children is further support for the notion that the pueblo was a composite of different ethnic groups and that women married into the local population at Grasshopper.

The variable treatment of children in death indicates the probable presence of multiple ethnic or social subgroups, each with its own particular approach to death. Similarities in the treatment provided women and children also indicate gender to have been a primary factor structuring social roles and statuses, particularly because Grasshopper's sociopolitical organization appears to have been based on ceremonial knowledge and performance, in which neither women nor children participated to any degree. Yet as discussed elsewhere (Whittlesey 1999), there is no indication that women and female children were treated poorly or regarded as inferior. Their lower social standing was evidently a product of their operation within kinship rather than ritual spheres. And although some women and their children were less well fed than others, there is no indication that male children were given preference over female children. The incidence of stress markers is about equal among children that Hinkes (1983:148) was able to identify as male and female.

How do these interpretations compare with those derived using mortuary and bioarchaeological data from contemporaneous prehistoric sites? We can look to two other large mortuary collections to examine how people of different cultures or ethnic groups treated their children.

Arroyo Hondo Pueblo

Arroyo Hondo Pueblo, located south of Santa Fe, New Mexico, is a prehistoric Rio Grande pueblo representing Anasazi (Ancestral Pueblo) culture. It was excavated and analyzed with modern techniques by the School of American Research during the early 1970s. The site was broadly contemporaneous with Grasshopper, although it was occupied somewhat longer (Schwartz 1980). The pueblo was established at precisely the same time as Grasshopper, at A.D. 1300, and it was abandoned except for a

small remnant occupation by A.D. 1345. After a hiatus, there was a reoc-
cupation termed Component II that lasted from sometime in the A.D.
1370s to about A.D. 1430 (Schwartz 1980). Unfortunately, the burial sample from Arroyo Hondo is not as likely to be representative of prehistoric
patterns as that from Grasshopper Pueblo. The site is twice as large as
Grasshopper—an estimated 1,000 rooms—and was occupied longer. Yet
only 120 burials were recovered, the majority from the earlier component
dating between A.D. 1300 and 1370 (Palkovich 1980).

The age distribution at Arroyo Hondo was almost identical to that at
Grasshopper: 55.8 percent of the interments were subadults. There was
also a predominance of female adults (60 percent of sexable adult skeletons). As at Grasshopper the majority of subadults were under the age of
5 (80.3 percent; Palkovich 1980:Table 5).

Mortuary practices differed substantially. The predominant interment
mode was flexed inhumation in a formal pit with the body placed on the
side. This was true for all ages and both sexes. Burials were placed primarily in plazas, but because the excavation strategy targeted extramural
areas and focused less intensively on rooms than at Grasshopper, it surely
influenced this distribution considerably. Of the subfloor room interments,
79.2 percent were subadults, contrasted with 64.3 percent of the plaza
burials (Palkovich 1980:Table 1).

Burial accompaniments differed from those at Grasshopper Pueblo.
Although about three-fourths of the subadults had grave goods, they were
typically perishable items such as matting, blankets, or food remains. Only
subadult burials contained shell ornaments, and few burials were accompanied by ceramic vessels, regardless of age (Palkovich 1980:16–17).

Mortality was high for the subgroups below age 10, and survivorship
and life expectancy were low (Palkovich 1980:36). Life expectancy at
birth was only about 16 years; individuals who survived to the age of
15 could expect to live another 19 years, however (Palkovich 1980:31).
A. M. Palkovich (1980:36) speculates that individuals who survived the
disease stresses of childhood were better able to cope with illness as young
adults.

The overall health status of the Arroyo Hondo population seems
poorer than what we infer for the people of Grasshopper. Forty-four percent of the Component I population displayed various skeletal pathologies, and 63.3 percent with these pathologies were subadults. Nutritional
stress was indicated by several anomalies; the incidence was much higher
among subadults. For example, no adults were observed to display porotic
hyperostosis; all 14 occurrences were among subadults. Palkovich (1980:25)

writes: "The incidence of pathologies in the subadult and adult age groups indicates a marked difference in the health status of these two segments of the population. Subadults showed nearly equal or greater incidence of each type of pathology than did the adult population of Component I. Greater susceptibility to disease and undernutrition probably created severe health problems in the younger age groups."

The incidence of porotic hyperostosis, endocranial lesions, cribra orbitalia, and generalized bone porosity among children younger than 5 suggested to Palkovich the effects of malnutrition, specifically iron-deficiency anemia. She proposed that "malnutrition, acting in combination with infectious disease, was at least partially responsible for the high level of mortality among infants and young children at Arroyo Hondo" (Palkovich 1980:47). Malnutrition may have been the product of infant diet and feeding practices, a general emphasis on high-carbohydrate foods, and farming shortages created by drought or other factors (Palkovich 1980:47).

Palkovich also examined the Arroyo Hondo burials in light of Alfonso Ortiz's (1969) ethnographically based model of age grading among Eastern Pueblos. She found some differences between the group less than 6 years of age and the group more than 6 years old, sufficient to suggest that the birth-to-6-year group "was recognized as a separate status group by the Arroyo Hondo individuals." She also found evidence for high status among adult males based on ritual knowledge and performance and some indications that status was ascribed based on kinship. Two of these patterns were similar to those described by Ortiz (1969); the last has no ethnographic parallel among the Eastern Pueblos. This comparison suffers from direct ethnographic analogy; a dated processual approach to status, prestige, and role; and problems in sample size and representativeness; but it suggests generalized patterns that could be explored with larger data sets.

The Arroyo Hondo subadult data are similar to those of Grasshopper Pueblo in indicating poor subadult nutritional and health status, which can be correlated with poor maternal nutrition and health; in having a similar pattern of respect for and treatment of children; and in showing some distinctions between adult and subadult mortuary treatment that reflect the different achievements of these segments of the population and correspondingly different recognition in death as well as life. Certainly the basic mortuary ritual suggests major differences that can only be ascribed to cultural or ethnic distinctions among the two populations—Anasazi or Ancestral Pueblo versus Mogollon or Western Pueblo peoples.

It is tempting to link the increased incidence of skeletal abnormalities and inferred poor nutritional status to maize dependence among the

Arroyo Hondo residents. Maize dependence is traditionally viewed as characterizing Anasazi or Ancestral Pueblo people; Mogollon or Western Pueblo people appear to have subsisted largely on game and wild plant foods supplemented by agricultural products. This was certainly true of Grasshopper Pueblo, at least until late in the pueblo's history, when the transition to agricultural dependence took place (Reid and Whittlesey 1999). We suspect that, as the master dry farmers of the Colorado Plateau, it was the Anasazi immigrants who were largely responsible for the conversion of the local Mogollon Pueblo people to maize dependence.

Pueblo Grande

Pueblo Grande is a large, adobe-compound village located in metropolitan Phoenix, Arizona. Although it was occupied primarily during what has been labeled the Hohokam Classic period, the later portion of which (Civano phase) was contemporaneous with the occupation at Grasshopper Pueblo after A.D. 1300, there was also a substantial pre-Classic Hohokam occupation. The site had a long history of investigation beginning in the early years of southwestern archaeology; it was investigated most intensively and recently for the Arizona Department of Transportation by Soil Systems, Inc., whose excavations focused on the Classic period occupation. A number of walled, residential compounds and a platform mound represent the Classic period occupation. More than 800 burials were excavated. Both cremation and inhumation burial were practiced, which is common among Classic period populations, and the dead were placed in discrete cemeteries associated with habitation areas (Mitchell 1994).

The cultural affiliation of the Pueblo Grande residents has been the topic of considerable debate. The early view labeled them Salado, a cultural group thought to represent Puebloan immigrants from the north who settled in the Phoenix area and displaced the original Hohokam inhabitants. Beginning in the 1970s, a fresh wave of intensive archaeological investigation in desert Arizona brought a new interpretation of continuity between pre-Classic and Classic period Hohokam. Today the interpretive climate is shifting again toward a view of demographic movement and lack of continuity between the people living in these two intervals of prehistory (see discussion in Reid and Whittlesey 1997). Regardless of the model of cultural affiliation to which one subscribes, the parallels between the mortuary practices of the people living at Pueblo Grande during the Classic period and those of the contemporaneous inhabitants of Grasshopper Pueblo (and elsewhere in central Arizona) are remarkable (Whittlesey and Reid 2001).

In particular, many aspects of the treatment of children are parallel. Subadult burials exhibited less formal grave preparation and more variable body positioning than adults. Children, particularly infants, were buried with fewer artifacts than adults. They were accompanied by many fewer ceramic vessels and utilitarian objects; certain ornament types, particularly turquoise and shell pendants, were not found with infant burials. The absence of tools with subadults indicated to D. R. Mitchell (1994: 154) an adult-subadult role distinction: "Infants and children/adolescents would not be expected to be associated with these items because they have not yet taken on their adult social roles."

Bioarchaeological data indicated a population experiencing nutritional stress and disease. Among the comparisons made by D. P. Van Gerven and S. G. Sheridan (1994c), mortality at Pueblo Grande was exceeded only by two other sites, one of which was Grasshopper Pueblo. Infant mortality was high; "the modal age at death was birth" (Van Gerven and Sheridan 1994c:9). A second peak in mortality at 3 years of age suggested weaning trauma and was followed by improved health. These phenomena were paralleled at Grasshopper Pueblo. Van Gerven and Sheridan (1994c:16) write that "the people of Pueblo Grande experienced high levels of subadult stress and mortality. If, as has been argued, subadults are a sensitive barometer of the biological well-being of the general population . . . then the people of Pueblo Grande appear to have experienced a high level of stress." Also as at Grasshopper, survivorship decreased through time (Van Gerven and Sheridan 1994c:18). In contrast to Grasshopper Pueblo, male and female mortality patterns were similar, with females experiencing slightly higher mortality during the reproductive years (Van Gerven and Sheridan 1994c:17).

Other data supported the paleodemographic analysis. Ninety-nine percent of the individuals examined exhibited dental hypoplasias (Karhu and Amon 1994:29). Bone loss, as measured by cortical reduction, was high for individuals between the ages of birth and 4 years, and loss was especially rapid after age 12. Van Gerven and Sheridan (1994b:52) interpret this finding as an indication of physiological stress, most likely nutritional in nature. Only isolated instances of porotic hyperostosis could be observed because of the fragmentary nature of the crania, but they were sufficient to document "the existence of severe subadult anemia at Pueblo Grande" (Mittler and Van Gerven 1994:61). Fifty-four percent of examined adults exhibited porotic hyperostosis (Mittler and Van Gerven 1994:61), reflecting a high frequency of childhood anemia. It was more frequent among young adult females than males (Mittler and Van Gerven 1994:68). Diploic thickening also indicated that adult females were more anemic than males (Mittler and Van Gerven 1994:69). Trace-element analysis provides an explanation: the diets of females were consistently higher in plant products than those of males (Jones and Sheridan 1994:85). In addition, the amount of animal protein in the diet evidently decreased through time.

Van Gerven and Sheridan (1994a:128) conclude that the people of Pueblo Grande were "living on the edge of survival, nutritionally and reproductively stressed and struggling to maintain their numbers." The information from Pueblo Grande suggests several parallels with Grasshopper Pueblo. Children were nutritionally stressed, probably as a consequence of poor maternal nutrition and health. The diets of men and women differed, and the greater amount of plant foods in women's diets contributed to anemia, bone loss, and reproductive inefficiency. These health problems were exacerbated through time, perhaps because of increasing maize dependence or a decline in hunting or game populations, and may have been associated with decreasing amounts of arable land or declining soil fertility. The variables influencing mortuary treatment and inferred life-cycle events appear to have been similar to those of Grasshopper Pueblo. Not unexpectedly, women's and children's lives and health appear to have been closely related.

It is appealing to explain the poor health of the Pueblo Grande population in terms of immigration. The pueblo dates to a time of demographic shifts and population movement probably related at least in part to deteriorating environmental conditions on the Colorado Plateau. People moved southward into the mountain Transition Zone, where they coresided with the indigenous Mogollon people at Point of Pines, Grasshopper, and Chodistaas Pueblos (Reid 1989). Other Puebloan groups moved into the Tonto Basin (Clark 1995; Reid and Whittlesey 1997; Whittlesey and Reid 1982). Some populations continued moving farther south along the San Pedro River and other corridors into southern Arizona (Di Peso 1958; Woodson 1995). The "Classic period Hohokam" residents of Pueblo Grande may have been one such immigrant group. Such populations, already experiencing poor health as a probable consequence of food shortages, may have found the better agricultural lands in their new homes already taken. Competition may have exacerbated an economy already stressed by population increase, climatic deterioration, and reduced soil fertility, with profound impacts on nutrition, health, and mortality.

CONCLUSIONS

In the children of Grasshopper Pueblo we see reflected a multiethnic population trying to adapt to the stresses of high population density, depleted or insufficient farmland, and inadequate nutrition. We also see a people who, while watching their babies and young children succumb in ever-increasing numbers to simple infectious diseases, evidently tried to offer them the best possible care. We glimpse the importance of kinship and family as the nucleus of Grasshopper social organization. It appears to have been the poor health and nutrition of Grasshopper's mothers that contributed in large measure to high fetal and infant mortality, and this may have been in part a product of traditional differences in the diets of women and men.

Comparisons with Arroyo Hondo Pueblo and Pueblo Grande indicate that these patterns were pervasive in the Southwest. Whereas Arroyo Hondo is distinctive for its mortuary practices, which appear to reflect the cultural affiliation of its residents, all three populations were similar in high degrees of subadult mortality and skeletal defects linked to nutritional stress. There were some differences, however. Although mortality was high in all groups, the incidence of nutritionally related defects such as porotic hyperostosis differed among the three populations. This may reflect differential maize dependence and other dietary, weaning, and feeding practices. The lower incidence at Grasshopper, for example, may reflect the traditional Mogollon emphasis on wild plant foods and game in the diet.

All three groups show a close link between women and children that went beyond the simple mother-child social relationship. Maternal health affected the health and survival of children profoundly, as did child-rearing, weaning, and postweaning dietary practices. Similarities in the treatment of women and children at death suggest the importance of the mother-child bond and family relationships in structuring social life. One of the more interesting patterns to emerge from the comparison is the widespread difference between the diets of men and women and their corresponding influence on infant health. Thus, in the parallels between the treatment in death of women and children as well as their health status, we glimpse the importance of gender in structuring everyday life. Future research would benefit from intensive exploration of these relationships, particularly the correlations among mortuary practices of children, their health and nutritional status, and their presumed ethnic membership.

ACKNOWLEDGMENTS

I would like to thank Kathy Kamp for inviting me to participate in the symposium, for her subsequent patience in getting the chapter to press, and for suggesting helpful additions. Jeff Reid provided invaluable assistance and his usual wry commentary. Grasshopper Pueblo is located on the White Mountain Apache Reservation, and the research there by the University of Arizona Archaeological Field School was made possible by the forbearance and hospitality of the Apache people. The National Science Foundation provided support for the field school during the 1960s and early 1970s. The staff and students who worked at Grasshopper deserve thanks for helping collect the data for this and so many other research efforts over the years. Madeleine Hinkes, wherever you are, I hope I haven't distorted your work too badly. Errors of fact and substance are mine alone.

9

Thoughts Count

Ideology and the Children of Sand Canyon Pueblo

CYNTHIA S. BRADLEY

In what ways can beliefs affect children's well-being for better or for worse? Material, environmental influences on children's health have been well demonstrated in studies of living children, and the investigation of physical stressors is a hallmark of current bioarchaeological research (Armelagos and Goodman 1991). So far, the world of ideas has received much less emphasis. Ideological tenets, however, play a powerful role in forming and altering adult behaviors toward children, producing both favorable and adverse health effects. Moreover, in recent years Native Americans such as Pueblo members Rina Swentzell (1992) and Gregory Cajete (2000) have challenged archaeologists to broaden their traditional research philosophies, predominantly reliant on a materialist approach, and adopt a holistic viewpoint that would incorporate the spiritual aspects of human existence. As demonstrated by David McClelland's (1981) study of ideology and child rearing in living children, ideational perspectives and scientific approaches based on observation, inference, and quantitative data are not mutually exclusive.

In this chapter I discuss the ways ideology might have influenced the well-being of the children of Sand Canyon Pueblo, a large thirteenth-century village. Since the specific cosmological, political, and religious beliefs of these prehistoric people are unknown, ideology is broadly defined here as being related to ideas. I have found no bioarchaeological studies that address the relationship between ideology, child rearing, and children's health in past societies. My research thus involves an eclectic, synthetic, cross-cultural approach and draws on a wide variety of documentary evidence. This information, discussed in more detail in my Master's thesis (Bradley 1998), is derived from historic, ethnographic, biological, biocultural, and child development studies.

The skeletal remains of 30 individuals, including 20 children, were discovered during archaeological research at Sand Canyon Pueblo. Skeletal indicators suggest that these Ancestral Pueblo children were basically healthy and apparently better nourished than children from comparable populations (Bradley 1998). I attribute their health to the enhanced nutrition that resulted from residence in a community that acted as a ritual center and thus was frequently the location of ritual feasting. Adult beliefs about the appropriateness of including children in such activities seem to have had a positive effect on the health of Sand Canyon Pueblo children.

Growing up at Sand Canyon Pueblo had risks as well as advantages, however. At least 20 children and adults, many with severe perimortem cranial trauma, apparently did not die from natural causes. Adolescents are overrepresented among the dead. A comparison of the skeletal and mortuary evidence to cross-cultural patterns of status and child well-being during material and ideological crises suggests that these Sand Canyon Pueblo youths died during an episode of violence at the end of the pueblo's occupation. Even though a major and controversial issue in the Southwest concerns lethal violence involving multiple victims (Bullock 1998; Kuckelman et al. 2000; Lipe 1995; White 1992), adult-initiated violence toward subadults has not been comprehensively addressed.

Currently, both cross-cultural considerations of warfare in pre-state societies (Ferguson and Whitehead 1992; Haas 1990) and considerations specifically of Puebloan violence (LeBlanc 1999; Wilcox and Haas 1994) usually explain violence in terms of material needs (but see Darling 1999 and Margolis 2000 for exceptions). This prevailing viewpoint occurs despite historical and ethnographic evidence demonstrating that, worldwide and among Puebloans, individuals often consider adherence to their society's norms to be of paramount importance (Dixon 1992; Dunn 1974; Ortiz 1969; Sagan 1985). Although all conflicts involve multiple causes and conditions, and ideals and physical needs can become intertwined at both the conscious and unconscious levels, people often rank either ideology or material causes as more important in a particular circumstance (Robarchek 1990:75). Cultural processes, which include adult-child interactions, help shape how individuals and groups perceive and characterize a threat as well as delimit acceptable reactions. A stressor envisioned as related primarily to material needs may produce one type of behavior, and a conflict involving ideology, another (Strauss and Howe 1991). My analysis of the patterns of violence and their distribution among age categories suggests that the violence occurring at the end of Sand Canyon Pueblo's occupation and claiming the lives of so many adolescents may well have been due to ideologically based factionalism.

WHO ARE CHILDREN?

Research concerning children has long been complicated and compromised by the lack of a standard definition of children. As detailed in *Centuries of Childhood* (Ariès 1962), *Generations: The History of America's Future* (Strauss and Howe 1991), and *Chinese Views of Childhood* (Kinney 1995), a society's scientific and social concepts of an individual's status as a child can vary from one time to another. Also, as occurred in American pioneer families, circumstance can thrust a child into taking on adult responsibilities but not necessarily imbue him or her with the status of one whose opinions are deemed worthy of consideration (Hampsten 1991; West 1989).

Given these inconsistencies, a standard definition of children is essential for understanding the cross-cultural factors that affect children's health. Barry Bogin and B. Holly Smith (1996) integrate scientific (innate developmental) and cultural (social status) perspectives in their human life-cycle theory, which includes a biocultural definition of children as anyone under about 20 years of age. Their model is derived from biological, psychological (primarily Piaget's theory of cognitive development), and evolutionary information, as well as ethnographic and historic data from several genetically and socioeconomically diverse societies. As it happens, their definition corresponds with the threshold between adults and subadults in the *Standards for Data Collection for Human Skeletal Remains* (Buikstra and Ubelaker 1994), hereafter referred to as *Standards*.

According to the Bogin and Smith model, human growth and development after birth can be divided into five universal, evolutionary stages: infancy, childhood, juvenile, adolescence, and adulthood. Each stage represents a combination of morphological, physiological, psychological, and behavioral attributes, with health and risk factors varying per developmental period. Infancy (birth to 3 years) is the time when the mother provides all or some nourishment to her child through lactation, ending with weaning at an average age of 36 months in preindustrialized societies. Childhood (3 to 7 years) is the period after weaning when children are still dependent on older people for protection and feeding. The juvenile

(7 to 12 years) stage consists of prepubertal individuals who are capable of obtaining their own food and protecting themselves adequately from disease and predation. The use of the childhood and juvenile stages provides more meaningful categories than the category of child in *Standards* since the needs and risk factors particular to young children and preadolescents are substantially different.

Of all the terms applied to subadults, *adolescence* is by far the most variable. In modern America the onset of puberty is often seen as beginning the last stage of childhood, but in other societies it may be viewed as the entry into adulthood (Ariès 1962; Dixon 1992). Bogin and Smith designate adolescence (12 to 20 years) as beginning with the onset of puberty and ending on reaching adult stature and complete reproductive maturity at an average age of 19 years in women and 21–25 years in men. They define reproductive maturity, but not necessarily capability, as the coalescence of "physiological, socioeconomic, and psychobehavioral attributes" (1996:706).

Especially in regard to the troublesome definition of adolescence, there is confusion between ritual adulthood and full adulthood. The early teen years, sometimes regardless of the onset of reproductive ability, commonly involve an adult status that is limited to the realm of ritual rights and responsibilities. In contrast, the late teens to early twenties usually mark the entry into the status of full adulthood, involving economic, ritual, social, and political responsibilities and status. As an example, several historic Pueblo groups whose children took part in ritual "finishing" initiations at about 12 years of age associated full adult status only with marriage, which typically occurred at about age 20 for both males and females (Beaglehole 1935; Ortiz 1969), or with initiation into a ritual group during the late teens to early twenties (Dennis 1940; Schlegal 1973). Only males were initiated in some Pueblo communities whereas other Pueblo groups inducted females as well (Ortiz 1969).

We do not know how the Ancestral Pueblo grouped or defined children, but there is no compelling reason to assume that their classification scheme would have been drastically different from the stages proposed by Bogin and Smith. This model thus forms the basis for the age classifications I use here.

SAND CANYON PUEBLO AND ITS CHILDREN

Ancestral Pueblo people built and occupied Sand Canyon Pueblo, located in the Mesa Verde region of southwest Colorado, in the mid to late A.D.

1200s (Figure 9.1). This 2.5-acre village was the largest Pueblo III site in the region. Because of its size, D-shaped layout, and communal structures, Sand Canyon Pueblo is widely considered to have been a significant ritual center. Archaeological evidence also indicates residential areas. The village had an estimated maximum population of 225 people (Adler 1992), and it contained about 400 surface rooms, 100 kivas, and 14 towers. It also included nondomestic, kiva-dominated units as well as a room-dominated section. In addition to farming and performing common domestic activities, the villagers expended a great deal of effort to build an enclosing wall, a great kiva, and a large, D-shaped, bi-walled building. Tree-ring samples date to the mid-1270s, later than those from any sites in the vicinity (Adler 1992).

Bruce Bradley (1992, 1993, 1996; Bradley and Churchill 1995) directed the sampling of about 12 percent of the village for Crow Canyon Archaeological Center. This sampling involved complete excavation of

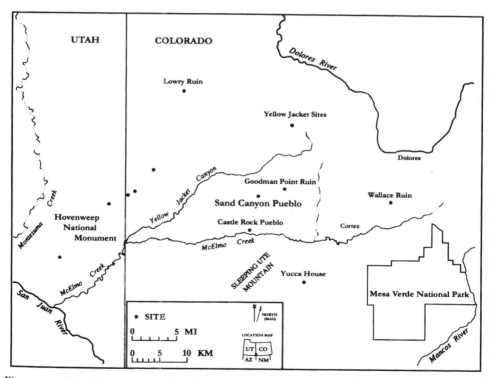

Figure 9.1. Sand Canyon Pueblo and other regional Ancestral Pueblo sites. Map by Bruce Bradley, adapted from Lightfoot and Kuckelman 1993.

eight kiva suites (a kiva and all associated rooms and open spaces), the testing of fourteen kivas and two communal structures, and numerous test squares. Bradley (personal communication 1997) infers from artifact assemblage and stratigraphic data that the village was rapidly vacated by about the early 1280s, several years into a major drought. There is no evidence that any group lived in the village's vicinity after its evacuation, which took place at about the same time as the well-known migrations from the region.

The Sand Canyon Pueblo skeletal population, excluding isolated bones, consists of 30 individuals, of whom 20 are less than 20 years of age. Michael Hoffman, Anne Katzenberg, Nancy Malville, Debra Martin, and Alan Goodman collected data on the curated skeletal and dental remains, and I performed the in situ analyses. The skeletal assessments conform to the criteria set forth in *Standards*. Using these evaluations, I performed an intensive analysis of the children's remains, employing six markers of skeletal stress: dental enamel hypoplasia, porotic hyperostosis, primary periostitis, stunting, infectious caries, and skeletal trauma. Kristin Sobolik's chapter in this volume provides background information on most of these indicators.

The specific identity of the population using Sand Canyon Pueblo is unknown. Although the pueblo could have served as a pilgrimage destination, as perhaps did the great houses of Chaco Canyon (Judge 1989), the dearth of nonlocal goods suggests a domestic or, at the most, a regional population. Lacking evidence otherwise, I assume that all the individuals discovered were village inhabitants. Apparently, these people died during two different periods: during village occupation and about the time the village was evacuated. This distinction is based on the combination of mortuary, stratigraphic, and artifact assemblage evidence. Of particular note is the presence of at least 20 individuals, adults and children, in atypical mortuary contexts (defined below) that are dispersed across the village (Figure 9.2). Cultural fill covered only one of these individuals, an adult male. Many room floors and courtyard areas were left with in-use artifact assemblages. Apparently, with the exception of the covered adult, all the individuals in atypical mortuary contexts died at the abrupt end of village occupation in about the early 1280s.

This archaeological and skeletal evidence has generated two hypotheses, which I evaluate in terms of Ancestral Pueblo participants only. Bruce Bradley (personal communication 1997) infers a conflict between two religious factions whereas Lightfoot and Kuckelman (1994) propose that it involved raiding. Rather than test these hypotheses, I use the Sand Canyon

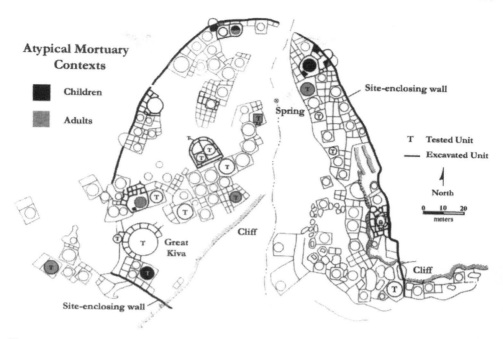

Figure 9.2. Locations of Sand Canyon Pueblo atypical mortuary contexts at the end of village occupation. Map by Bruce Bradley, adapted from Lipe 1992.

Pueblo information to offer a theoretical framework. In order to limit variables, I use information solely from Sand Canyon Pueblo even though there is skeletal evidence of violence at Castle Rock Pueblo, a contemporary PIII community about 10 kilometers (6 miles) to the south (Kuckelman et al. 2000).

Instead of the interpretive terms commonly used in mortuary analysis, such as *formal/nonformal burial* (LeBlanc 1999:85) or *considerate/abnormal burial* (Turner and Turner 1999:39), I prefer a descriptive approach. Every mortuary context involves the combination of skeletal positioning and location but, as discussed by Stephanie Whittlesey in this volume, not necessarily grave goods. In essence, typical mortuary contexts consist of systematic positioning, mainly semiflexed in the PIII period, in secure locations such as middens, cliff crevices, sealed rooms, or under floors. Individuals, especially children, may or may not be buried with grave goods. When discovered in kivas, human remains are normally located within cultural fill deposits (Cattanach 1980:Table 6; Martin et al. in press), indicating that the structure was being used as a midden. In contrast,

atypical mortuary contexts involve human remains that are irregularly positioned and in unprotected and/or unusual locations. Such remains are
usually sprawled, often face-down, and in locations such as on roofs, in
unsealed rooms, on courtyard surfaces, and on kiva floors. Individuals in
atypical mortuary contexts commonly show perimortem trauma (Martin
et al. 2001; Turner and Turner 1999).

Although there are 30 individuals from Sand Canyon Pueblo, one adult
in an atypical mortuary context is not further considered since stratigraphic evidence indicates that he died during village occupation; this
leaves a total of 29 individuals from all mortuary contexts. Thirty-one percent (9/29) of the individuals are in typical mortuary contexts. Most of the
"typical" children (6/8) were infants (see Table 9.4). The children's positioning, regardless of age, was either semiflexed or indeterminate. Two infants, a young child, and an adolescent had grave goods, but 4 infants did
not. Moreover, the children's mortuary treatment was very similar to that
of a young adult female and the only typical adult found at Sand Canyon
Pueblo. She was interred in the fill of a surface room, placed on her right
side/back in a semiflexed position, and accompanied by a vessel.

In contrast, 69 percent (20/29) of the individuals are in atypical mortuary contexts. Forty-five percent (5/11) of the "atypical" children and 75
percent (6/8) of the "atypical" adults are on kiva floors. They are either
underneath the (then) area of the hatchway or lying between the ventilator
tunnel and the deflector. Their location and positioning suggest that they
fell or were dropped through the hatchway. Of the remaining atypical individuals, 6 children and 2 adults were found either on kiva/courtyard
roofs or in rooms open to the elements. In terms of subadult developmental stages, 75 percent of the children found in atypical contexts are adolescents. One 5-to-6-year-old child is in an ambiguous mortuary context; he
or she is in a face-down, semiflexed position, on top of the ashy fill of a fire
pit and scrunched in the corner of an unsealed room. This individual's
skeletal data are grouped with the atypical-context, evacuation-period
children since the evidence is more suggestive of an unusual circumstance
than a formal burial.

Charles Adams (1983) and Bruce Bradley developed the Sand Canyon
Pueblo research design to investigate various aspects of large, late Pueblo
III communities in which human remains data played only a minor role.
This design did not involve the intentional discovery of human remains,
and in fact common Ancestral Pueblo burial locations were generally
avoided. The result of this decision is that we do not know if the excavated
skeletons of those dying during occupation are representative.

I assume, however, that those individuals associated with kiva roofs and kiva floors represent the sex/age groups of those dying at the time the village was vacated. This premise is based on the fact that archaeologists sampled about 23 percent of the kivas, in locations selected across the village. This rate lends confidence that the evidence associated with kivas is reasonably representative in terms of type and frequency. Since kivas are not typical mortuary locations, there is no reason to expect either age or sex grading. This expectation of randomness means that it is even more likely that the skeletons associated with kivas are representative of those dying at the end of village occupation.

Beliefs, as well as the desire to establish a social hierarchy (Potter 2000), are expressed through ritual occasions that are highly associated with family or community feasting. Alternatively, particular individuals or groups are granted access to specific foods presented as ritual offerings. In the Southwest, as in other areas, ritual foods are often large-game meats such as venison (Muir 1999), which has almost twice the iron of poultry and rabbit. Robert Muir's (1999) study of the animal remains suggests that there was more feasting on large game, especially deer, at Sand Canyon Pueblo than at contemporary regional sites. The provenience of the faunal remains suggests that the venison was initially processed in specific locations within the village and then evenly distributed. Scott Ortman's (2000) examination of vessel size and exterior bowl decoration also suggests a higher incidence of feasting at Sand Canyon Pueblo.

THE OVERALL HEALTH OF SAND CANYON PUEBLO'S CHILDREN

Studies on living children show that their skeletons are quite responsive to physiological stressors. As detailed in this volume by Sobolik, skeletal remains can provide multiple lines of evidence about the health of past children since the skeletal system is directly involved in several bodily functions. Children, because of their developmental needs, are particularly responsive to pathological and nutritional problems that disrupt growth and development. Also, since they are usually physically, intellectually, and socially less powerful than adults, they are vulnerable to skeletal trauma from adult-initiated violence.

The 307 postfetal children's remains from the village of Grasshopper Pueblo in east-central Arizona serve as the primary comparative population, with most of the information derived from Madeleine Hinkes's (1983) dissertation research. In addition to having a large, well-documented skeletal population, the inhabitants of this large Pueblo IV village, occupied from about A.D. 1275 to 1400, may have faced stressors similar to those at Sand Canyon Pueblo (see Whittlesey, this volume).

Hinkes considers the Grasshopper Pueblo skeletal remains to be a representative sample. Their morbidity (illness) and mortality patterns correspond to those of existing children from non-antibiotic societies living under normal conditions, that is, high infant illness and mortality rates that begin to decline during the childhood years, then decrease even further during the juvenile period until illness and death reach their lowest point in early adolescence. The adolescent death rate of about 5 to 10 percent then slowly rises, but it is still usually less than about 20 percent at the end of adolescence; much of this upsurge is attributed to death during childbirth. Children usually die from illness, exacerbated by undernutrition. Death rates from accident or homicide are not usually delineated in public health data from developing societies. Cross-cultural information indicates that these rates are low, however.

Most of the Sand Canyon Pueblo skeletons, including those of several infants, were in good condition; this circumstance allows a high level of confidence in the reliability of the observations. Because of the research strategy and the small sample size, it is possible that these human remains, and the physiological stress exhibited by them, are not representative. The following data should be considered particular to these 20 Sand Canyon Pueblo individuals. For these reasons, as well as issues addressed by Sobolik in this volume, I use frequency analysis only. Information from the childhood and juvenile stages is especially limited. There are an unusual number of adolescents, however, many of whom apparently did not die of natural causes. The adolescent data may be used, guardedly, to assess this group's health while in previous developmental stages.

To evaluate the nutritional status of the Sand Canyon Pueblo children, I assess anemia and stunting. Linear enamel hypoplasia (LEH) data are not included since such defects are nonspecific indicators. They may represent episodes of malnutrition, infection, or perhaps psychological stress (Hillson 1986).

Owing in part to their iron-poor, maize-reliant diets, Ancestral Pueblo children's remains commonly show porotic hyperostosis (PH), the skeletal reaction to anemia. Anne Katzenberg's isotope analyses (1992) indicate that the Sand Canyon Pueblo villagers were as maize-reliant as other regional populations, yet, as shown in Table 9.1, no subadult has active PH. Four of 14, or 29 percent of the individuals, exhibit well-healed lesions. These reactions are of mild to moderate severity and more suggestive of

TABLE 9.1. SAND CANYON PUEBLO NUTRITIONAL INDICATORS PER
INDIVIDUAL, BY SUBADULT DEVELOPMENTAL STAGE.

Developmental Stage/Years	Actice Porotic Hyperostosis	Growth Retarding	Tallness
Infancy (birth to 3)	0% (0/4)	0% (0/7)	33% (2/6)
Childhood (3 to 7)	0% (0/2)	0% (0/1)	0% (0/1)
Juvenile (7 to 12)	0% (0/1)	0% (0/1)	0% (0/1)
Adolescence (12 to 20)	0% (0/7)	0% (0/9)	45% (4/9)
Total subadult (birth to 20)	0% (0/14)	0% (0/18)	35% (6/17)

single than chronic episodes. Three adolescents and 1 juvenile are affected,
but their enamel hypoplasia data raise the possibility that each individual
acquired his or her PH while in the childhood stage. Regardless of when
these lesions developed, their mild to moderate expression suggests that
anemia was not a pervasive problem.

These Sand Canyon Pueblo children exhibit low to moderate rates of PH
compared with similar groups (Table 9.2). Grasshopper Pueblo children 3 to
16 years old exhibit active PH at an average frequency of 13 percent, although most of the affected children are under the age of 5 (Stodder and
Martin 1992). Mesa Verde region children show active lesions at an average
rate of 67 percent for both newborn to 3-year-olds and 3- to 16-year-olds.

TABLE 9.2. SKELETAL EVIDENCE OF SUBADULT NUTRITIONAL STRESS PER
INDIVIDUAL, BY SITE AND TIME PERIOD.

Site/ Time Period	Active Porotic Hyperostosis	Healed Porotic Hyperostosis	Stunting	Tallness
Sand Canyon Pueblo A.D. 1250–1280±	0% (0/14)	29% (4/14)	0% (0/17)	35% (6/17)
Sand Canyon Pueblo during occupation	0% (0/5)	0% (0/5)	0% (0/6)	16% (1/6)
Sand Canyon Pueblo at evacuation	0% (0/9)	29% (4/14)	0% (0/11)	45% (5/11)
Grasshopper Pueblo A.D. 1275–1350	13%[a]		6%[b] (birth to 10 years)	6%[b] (birth to 10 years)
Mesa Verde Region Pueblo III	67%[a]			

[a]Stodder and Martin 1992. Although several sources (see Sobolik, this volume) provide information on the Mesa verde region, I use Stoddard and Martin because Martin also analyzed the
Sand Canyon data.
[b]Hinkes 1983.

When I use Hinkes's age category of birth to 10 years, Sand Canyon Pueblo children have a combined (active and healed) PH rate of 14 percent (1/7). The only affected child, a juvenile, has very mild and well-healed lesions suggestive of a single episode of anemia. This frequency is similar to the Grasshopper Pueblo birth-to-10 combined rate of 15 percent. Some of these Grasshopper Pueblo children had active lesions, however, whereas the Sand Canyon Pueblo children did not. The regional combined frequency for children in the birth-to-10 category is a much higher 79 percent, primarily owing to a high rate of active lesions. Even when I consider the possibility that all healed episodes of anemia occurred before the age of 10, the Sand Canyon Pueblo rate is still only 29 percent. These figures suggest that the Sand Canyon Pueblo children, apparently through all developmental stages and regardless of chronological grouping, were much less troubled by factors causing anemia than the regional children. A key finding is that the lack of active lesions in any child from an atypical mortuary context indicates that anemia was not a significant stressor in the months or so preceding the end of occupation.

The Sand Canyon Pueblo children were also appraised for growth retardation, defined by Hinkes (1983:95) as less than one standard deviation below the mean long-bone diaphyseal length per age group. I used Hinkes's (1983:95) Grasshopper Pueblo data to assess the preadolescents and R. I. Sundick's findings from Indian Knoll, Kentucky (in Ubelaker 1989), to evaluate the adolescents. Even though from a completely different Precolumbian group, the Indian Knoll growth curves are similar to those from Grasshopper Pueblo. Relatively few Grasshopper Pueblo children, 10 years and younger, are stunted, but no Sand Canyon Pueblo child of that age shows growth retardation. In fact, two Sand Canyon Pueblo children, birth to 10, are more than one standard deviation taller than average, for a tallness rate of 25 percent, compared with the 6 percent tallness rate at Grasshopper Pueblo. Recent research on living children (Khan et al. 1996) shows that stunting is most reliably assessed when defined as falling below the second standard deviation from the mean. Even when using this more restrictive definition, no Sand Canyon Pueblo individual aged birth to 10 years is stunted. Unfortunately, Hinkes's format does not allow the reassessment of Grasshopper Pueblo children.

Although Hinkes did not evaluate stunting in children over 10 years of age, Sand Canyon Pueblo teens are also taller than those from Grasshopper Pueblo. I found no regional population stunting assessments, but the Sand Canyon Pueblo average adolescent female stature of 160 cm exceeds the regional average by about 5 cm. When compared with Sobolik's data in this volume, the average stature of the Sand Canyon Pueblo adolescent females is closer to the 162–cm stature of Pueblo Bonito females than that of any other group. Sample size problems that affect both sites warn against overinterpretation, but this is intriguing given Nancy Akins's (1986) inference of hereditary elitism at that Chacoan great house. Regardless of the comparative group, the evidence suggests that these Sand Canyon Pueblo children were average to moderately above average in height through each developmental stage.

INTERPRETING THE GOOD HEALTH OF THE SAND CANYON PUEBLO CHILDREN

There are several possibilities for interpreting the relatively good health of the Sand Canyon children. Environmental interpretations might suggest that the villagers lived in a more stable and productive microclimate during a time of climatic stress. Or the good health could reflect sample size discrepancy. It is entirely possible, however, that their well-being represents the role of ideas in children's lives.

Obligatory relationships rooted in ideology help shape the child's status as an individual, resulting in both beneficial and detrimental health consequences. Individualistic ideologies that recognize the *specific status* of every person often stress meeting each child's developmental, and thus dietary, needs. As documented by historic and ethnographic sources (Ariès 1962; Furth 1995; Hewlett 1991; Strauss and Howe 1991) as well as research on living children (Bogin and Loucky 1997; Flinn and England 1995; May et al. 1993), groups or eras that emphasize meeting each child's developmental needs show increased levels of child health. In societies having a collective ideology, in which obligations to the group are more important than obligations to individuals, children have a *communal status* and usually eat what everyone else is eating regardless of suitability. Depending on the available foods, their diet could be very good, adequate, or poor (Dunn 1974; Gies and Gies 1991). Finally, some children within a group may have an *exclusive status*, enabling them to be well fed because of beliefs expressed through rank, privilege, or ritual practice. Infants and young children with elite status tend to be better nourished, be less sickly, and have a higher rate of survival than their non-elite peers (Ariès 1962; McLaughlin 1974). Exclusive status can be hazardous, however, to even young teens when heightened family and social expectations engage them in high-risk activities such as military service (Ariès 1962; Shulamith 1990).

Both historic and ethnographic evidence demonstrate that a tightly woven collective ideology permeated and controlled virtually all aspects of Pueblo society. This ideology did not involve personal relationship with a deity, moralistic values, or even institutionalized coming-of-age "vision quests" (Benedict 1934) that would allow some measure of individualism. Instead, parents and communities employed extremely uniform, often co-ercive child-rearing practices to develop the conformist adult personality needed to take over community subsistence responsibilities and sustain the social expression of Pueblo world view (Dozier 1970; Goldfrank 1945). Although ideology is highly influential in child rearing in all societies, Pueblo ideology, as a system that fully integrated subsistence, social, and intellectual concerns, had an extreme impact. Child-rearing patterns were an intentional product of Pueblo ideology, with obligations to ideology and the group ranked well above obligations to the child as an individual.

The direct application of historic Pueblo beliefs and customs to the Ancestral Pueblo is inappropriate, given the changes that have occurred over time and the degree of observed diversity among existing communities. Nevertheless, Pueblo child-rearing behaviors, and the attitudes of obligation shaping those behaviors, are both remarkably consistent and in keeping with those from similar societies (Bradley 1998). Given this uniformity, it is reasonable to infer that the Ancestral Pueblo dynamic of ideology, child rearing, and children's health would have been similar.

The skeletal evidence suggests that these Sand Canyon Pueblo children had some type of exclusive status relative to peers in contemporary communities and that this status resulted in a moderately higher level of nutritional adequacy. Even though most of the children beyond the infancy stage were alive during the time of the Great Drought, their skeletal indicators suggest that they had been buffered, in contrast to the common finding that Ancestral Pueblo children from this period exhibit increased skeletal stress (Martin 1994; Sobolik, this volume).

Adolescence is a developmental stage requiring adequate nutrition to sustain its high linear growth velocity. The finding that no adolescents were stunted provides insight into their last years of life. Their average to above average diaphyseal lengths and final stature indicate that nutritional stress had not been a significant or unusual problem for them during the years preceding the end of village occupation. This inference of nutritional advantage is guarded, however, given the small number of evaluated Sand Canyon Pueblo children. It is unfortunate that there is not a comparative regional population, along the lines of Grasshopper Pueblo, that can be as closely associated with this particular ecological stressor, but it appears likely that the Sand Canyon Pueblo population as a whole was buffered by its village's special ritual status.

Even though Katzenberg's bone-chemistry analyses indicate that the villagers had a typical Ancestral Pueblo diet, the opportunity to consume deer/artiodactyl meat occasionally may have helped prevent or moderate the anemia so prevalent in the regional populations. In turn, fewer bouts of anemia may have contributed to their average to above average stature. In particular, the absence of active PH, as well as the villagers' apparently smooth growth trajectories through all developmental stages, provides support for Muir's contention that the unusually high frequency of deer bones at Sand Canyon Pueblo reflects some sort of differential access to iron-rich, high-quality game. Additionally, regardless of their location within the village, mortuary context, or time of death, the children's uniform skeletal health suggests that they did not belong to a particular village subgroup. This finding corresponds to Muir's conclusion that once artiodactyls were initially processed in specific locations, they were "apportioned relatively equally throughout the community" (1999:14).

Alternatively, the Sand Canyon Pueblo children's low level of ambient physiological stress could represent an increased attention to children in their own right. Since individuals who have a specific status tend to show comparatively higher levels of child health, it is possible that the Sand Canyon Pueblo children's good health derived from life in a village having an ideology catering to the particular needs of individual children. Though low in frequency, the presence of some porotic hyperostosis suggests that children's diets may not have always been developmentally appropriate, however. Further, the mild yet pervasive occurrence of LEH indicates that health stressors were common, albeit at low levels. Both these circumstances raise the possibility that at least some physiological stress may have been readily preventable. I suggest that as in historic Pueblo communities, the Sand Canyon Pueblo children's level of health most likely involved beliefs that did not emphasize the individual, and that children's basic needs were met by obligatory, reciprocal relationships present in extended family and/or formalized community networks.

ENHANCED RISK FOR VIOLENCE

During an ideological conflict, adolescent mortality from adult-initiated violence rises dramatically regardless of the belief system. This outcome is due to one of two factors. The first involves the issue of adolescent cognitive development. According to Jean Piaget, adolescent cognition is abstract, deductive, idealistic, egocentric, and peer-oriented (Lowrey 1974). Erik Erikson considers ideology an intrinsic part of adolescent identity formation; it helps give adolescents a sense of purpose and a connection to the future as they strive to make logical sense of the world around them (Santrock 1998). Neither Piaget's nor Erikson's theories are based on cross-cultural research. Nevertheless, the worldwide prevalence of adolescent coming-of-age ceremonies suggests the common recognition that teens have developed some ability to comprehend abstract societal beliefs.

There is also ample historical evidence that teens tend to convert strongly to a cause or a belief system. As occurred at U.S. anti-war and civil rights protests in the 1960s, youthful demonstrators may suffer injury and even death because of their ideological nonconformity, especially when they also lack the experience to know when to back down. This pattern of idealistic fervor and an increased level of adolescent mortality due to violence occurs in non-Western societies as well. The impact on adolescent mortality in the Chinese political factionalism involving the 1960s Red Guard as well as the pro-democracy dissidents of Tiananmen Square has been well documented (Lupher 1995). In a less well known example, adolescent converts to Islam, then Christianity, were martyred when they refused to follow their ruler's lead and reconvert to the traditional Bugandan belief system (Sagan 1985). In such cases the adolescent death rate but not the adult death rate increases; adults' nonconformist behaviors are frequently moderated by their established family or community obligations as well as discretion gained through experience.

Perhaps more commonly, conforming adolescents may be threatened simply because of their membership in a group. In many cultures, including historic Pueblo communities, children are initiated into religious associations at about 12 to 14 years of age. They are then considered ritually accountable adults even while viewed as economically dependent children. Thus, during an ideological conflict between factions, children old enough to be initiated face the same risk of violence as full adults, and often regardless of gender. Oral histories report that traditional Hopis killed male adolescents and adults who were members of Awatovi's Christian faction (Fewkes 1898). These sources and others (Darling 1999; Dozier 1970; Turner and Turner 1999) indicate that initiated, nonconforming Pueblo females were also subject to physical, and sometimes lethal, disciplinary action. At Awatovi, adolescent inexperience may not have been a risk factor since adults were also killed. Regardless of whether the catalyst involves adolescent fervor or ritual factionalism, the evidence suggests that societies having collective ideologies are quite intolerant of ideological nonconformism, even to the point of extreme violence toward previously protected children, but especially teens.

For groups with elitist ideologies, Mary Lucas Powell (1991) expected that in the Southeast elite males would show higher frequencies of skeletal trauma than non-elites, since among southeastern late-prehistoric groups, social advancement was tied to participation in warfare. In her research on the Mississippian inhabitants of Moundville, however, Powell (1991) determined that antemortem fractures occurred in 34 (of about 400) adults but no children under the age of 20. This suggests that even in an obviously ranked society, subadults may not customarily face increased physical risk.

Powell's finding is similar to cross-cultural information from non-ranked societies. Bruce Knauft (1987) describes violence among the Gebusi, a Southeast Asian band-level group in which youths were neither participants nor targets in socially patterned raiding. Keith Otterbein's (2000) research on the killing of captured enemies indicates that uncentralized societies were likely to spare and incorporate children. Though only suggestive, these sources indicate that small-scale assaults in band-to-tribal-level groups rarely involved subadults. As at Moundville, attackers and victims were usually adult males.

In skeletal remains, enhanced risk is best assessed by analyzing mortality patterns and skeletal trauma per developmental stage. Under normal conditions the expected Sand Canyon Pueblo mortality pattern would approximate that of Grasshopper Pueblo. Hinkes and I did not use the same developmental stages, so, using the raw data she presented in Table 1 and Appendix B, I adjusted her categories to correspond with mine. The 100 fetal remains from Grasshopper Pueblo are not included in this analysis. As shown in Table 9.3, both groups conform to the expected pattern of declining mortality through the first three developmental stages.

TABLE 9.3. GRASSHOPPER PUEBLO AND SAND CANYON PUEBLO MORTALITY, BY SUBADULT DEVELOPMENTAL STAGE.

Developmental Stage/Years	Grasshopper Pueblo Mortality	Sand Canyon Pueblo Mortality
Infancy (birth to 3)	53% (162)	35% (7)
Childhood (3 to 7)	28% (85)	10% (2)
Juvenile (7 to 12)	9% (28)	5% (1)
Adolescence (12 to 20)	10% (35)	50% (10)
Total subadult (birth to 20)	100% (307)	100% (20)

There is a major discrepancy with regard to the high Sand Canyon Pueblo adolescent mortality rate, however. When the rate is classified by mortuary context (Table 9.4), deviations from the expected pattern are even more pronounced. Although it is unknown if the typical group is representative of the Sand Canyon Pueblo population, its mortality pattern follows the Grasshopper Pueblo characteristic of declining child mortality through the subadult developmental stages. Adult mortality is lower than expected, probably owing to the archaeologists' decision to avoid common burial locations.

In contrast, the atypical group's mortality pattern characteristics are almost exactly the opposite of those seen in the typical pattern; they involve low infancy, childhood, and juvenile death rates but a very high adolescent death rate. It is remarkable that 10 of the 30 (33 percent) Sand Canyon Pueblo individuals are adolescents, when only 32 adolescents, out of 508 (6 percent) postfetal remains, were found at Grasshopper Pueblo. As discussed previously, it is unlikely that this anomaly is primarily due to sampling bias since most of the atypical-context individuals were associated with kiva floors or roofs. When differential risk is assessed by subadult stages only, the 75 percent adolescent mortality rate is extraordinary, especially since this is a momentary death rate. Under normal conditions an *annual* death rate for adolescents should be in the 5 to 10 percent range.

What caused this variation, given that adolescents are the least likely of all age groups to die suddenly? Table 9.5 shows that five children, or 25 percent, have perimortem fractures. Four of these individuals, three adolescents and one juvenile, have severe (penetrating both cranial tables) depression fractures, in "fight or flight" locations; two of the teens are young adolescents about 12 to 15 years of age, and the third is about 18 to 20

TABLE 9.4. SAND CANYON PUEBLO MORTALITY RATES, BY DEVELOPMENTAL STAGE, MORTUARY PATTERN, AND CHRONOLOGICAL PERIOD.

Developmental Stage/Years	Typical Mortuary Context During Village Occupation	Atypical Mortuary Context at Village Evacuation
Infancy (birth to 3)	67% (6/9)	5% (1/20)
Childhood (3 to 7)	11% (1/9)	5%[a] (1/20)
Juvenile (7 to 12)	0% (0/9)	5% (1/20)
Adolescence (12 to 20)	11% (1/9)	45% (9/20)
Adulthood (20+)	11% (1/9)	40% (8/20)
Total (birth to 20+)	100% (9)	100% (20)

[a] Ambiguous mortuary context.

years old. One of the adolescents has a blunt-impact blow to the cranial base that could have been caused by striking fallen wall stones, possibly from being dropped or pushed from a tower into the roofless ground-story room. Two teens and one juvenile have at least one blunt-object, cranial depression fracture whose shape is indicative of a hand-held weapon, possibly a stone ax. Sutural separation that may have been coincident with the depression fracturing is present in three of these children. Postmortem sutural separation can occur in juveniles and young adolescents even without trauma, depending on the complexity of the sutures (J. M. Hoffman, personal communication 1998). At Sand Canyon Pueblo, however, no adolescent without depression fracturing exhibits sutural separation, and no other juveniles were present for comparison. One adult male in an atypical mortuary context has a severe blunt-object, cranial depression fracture. When this person is included, the Sand Canyon Pueblo perimortem fracture rate for those individuals (6/20) dying at the end of the occupation is 30 percent, with a total perimortem cranial trauma rate of 21 percent.

The postcranial perimortem skeletal trauma is insignificant and does not conform to a pattern indicating defensive positioning (parrying fractures), active participation in risky/aggressive actions, or intentional postmortem processing. The mortuary context of each of the affected individuals involves stone architectural features (wall fall or a deflector), so the damage could well be related to depositional circumstances rather than violent intent.

The cranial injuries are consistent with the intentional lethal blows evidenced in current populations, and they affect only the individuals who died at the end of occupation. The incidence of skeletal trauma is high in

TABLE 9.5. SAND CANYON PUEBLO CRANIAL TRAUMA, BY
DEVELOPMENTAL STAGE.

Developmental Stage/Years	Perimortem Cranial Trauma	Antemortem Cranial Trauma
Infancy (birth to 3)	0% (0/5)	0% (0/5)
Childhood (3 to 7)	0% (0/2)	0% (0/2)
Juvenile (7 to 12)	100% (1/1)	0% (0/1)
Adolescence (12 to 20)	43% (3/7)	43% (3/7)
Total subadult (birth to 20)	27% (4/15)	20% (3/15)
Adulthood (20+)	25% (1/4)	25% (1/4)

comparison with other Ancestral Pueblo groups. No children from Grass-hopper Pueblo (Hinkes 1983), Mesa Verde National Park (Debra Martin, personal communication 1997), or Chaco Canyon (Akins 1986) exhibit perimortem cranial fractures. When present in Ancestral Pueblo groups, cranial fracture rates are typically below 8 percent (Martin et al. 2001), but these rates include all types of cranial trauma, healed and unhealed, and (apparently) predominantly involve adults. It is possible that Ancestral Pueblo adolescents older than 16 years have been analyzed and counted as adults by bioarchaeologists, but two of the three affected Sand Canyon Pueblo adolescents are less than 15 years of age. Additionally, as perimortem trauma is present only in the atypical mortuary group, these fractures apparently occurred within a narrow time frame. I consider it very unlikely that three to four children would have suffered accidental, lethal cranial trauma within such a discrete period.

It is probable that this already high rate is an underestimate. Forensic data show that lethal knife wounds frequently do not harm the skeleton, and infants and young children are especially susceptible to lethal blows to the abdomen (Cohle et al. 1995; Fossum and Descheneaux 1991). Unfortunately, the six remaining adolescents found in atypical contexts could not be observed for cranial trauma, so their manner of death is not as conclusive. Skeletal evidence indicates that they did not suffer from chronic disease or starvation, although they could have succumbed to an acute illness that left no trace. Adolescents have the most-developed immune systems of all children, however, and are the least likely to die in an epidemic.

Comparing all the individuals, children and adults, with observable crania provides a more plausible explanation. Perimortem cranial trauma is present in the evacuation-era group only, affecting five of nineteen, or 26 percent. Among the Ancestral Pueblo, atypical mortuary contexts, especially kiva floor locations, are commonly associated with perimortem trauma (Turner and Turner 1999). Based on this relationship, I consider it most likely that these six adolescents, for a total of nine, as well as eight adults, were victims of violence. In sum, objective and inferential evidence indicate that nine adolescents, one juvenile, eight adults, and probably an infant and a young child suffered violent deaths at about the time the pueblo was vacated.

The children's antemortem trauma data generally support the finding of a single episode of intentional violence. Three of eighteen (16 percent) children have healed fractures, and they are present in terminal-phase adolescents only. A total of six lesions involve cranial bones only. These injuries are very well healed and could have occurred in previous developmental periods. Four of the wounds are incidental and in locations that, in children, probably indicate accident or roughhousing (Bradley 1998). Interestingly, the only individual with lesions indicative of intentional, nonlethal violence is an older adolescent female, and her two wounds' degree of healing suggests injury at least a few years before death. No individuals have postcranial metaphyseal, rib, or parrying breaks that commonly result from either adult-initiated domestic (Krogman and Isçan 1986) or warfare/raiding violence (Powell 1991).

Their fractures' well-healed conditions suggest that the children suffered these breaks several years before the end of the village's occupation. Their degree of healing also indicates that adult-initiated violence toward children did not increase in the year or so before the end of village occupation. Overall, the antemortem trauma data suggest that the Sand Canyon Pueblo teens had not faced increased risk from status-based activities during village occupation and that their high adolescent death rate due to violence was an aberration.

MOTIVES FOR VIOLENCE: A THEORETICAL APPROACH

The Sand Canyon Pueblo children lived in a community organized around both ritual and subsistence concerns. Does their skeletal and mortuary evidence suggest the preeminence of an ideological or material motive for violence? Bruce Bradley (personal communication 1997) proposes that a sudden, intense, violent, and occupation-ending episode took place at Sand Canyon Pueblo in the early 1280s, that this attack resulted from either intervillage or intravillage social/ideological disintegration, and that it probably occurred in reaction to a specific but indeterminate ideological crisis. He suggests that the conflict could have involved two factions: the "Chaco Revivalists," who emphasized beliefs involving obligation to the lineage, and the "New Communalists," who adhered to beliefs associated with obligation to the community, as in historic Rio Grande Pueblo social organization and values. In essence, conformist, tradition-oriented Chaco Revivalists had become the Ancestral Pueblo nonconformists as most communities began to follow the Kachina phenomenon, soon to dominate Ancestral Pueblo/Pueblo society.

Alternatively, although they do not suggest a motive, Ricky Lightfoot and Kristin Kuckelman raise the possibility that these individuals died during "long-term, small-scale conflict" (1994:9). By the early 1280s the period known as the Great Drought, which archaeologists infer seriously compromised food resources, had been ongoing in the Four Corners region for several years. Yet the human remains and the information on fauna (Muir 1999) and flora (Adams and Bowyer 1999) indicate that these Sand Canyon Pueblo villagers had sufficient access to food. Assuming that regional nutritional resources had diminished, it is possible that the village's differential access to high-quality foods provided an impetus for competition-based raiding by other Ancestral Puebloans.

The extensive research of Christy Turner and Jacqueline Turner (1999) demonstrates that Ancestral Pueblo individuals of all ages experienced violent deaths. Overall, though, neither those scholars nor archaeologists provide thorough discussions that consider children. Subadults tend to not be mentioned or are relegated to the ubiquitous category "women and children," or researchers make unreferenced comments that older adolescent males were either active participants or the most likely victims. Pueblo oral tradition (Haas and Creamer 1997; Malotki 1993), historic accounts (Bayer et al. 1994; Jones 1966; Sando 1992; Spicer 1962), and ethnographic sources (Dozier 1970; Ellis 1951) are equally uninformative. Thus, analyses that address the risk factors faced by Ancestral Pueblo children at different developmental stages are practically nonexistent. Given the significant relationship among ideology, child rearing, and enhanced risk, how can we begin to develop a process for identifying and understanding these circumstances in the lives of past peoples?

Documentary evidence shows that different types of stressors can produce distinctive patterns of violence. Unfortunately, since many ancient stressors are inferred rather than observed, they may not be discernible from the archaeological record. Historic and ethnographic information, however, indicates that mortality patterns involving children follow fairly specific cross-cultural tendencies, depending on the type of stressor and the type of society (Bradley 1998). The significant attributes of these trends are presented in rows 1 and 2 of Table 9.6. This table describes the ways adults within a community or society react to internal stressors, not to the actions of a completely different group. In other words, for the Sand Canyon Pueblo example, I assume that all aggressors and victims were Ancestral Puebloans, from within Sand Canyon Pueblo itself or including neighboring villagers, or even people from more distant Puebloan areas, but not non-Puebloan individuals.

R. Brian Ferguson (1992:26) defines warfare as "organized, purposeful group action, directed against another group . . . involving the actual or potential application of lethal force." Ideological factionalism is a type of civil warfare in which one group within a society initiates a violent response to eradicate an opposing faction and/or its beliefs. It occurs when there is extreme disagreement about social norms or values or about the

TABLE 9.6. STRESSOR CHARACTERISTICS, BY SUBADULT DEVELOPMENTAL STAGE AND
SAND CANYON PUEBLO CHRONOLOGICAL PERIOD.

Stressor/Type Chronological Period	Developmental Stage with Highest Mortality	Perimortem Violence Rate	Mortuary Context
IDEOLOGICAL CONFLICT Religious factionalism	Adolescence	High	Atypical
CIVIL RAIDING Material concerns	Possibly slight increase, all subadult stages	Low	Typical
SAND CANYON PUEBLO During village occupation	Infancy	Absent	Typical
SAND CANYON PUEBLO At village evacuation	Adolescence	High	Atypical

perception of what is essential for the larger group's collective survival. Although material stressors may also exist, issues or needs are perceived and expressed in ideological terms. The massacre of the nonconformist, pro-Christian faction at Awatovi by other Hopis represents an acute episode of intervillage factionalism. As in that situation, ideological factionalism typically involves high levels of emotional intensity and zealotry that can provoke otherwise unacceptable behaviors.

Cross-cultural information on children indicates that mortality rates for the infant and childhood categories will be low during an ideological conflict. A slight increase in juvenile mortality may occur, but the death rate will sharply escalate among adolescents, especially but not exclusively males. As at Awatovi, the affected children will not be buried according to a typical mortuary pattern; the level of violence, and the consequent widespread social disruption, will exceed the ability of the community or the survivors to maintain traditional practices.

Although researchers use a range of definitions, small-scale conflicts are commonly construed as raids rather than full-scale warfare. This interpretation falls within Florence Hawley Ellis's (1951) and Laura Bayer and others' (1994) documentation of such actions in Pueblo oral traditions. For the most part, this type of civil raiding consisted of competition-based actions intended to obtain needed or desired material objectives, such as supplies, mates, slaves, or control of resources, that is, secular stressors. Lethal violence may accompany such raids, but it was not the primary focus.

Cross-cultural information regarding the impact of small-scale conflicts on children is especially deficient. It is unclear if this data void occurs because children have been generally unaffected or because adults, once again, have not included material involving children in either their histories or research. The available information suggests that children's daily level of health may decrease dramatically, very little, or not at all, especially since, cross-culturally, raiding activities are often not related to nutritional stressors. Data collected by Ellis (1951), Knauft (1987), and Otterbein (2000) suggest that children below the age of adolescence rarely suffer violence during small-scale conflicts, and it is unlikely that adolescents, especially younger ones, are affected either. Nevertheless, there could be a slight increase in antemortem skeletal trauma in children of all ages. Perimortem fracture and mortality rates in all developmental age groups could increase slightly. Inter-pueblo raiding during the protohistoric and historic eras did not occur at a level that completely disrupted a targeted community (Ellis 1951), so it is likely that settlements in the prehistoric period were similarly affected. Thus, it is reasonable to expect that Ancestral Pueblo individuals killed during a raid would receive a burial in keeping with traditional mortuary practices.

The Sand Canyon Pueblo stressor attributes when the village was evacuated more closely follow the characteristics of an incidence of ideological factionalism (Table 9.6). Of the individuals located, nine adolescents, one juvenile, and eight adults were apparently killed in the attack. One infant and a young child may have been victims of violence as well, although the case for them is not compelling. The juvenile may have been viewed as a ritually responsible adult since the age variation in Pueblo "finishing" initiations allows for this possibility. But the juvenile rate is the same as the 5 percent rates for atypical mortuary context infancy and childhood stage children; these low rates comply with the potential for the unintentional deaths of ritually innocent children during an ideological crisis.

Gender analysis, although provisional because of osteological methodology and sample size issues, adds support to the likelihood of an ideological upheaval. At least four of the eleven individuals who could be sexed are females or possible females who were either at or soon would be at optimum reproductive maturity. As documented by Ellis (1951) and Bayer and others (1994), Pueblo males commonly participated in raids to obtain or keep mates, not kill them. The presence of both male and female adolescents is not unexpected in an ideological crisis, although males are more frequently victims. Both sexes are considered ritually responsible in historic Pueblo communities, and at least one young adult female was killed at Awatovi (Turner and Turner 1999).

B. Bradley (personal communication 1997) infers that most of the villagers were killed during the attack. His reasoning is based on the number of atypical mortuary context individuals (20), multiplied by the percentage of the structures excavated (10–12 percent), yielding a figure of about 200 to 240 villagers. This possibility is reasonable, given the maximum population estimate of 225 people. When the estimate is calculated using the known frequency of individuals per developmental stage, however, the comparatively low number of infants, young children, juveniles, and (perhaps) older adolescent and adult males argues that not all villagers died during this event. If any older adolescent and/or adult males survived, they may have gathered other survivors and quickly moved away. Or the survivors, potentially related to the attackers as kin or community members, may have been taken away and incorporated as fellow villagers, as at Awatovi, or perhaps enslaved, as possibly occurred at La Plata Valley (Martin et al. 2001).

Regardless of the actual number of people killed, the presence of at least twenty people in dispersed, atypical mortuary contexts by itself argues for a severe social disruption, a more common characteristic of intense factionalism than raiding. Many societies, including the historic Pueblo, perform very specific burial rituals to ensure the continuance of the natural order and/or to control otherwise dangerous forces. The abrogation of such rituals in a community that had heretofore followed traditional Pueblo III mortuary rites, regardless of the individual's age, is laden with meaning. It implies that the survivors were either overwhelmed by the circumstance or incapable of carrying out traditional, and presumably highly obligatory, responsibilities.

IDEOLOGY, PLACE, AND WELL-BEING

The children of Sand Canyon apparently participated in at least periodic community feasting on large, iron-rich game, giving them a moderately higher level of nutritional adequacy than other Ancestral Pueblo children. Of the subadults, however, the adolescents especially suffered quite unusual trauma and mortality rates. The combination of these circumstances suggests some type of differential status. The Sand Canyon Pueblo teens' lethal trauma could indicate that they were involved in status-building conflicts as members of a ranked society, yet their antemortem trauma patterns are not suggestive of involvement in risky activities. This possibility is further weakened since at least three of the older adolescents were females or possible females. Also, even if some of the 12-to-14-year-old teens were males, their conventional participation in such dangerous activities would be unusual. Young male teens are apparently rarely involved as aggressors in lethal hand-to-hand combat, perhaps because they tend to lack the necessary strength, stamina, or cognitive ability. Although not conclusive, the adolescents' skeletal evidence does not suggest ranked status.

The uniformity of the children's skeletal stress suggests that they were not members of a particular village subgroup with an enhanced status. Apparently, their differential status reflects ritual complexity rather than social hierarchy, the special status of their community rather than differentiation within it. This is in keeping with the archaeological information, which shows no evidence of the unequal accumulation of domestic or exotic goods or of variation in residential building quality (Lipe et al. 1999).

It is impossible to know if the adolescents were targeted and killed because of their membership in a family, faction, or community, because they steadfastly refused to give up their beliefs, or because they were active defenders or aggressors. It could well be that their deaths were due to a variety of these possibilities. No objects that may have been weapons were found with them, however, and their observed injuries are more suggestive of "flight" than "fight." Assuming that all the individuals from atypical mortuary contexts died near where they were found, their locations show that they had not been gathered together for execution.

The dynamic between high mortality and lethal violence is duplicated in both the adults and teens. It thus conforms more closely to the cross-cultural pattern involving ideological factionalism. That is, during an ideological upheaval, economically dependent adolescents are viewed as ritually responsible adults; when perceived as ideological nonconformists, they too experience increased levels of intentional and lethal violence. Overall, the skeletal evidence points to the children's communal status in a village that apparently itself held a distinctive, ritual position. This circumstance of place proved to be both beneficial and detrimental, apparently buffering the children in life but ultimately contributing to their violent deaths.

Infant health is accepted as a sensitive marker of material stressors in past societies. Although further research is in order, escalated adolescent mortality due to violence may prove to be an accurate indicator of ideological conflict. I submit that an understanding of how beliefs affect children's well-being, and what their health status thus conveys about social conditions, needs to be more fully addressed in both archaeological and bioarchaeological research. But even though the issue of Ancestral Pueblo violence is currently a prominent subject of debate, it would be insufficient to consider only the negative effects of ideological concerns. Cross-cultural patterns show that, as apparently occurred at Sand Canyon Pueblo, beliefs can also enhance children's well-being. Holistic approaches are needed to understand issues related to children's health regardless of society, time, or place.

ACKNOWLEDGMENTS

This chapter includes material presented at the 2000 Society for American Archaeology symposium on Ancestral Pueblo children. I extend my sincere thanks to Kathryn Kamp for organizing that forum and for her thoughtful and constructive appraisals of this chapter as volume editor. The comments of Nan Rothschild, Michelle Hegmon, and an anonymous reviewer were also most helpful. I especially wish to acknowledge the contributions, comments, and maps provided by Bruce Bradley, the director of research at Sand Canyon Pueblo. Finally, Michael Hoffman's insightful critique and encouragement of my research on the relationship between obligation and child health have been invaluable.

10

Wearing a Butterfly, Coming of Age

A 1,500-Year-Old Pueblo Tradition

KELLEY HAYS-GILPIN

When a Pueblo girl experiences her first menses, her mother puts her hair in "butterfly" whorls, which she wears on ceremonial occasions until marriage. Depictions of hair whorls appear by about A.D. 500 in rock art and a little later in painted pottery. Contextual analysis of rock art, pottery, and oral traditions suggests the long-standing symbolic significance of an important life stage between "girl" and "woman," a stage often translated from Hopi as "maidenhood."

STUDYING GIRLS' PUBERTY IN THE WESTERN UNITED STATES

Anthropological attention to girls' puberty rites has flourished in the western United States ever since Franz Boas launched detailed studies of western Indians, facilitating Alfred Kroeber's monumental *Handbook of California Indians* (1925). Kroeber described girls' puberty rites for nearly every tribe in that state, providing data for Harold Driver's 1941 comparative study of girls' puberty rites in western North America. Driver's stated purpose was not to explain puberty rites but to use the unusually detailed data set about them to demonstrate appropriate statistical methods for comparing cultures using culture trait lists. Joseph Jorgensen's 1980 assessment of the topic draws on Driver's data but uses them to reveal historical connections among tribes and to explore links between the economic bases of western Indian cultures and patterns of ritual practice.

Systematic comparison of western tribes' puberty rites identified a few features that most hold in common: belief that menstrual blood is dangerous and polluting to spiritual things, hunting, and fishing, and that menstrual blood offends bears and invites bear attacks; group performance of a dance; use of a head scratcher; and abstention from meat, often with other dietary restrictions. Among other features noted in at least some groups are seclusion, usually seclusion to a special structure; food taboos or restrictions, usually including meat; use of designated objects such as food and water containers; instruction from older women about morals and behavior; body molding (older women massage or knead the girl's body to make her strong and straight); running or racing; preparing special foods for family members; craft activities that demonstrate skills valued as women's work; obtaining spirit helpers; body positioning (the girl lies in a pit with hot rocks, on warm sand, or in a trench she digs herself); and storing food in baskets or buried in pits where trails cross. Comparative studies conclude not that puberty rites are universal but that in western North America they have ancient historical roots and ideological connections with hunting and fishing economies.

Driver found that most of these features are absent in the Puebloan region of northern Arizona and New Mexico. Jorgensen (1980) attributes the low visibility of Pueblo puberty rites to differing cultural-historical trajectories and different economic bases. Far western girls' puberty rites emphasize the adverse effects of menstruating women on hunting and fishing. The Pueblos are resolute agriculturalists, he notes, and Pueblo women observe no menstrual taboos. Anthropologists, then, have used accounts of puberty rites as evidence for historical and economic commonalities and cleavages among ethnic groups in the western United States. They have accorded little attention to the social and symbolic contexts of puberty rites within cultures, the meanings of puberty in native cosmologies, or individual experience.

Recently, combined ethnographic and archaeological research that stresses sacred landscapes, including rock art, suggests that most western tribes' puberty training periods and initiations rest on a shamanistic foundation that stresses obtaining spirit helpers and manipulating spiritual power (Hays-Gilpin 2001; Whitley 1994, 1998, 2000). Among the Columbia Plateau tribes, for example, an individual of either sex goes to remote locations alone and with mentors and may dream of any number of helping spirits; initiates probably enter altered states of consciousness (ASCs) in this process. In the larger, densely populated Luiseño villages of southern California, initiation is a more public matter, taking place in and near the village. The obtaining of helping spirits is guided not only by elders of an opposite clan or village but by manipulating symbols of gender inversions. Girls paint rattlesnake designs because this masculine symbol is a potent spirit helper for women; likewise, female bears are important helpers of male initiates. ASCs may or may not play an active role for any given individual, but puberty practices have a shamanistic foundation.

Again, Pueblo practice stands out as different from that of northern and western neighbors, but we should ask not only why agriculturalists downplay puberty and shamanism but also what puberty means for Pueblo cultures and what girls experienced in the distant as well as the recent past. In spite of the lack of public Pueblo puberty fanfare, pubescent girls are extremely important spiritually and symbolically. They represent the growing maize plants that will soon bear a harvest (Black 1984) and other aspects of fertility, abundance, and potentiality. As future lineage heads and clan mothers, "maidens" are in training to take on important social and ritual roles. They have been depicted in rock art, pottery, and kiva murals for more than a thousand years.

COMING OF AGE IN THE PUEBLOS

In most of the pueblos a girl's female relatives marked her first menses by setting her to grind corn for four days and then putting her hair up in two whorls on the sides of her head (Figure 10.1). At Hopi these whorls are called *poli'ini*. The verb form, *poli'inta*, means "wearing a butterfly" (Hopi Dictionary Project 1998:421). Hopi speakers, like most other speakers of Uto-Aztecan languages, associate butterflies with summer, flowers, fertility, water, and a utopian spiritual world (Hays-Gilpin and Hill 1999).

The most elaborate puberty observances among the Pueblos took place in the First Mesa Hopi village of Walpi. Alexander Stephen describes a Walpi puberty observance in January 1893:

> For four days . . . Küyimana [who belongs to the Patki clan] and, assisting at different times, nearly all the other girls of Walpi, have ground white corn meal in the house of Sikya'nümka of the Reed clan who is Kü'yi's father's sister. . . . A rabbit skin rug is hung up to conceal the grinding stones from the direct sunlight, which must not touch Kü'yi during the four days, nor must she touch salt or flesh for that time.

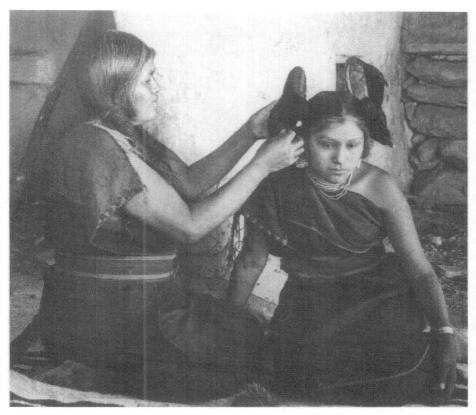

Figure 10.1. Hopi woman dressing the hair of an unmarried girl. Note U-shaped wooden stick in partly shaped hair whorl on left side of photo. Photographed by Henry Peabody, ca. 1900. National Archives and Record Administration catalog no. 79-HPS-6-3274.

> Her first menses have occurred and she is now qualifying herself to have her hair dressed in large whorls called *boli'inta*. It is in the evening of this occurrence that the maiden goes to the house of her father's sister. What is done then I have not yet discovered. (Parsons 1936a:139–140)

Stephen later discovers that the next morning other girls who have already had their hair whorled join Kü'yi to take turns grinding in the darkened room, and "matrons" (married women) bring gifts of cornmeal. Kü'yi's aunt's husband or her grandfather brings a head scratcher: "If the maid scratched her hair or body with her fingers during these days of observance, her hair would fall out." The girls "chatter and make light sport of what appears to one a very tedious and laborious occupation." Next the family calls a general feast for women friends. On the last morning Küyi's aunt washes her hair and dresses it in the whorls, rubs her face with white cornmeal, and takes her to a shrine with about eight other young girls. They deposit a basket of prayer meal and the head scratcher there (Parsons 1936a:140–143).

In other Hopi villages girls' puberty rites were less elaborate or not as well reported. In the Second Mesa village of Mishongnovi, Elsie Clews Parsons reports, "At her adolescence retreat the Mishongnovi girl is also kept in the shade; she fasts from salt and meat"; she is "like a baby" (1939:601); "on Second Mesa the girls go out with the hunters after an adolescence ceremony at which they have been grinding" (1939:25).

Helen Sekaquaptewa grew up in the Third Mesa village of Hotvela. She writes: "A girl wears her hair long and loose until she is fourteen or fifteen years old. After she menstruates, she puts her hair up in two whorls at each side of her head . . . I should say that her hair is put up for her" (1969:118). She does not mention undertaking a puberty seclusion but rather describes ritual grinding in the home of her future mother-in-law as part of the marriage ceremony several years later: "As a bride I was considered sacred the first few days, being in a room with the shades on the windows, talking to no one. All this time I was steadily grinding corn which was brought in by Emory's kinswomen" (1969:155; Emory was her husband-to-be).

In most other Pueblo villages, at first menstruation girls grind corn to help prepare for a family feast and have their hair put up, whereas darkened rooms and food taboos may be specific to Hopi, and scratching sticks and offerings at shrines may appear only at Walpi. These differences may be due to sparse ethnographic information about life-cycle events in the other pueblos, or as Jorgensen (1980) suggests, the First Mesa version of the puberty ceremony may have been influenced by Athapaskan-speaking Navajo neighbors, who retain the far western tribes' emphasis on elaborate female puberty rites and restrictions and arrived in Hopiland sometime in the 1700s. Likewise, Parsons notes that the Walpi puberty rite has some similarities (food taboos, seclusion, scratching stick) to the practices of California tribes and the Paiute (distant linguistic relatives of the Hopi), and not to those of the other pueblos (1939:58). In any case, even within the Pueblo culture area, ways of observing puberty vary, probably for historical reasons, and archaeologists might be able to discern some of this variation.

Arnold van Gennep's (1960 [1909]) three-stage ritual model of separation, transition, and incorporation applies to Puebloan observance of female puberty in that the puberty rite marks a "transition" via a "liminal" state between "girl" and a distinct social category, *maana*, often translated "maiden," which is complete in itself. Unlike the case among many tribes of the Far West, the separation phase does not involve seclusion. Even on First Mesa the initial stage of the ritual involves only a short journey to the home of an aunt of the girl's father's clan, where the girl is not alone but has a great deal of company during the corn-grinding ordeal, which may be said to constitute the transition phase of the ritual. On completing "incorporation" via the family feast, an individual holds the status of *maana* for several years, from puberty until the beginning of her lengthy marriage ceremony, when she becomes a *wuuti*, "woman" (as Sekaquaptewa suggests, some aspects of the wedding indicate another separation, transition, and incorporation sequence). In all the Hopi villages maidens appear as a group at public dances, and they are eligible for initiation into one of three women's ritual societies; usually, the maiden chooses the one her paternal aunt has joined. The Marau, Lakon, and Oaqöl societies closely parallel many of the functions and practices of men's sodalities and have similar initiations. These initiations do not mark puberty; rather, puberty is a prerequisite.

Although the observance of puberty for any individual Pueblo girl is downplayed compared with far western tribes, the symbolic importance of young, marriageable women in Pueblo religion and iconography is unparalleled. The butterfly hair whorls are the key symbol of maidenhood. This hairstyle change is well described for Hopi, Taos, and Zuni, and some version of hair whorls probably appeared in the other pueblos as well. Taos girls "wore a braid down the back which was changed after the first menstruation to the double cue [*sic*] arrangement" (Parsons 1936b:26). Zuni maidens, who ground corn for one day in the home of paternal relatives, wore hair whorls with a wooden frame left inside to hold their butterfly shape. Women wearing butterfly hair whorls appear in paintings on pottery and kiva walls, in rock art, and on painted wooden ritual paraphernalia. Many feminine kachinas wear butterfly hair whorls and at Hopi are called *katsinmana*. Only a few represent adult women, such as Spider Grandmother and Hahay'iwuuti, the mother of the kachinas, who symbolizes ideal womanhood. At Hopi, maize plants are called maidens until they become mothers by bearing mature ears (Black 1984), and Zuni and Keresan oral traditions are filled with corn maidens who flee mistreatment, only to be recovered by a masculine culture hero who lures them back with his flute-playing.

ARCHAEOLOGICAL EVIDENCE

Can studying prehistoric depictions of figures with butterfly hair whorls shed light on the long-term history of Puebloan puberty practices and beliefs? What is their distribution in space and time? Have hair whorls always indicated pubescent females? Can their contexts and associations tell us anything about variations in meaning accorded "maidenhood" in Pueblo cultures? Such figures appear often in rock art (Figure 10.2) and rarely but regularly on pottery and other media. Images on pottery (Figure 10.3) are especially interesting because pottery styles have known date ranges and production areas. Depictions of maidens on pottery are most frequent between about A.D. 600 and 900 and again between about A.D. 1350 and 1700.

Detailed study of human figures that have hair whorls, breasts, or genitals depicted suggests hair whorls frequently appear in rock art and pottery in northeastern Arizona and northwestern New Mexico. To the south, they appear just below the Mogollon Rim in the Payson and Grasshopper/Cibecue areas of Arizona but not in the Salt-Gila basin or in southern and western Arizona, with the exception of one possible hair-whorled figure north of Tucson. They appear along the San Juan River and may extend into the Fremont culture area to the north. A western boundary occurs somewhere around Prescott, Seligman, and the Grand Canyon, except for one figure in the Coso Range of California that appears to represent hair whorls. Hair whorl depictions are abundant in the Rio Grande region, especially after A.D. 1300, but do not seem to extend to the Plains. Equivocal figures in the Big Bend area of Texas and Durango, Mexico, bear further investigation.

To my knowledge, the earliest hair whorl depiction appears in Canyon de Chelly (Figure 10.4). Details of shape, technique, pigments, and associated figures suggest a date sometime between A.D. 200 and 600 because this painting resembles figures thought to date to this era in the Four Corners area (Robins and Hays-Gilpin 2000). A figure holding a U-shaped stick bends over a recumbent figure with square hair whorls and a triangular garment sometimes described as a "menstrual apron" (Cole 1990: 124). Strings attached to a waistband were pulled between the legs and tucked in back, forming a triangular shape over the pubic area; such aprons or string skirts occur only on female burials of this time period and sometimes bear stains of menstrual blood. Campbell Grant (1978:185) interpreted this scene as a shaman attending to a female patient, but it seems more likely that the U-shaped stick is the very same item used today to shape a Hopi maiden's hair whorls (called a *poli"inngölu*; a historic example is visible in Figure 10.1). Just to the left of this tableau appears a second pair of figures in the same style. The smaller has hair whorls, and the larger carries a *poli"inngölu*.

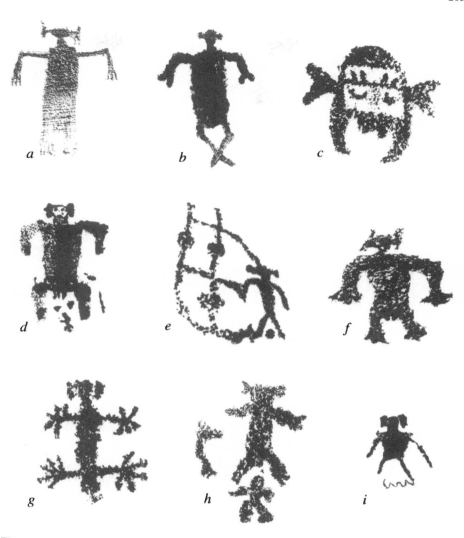

Figure 10.2. Figures with hair whorls in rock art from various localities (drawings/photo enhancements by Kelley Hays-Gilpin). Date unknown unless specified; petroglyphs unless specified. *a.* Arizona strip north of Grand Canyon; *b.* Morris Cave 4, Prayer Rock District, white paint, Basketmaker III period, ca. A.D. 600s; *c.* Petroglyph National Monument, near Albuquerque, on basalt, Pueblo IV period, ca. A.D. 1300–1700; *d.* Baird's Chevelon Steps site, near Winslow, Arizona, Pueblo IV period, ca. A.D. 1300s; *e.* near Holbrook, Arizona; *f.* near Winslow, Arizona; *g.* near Seligman, Arizona; *h.* near Payson, Arizona; *i.* near Cibecue, Arizona, black paint.

Figure 10.3. Figures with hair whorls on pottery (drawings by Kelley Hays-Gilpin); a and c. La Plata Black-on-white, Basketmaker III period, near Durango, Colorado (after Lister and Lister 1978:11); b. White Mound Black-on-white bowl sherd from NA 8939, Pithouse 3, near Houck, Arizona; associated tree-ring dates range from A.D. 785 to 837; d. Pueblo I period black-on-white pitcher, La Plata District (after Morris 1939:Plate 224l); e. Jeddito Black-on-yellow ladle base, Homol'ovi area, near Winslow, Arizona; Pueblo IV period, ca. A.D. 1350–1400 (Arizona State Museum); f. Figure from Jeddito Engraved bowl, late Pueblo IV period, ca. A.D. 1450–1700, Awatovi, Hopi Mesas (Harvard Peabody Museum, Awatovi Expedition catalog no. 5361).

Figure 10.4. Canyon de Chelly, Arizona. Figures with hair whorls paired with figures holding U-shaped stick; white, yellow, and red paint. Probably late Basketmaker II period, ca. A.D. 200–500. CDC-25 (enhanced photo by Robert Mark).

Figures with hair whorls appear regularly in rock art in Basketmaker III sites that date to the A.D. 600s and on black-on-white pottery from southwestern Colorado, northwestern New Mexico, and eastern Arizona. The pottery dates to the 600s–800s, probably later than the earliest rock-art depictions but easier to date. One pottery fragment from Houck, Arizona, was found in a pithouse whose timbers were tree-ring-dated to the late A.D. 700s and early 800s (Figure 10.3b; Hays-Gilpin and van Hartesvelt 1998:61–62).

Figures with hair whorls, then, are firmly associated with the distribution of ancestral Puebloan cultures, including the Mogollon and Hisatsinom (Anasazi). In the 600s–800s, villages made up of large pithouses surrounding early great-kiva structures appear throughout the Four Corners area. Matrilocal extended families probably became the primary residence unit during this period, together with ritual sodalities that integrated unrelated men who married into the small villages (Hays 1992; Robins and Hays-Gilpin 2000). A second florescence of hair-whorled figures appears on pottery dating between about A.D. 1350 and 1600, primarily in the Hopi area (Figure 10.3e and f). Community growth and increasing elaboration of the ritual system also characterized this period, albeit on a much larger scale.

Are the hair whorls associated with female figures and not with male figures? Numerous figures with hair whorls also have female genitalia; several with hair whorls have the string aprons worn by women in ancestral Puebloan cultures at least until the mid-1100s. Many figures with hair whorls have no indication of sex or gender, and I have found only two instances of figures with hair whorls and what might be penises (Figure 10.5). The possibly male figures are a petroglyph on Leroux Wash in the middle Little Colorado River drainage that probably dates to the mid-1200s (Hays-Gilpin 2000:171) and a pair of painted figures in Snake Gulch, near Kanab, Utah (Schaafsma 1980:119), which appear to be early,

Figure 10.5. Ambiguous figures with hair whorls. *a*. Near Holbrook, Arizona. Line between legs may represent a penis or menstruation (drawing by Kelley Hays-Gilpin); *b*. Snake Gulch, north of Grand Canyon, Arizona (Schaafsma 1980:119, courtesy of the University of New Mexico Press). Short lines between legs may represent male or female genitals.

perhaps Basketmaker II (before A.D. 500 or so). They have square shapes floating on each side of the head, barely above the shoulders, and may be simply one of many elaborate hairstyles and/or headdresses depicted in this area and possibly related Fremont figures to the north. If these shapes indeed represent hair whorls rather than some other hairstyle, and penises rather than female genitals or menstruation, which seems just as likely, these figures may represent males who chose to take on a feminine gender identity, as did a small proportion of males in nearly every traditional Native American society (Jacobs et al. 1997; Roscoe 1998). Because exceptions are so rare, the correlation between hair whorls and feminine gender identity is strong even in the earliest depictions.

Figures with hair whorls seem to represent females, but do they represent "maidens," females between puberty and marriage? First, many images have female genitalia and lack hair whorls, suggesting that not all females, but only a special category, wore this hairstyle. Second, a few figures with hair whorls seem to correlate with depictions of menstruation and courtship. Ethnographies suggest that first menstruation was marked by wearing hair whorls and the start of courtship, and in some Pueblo traditions corn maidens were courted by a flute-playing male culture hero. Possible representations of menstruation appear in the form of discontinuous, wavy, or otherwise elaborated lines between the figure's legs (Figure 10.6); many such depictions have hair whorls. Several hair-whorled figures are paired with flute players (Figure 10.7). One of these has hair whorls and a short line below her groin that may represent menstruation (Figure 10.7a), several have hair whorls and clearly female genitals, and the others are more equivocal. Of course, flute players and maidens appear in other contexts, and many other figures appear with flute players, but the consistent if rare appearance of depictions of menstruation and courtship suggests that hair whorls could have indicated "maiden" status in the past as well as the present.

Finally, if rock-art depictions of maidens are linked to Puebloan puberty rites, one must ask whether rock art offers any evidence that Puebloan puberty rites in the past involved trance and acquisition of spirit helpers, as in far western puberty rites. Images of "maidens" do not regularly occur with repeated geometric patterns that many researchers associate with entoptic imagery produced by the brain in trance (see Lewis-Williams and Dowson 1988). Such styles are found in the Southwest, but most appear to be very early and were probably produced by Archaic hunter-gatherers and early Basketmaker horticulturalists before the appearance of settled villages. Although some Pueblo priests, especially healers, practiced

Figure 10.6. Probable depictions of menstruation at Lyman Lake, Arizona. Photo by Kelley Hays-Gilpin.

trance in some contexts, we have very little evidence that vision questing or trance was a prominent part of Pueblo religion, and it plays no role in the public aspects of Pueblo ritual. Though entoptic forms and especially construals of later trance-phase imagery cannot be ruled out (significantly, scientific investigation has no way to rule them out in any case), most Puebloan rock art can be explained by other practices that emphasize not so much an individual's relationship to the spirit world but the relationship between social groups and the landscape. These practices include sun watching and other astronomical observation, boundary marking, marking the movement of social groups as in clan migrations, marking shrines used by particular sodalities, and depiction of kachinas and other immortal beings from oral traditions. Female beings include corn maidens, the mother of game animals, Spider Woman, and the maiden mother of the Hero Twins (Hays-Gilpin 2000). Life-cycle symbolism inheres in all these

Figure 10.7. "Maidens" paired with phallic flute players. *a*. Catron County, New Mexico (courtesy of J. Louis Argend-Farlow). *b* and *c*. La Cieneguilla, near Santa Fe (drawings by Kelley Hays-Gilpin).

beings, and each represents social and ceremonial relationships among members of different genders and generations. Therefore, I would argue that the key metaphor of Pueblo puberty rites and butterfly hair whorls is agricultural fertility. The primary functions of this process are signaling a young woman's marriageability, perhaps especially important in the villages of the A.D. 600s–900s, and her readiness to take on ritual responsibilities, most important in the large, aggregated, ritually complex communities of the 1300s and later.

Traditional stories are still told, and the traditional puberty ceremony sometimes still takes place. During almost any visit to a pueblo, we may see kachinas dancing in the plazas, visiting shrines, and handing out presents and punishments to children. We may see maidens lined up on the edge of the plaza at the Hopi Home Dance in late summer and entering the kivas for their sodality initiations. Butterfly hair whorls are a living tradition as well as an ancient one. At a "Girl Power" seminar held at the Hopi Cultural Center in December 2000, Lucinda Andreani presented her current Master's thesis research about butterfly hair whorls in rock art (see also Andreani and Kuyvaya 2000). Girls, mothers, and grandmothers enjoyed discussing traditional puberty rites and agreed that the ceremony should continue to help show community support for individual girls as they take new ritual responsibilities. Many were surprised to learn that this tradition has continued at least 1,500 years.

ACKNOWLEDGMENTS

Special thanks to Lucinda Andreani, Evelyn Billo, J. Louis Argend-Farlow, Margaret "Marglyph" Berrier, Marcia-Anne Dobres, Jane Kolber, Robert Mark, Patricia McCreery, Carol Patterson, Linda Powell, Polly Schaafsma, Claudette Piper, and all the others who have generously provided images for the rock art database and the source photographs of some of the drawings presented here. The Arizona State Museum, Museum of Northern Arizona, and Harvard Peabody Museum graciously provided access to pottery collections cited here. I extend my gratitude to the conference participants and anonymous reviewers who made helpful suggestions; any errors or omissions are mine.

References

Adams, E. C.

1983 Archaeological Research Design. Ms. on file, Crow Canyon Archaeological Center, Cortez, Colorado.

Adams, K., and V. E. Bowyer

1999 Subsistence and Human Impact on the Environment: The Thirteenth Century and Abandonment as Viewed from the Archaeobotanical Record. Paper presented at the 64th Annual Meeting of the Society for American Archaeology, Chicago.

Adler, M. A.

1992 The Upland Survey. In *The Sand Canyon Archaeological Project: A Progress Report,* edited by W. Lipe, pp. 11–23. Occasional Papers No. 2. Crow Canyon Archaeological Center, Cortez, Colorado.

Akins, N. J.

1986 *A Biocultural Approach to Human Burials from Chaco Canyon, New Mexico.* Reports of the Chaco Center No. 9. National Park Service, Santa Fe.

Ambler, R.

1989 *Anasazi: Prehistoric People of the Four Corners Region.* Museum of Northern Arizona, Flagstaff.

Andreani, L., and S. Kuyvaya

2000 Integrating Iconographic Studies with Ethnography to Document Puebloan Clan Migrations and Cultural Affiliation. Paper presented at the 6th Gender and Archaeology Conference, Flagstaff, Arizona.

Ariès, P.

1962 *Centuries of Childhood: A Social History of Family Life.* Alfred A. Knopf, New York.

Armelagos, G. J., and A. H. Goodman

1991 The Concept of Stress and Its Relevance to Studies of Adaptation in Prehistoric Populations. *Collegium Antropologicum* 15:45–58.

Arnold, C.

1992 *The Ancient Cliff Dwellers of Mesa Verde*. Clarion Books, New York.

Arnold, D. E.

1999 Advantages and Disadvantages of Vertical-Half Molding Technology: Implications for Production Organization. In *Pottery and People*, edited by J. Skibo and G. Feinman, pp. 59–80. University of Utah Press, Salt Lake City.

Ayer, E. H.

1993 *The Anasazi*. Walker, New York.

Babcock, B. A.

1986 *The Pueblo Storyteller*. University of Arizona Press, Tucson.

Baity, E. C.

1951 *Americans Before Columbus*. Viking Press, New York.

Baldwin, G. C.

1963 *The Ancient Ones: Basketmakers and Cliff Dwellers of the Southwest*. W. W. Norton, New York.

Bartlett, K.

1933 Pueblo Milling Stones of the Flagstaff Region and Their Relation to Others in the Southwest. *Museum of Northern Arizona Bulletin* No. 7. Flagstaff.

1934 *The Material Culture of Pueblo II in the San Francisco Mountains, Arizona*. Northern Arizona Society of Science and Art, Nos. 4–7. Museum of Northern Arizona, Flagstaff.

Bayer, L., with F. Montoya and the Pueblo of Santa Ana

1994 *Santa Ana: The People, the Pueblo, and the History of Tamaya*. University of New Mexico Press, Albuquerque.

Beaglehole, E.

1937 *Notes on Hopi Economic Life*. Yale University Publications in Anthropology No. 15. Yale University Press, New Haven.

Beaglehole, E., and P. Beaglehole

1935 Hopi of Second Mesa. *Memoirs of the American Anthropological Association* 44:5–14.

Beaglehole, P.

1935 Census Data from Two Hopi Villages. *American Anthropologist* 37:41–54.

Beem, J. A.

1999 Daily Life: Making the Most of Everything. *Cobblestone* 20(6):9–12.

Benedict, R.

1934 *Patterns of Culture*. Houghton Mifflin, New York.

Bennett, K. A.

1961 Artificial Cranial Deformation Among the Caddo Indians. *Texas Journal of Science* 13:377–390.

1973 *Indians of Point of Pines, Arizona: A Comparative Study of Their Physical Characteristics*. Anthropological Papers of the University of Arizona No. 23. University of Arizona Press, Tucson.

1975 *Skeletal Remains from Mesa Verde National Park, Colorado*. Publications in Archeology 7F, Wetherill Mesa Studies. National Park Service, Washington, D.C.

Bernbeck, R.

1999 Structure Strikes Back: Intuitive Meanings of Ceramics from Qale Rostam, Iran. In *Material Symbols: Culture and Economy in Prehistory*, edited by

J. Robb, pp. 90–111. Center for Archaeological Investigations Occasional
Paper No. 26. Carbondale, Illinois.

Berry, D. R.

1983 Disease and Climatological Relationships Among Pueblo III–Pueblo IV
Anasazi of the Colorado Plateau. Unpublished Ph.D. dissertation, Department of Anthropology, University of California, Los Angeles.

1985a Aspects of Paleodemography at Grasshopper Pueblo, Arizona. In *Health
and Disease in the Prehistoric Southwest*, edited by C. Merbs and R. Miller,
pp. 43–64. Anthropological Research Papers No. 34. Arizona State University, Tempe.

1985b Dental Paleopathology of Grasshopper Pueblo, Arizona. In *Health and
Disease in the Prehistoric Southwest*, edited by C. Merbs and R. Miller, pp.
253–274. Anthropological Research Papers No. 34. Arizona State University, Tempe, Arizona.

Biber, B.

1962 *Children's Drawings: From Lines to Pictures Illustrated.* Bank Street College of Education Publications, New York.

Bird, D. W., and R. B. Bird

2000 The Ethnoarchaeology of Juvenile Foragers: Shellfishing Strategies among
Meriam Children. *Journal of Anthropological Archaeology* 19:461–476.

Bird, E. J.

1993 *The Rainmakers.* Carolrhoda Books, Minneapolis.

Birkby, W. H.

1969 Appendix 1 in *Two Pueblo III Cradle Burials from Upper Glen Canyon,
Utah.* Museum of Northern Arizona. Report No. 14.354. Submitted to the
National Park Service. Copies available from the Museum of Northern
Arizona, Flagstaff.

1973 Discontinuous Morphological Traits of the Skull as Population Markers in
the Prehistoric Southwest. Unpublished Ph.D. dissertation, Department of
Anthropology, University of Arizona, Tucson.

1982 BioSocial Interpretations from Cranial Nonmetric Traits of the Grasshopper Pueblo Skeletal Remains. In *Multidisciplinary Research at Grasshopper Pueblo, Arizona*, edited by W. A. Longacre, S. J. Holbrook, and
M. W. Graves, pp. 36–41. Anthropological Papers of the University of Arizona No. 40. University of Arizona Press, Tucson.

Black, M.

1984 Maidens and Mothers: An Analysis of Hopi Corn Metaphors. *Ethnology*
23:279–288.

Blackman, M. J., G. J. Stein, and P. B. Vandiver

1993 The Standardization Hypothesis and Ceramic Mass Production: Technological, Compositional, and Metric Indices of Craft Specialization at Tell
Leilan, Syria. *American Antiquity* 58(1):60–80.

Blair, M. E., and L. Blair

1999 *The Legacy of a Master Potter: Nampeyo and Her Descendants.* Treasure
Chest Books, Tucson.

Blurton Jones, N., K. Hawkes, and P. Draper

1994 Differences Between Hadza and !Kung Children's Work: Original Af-
fluence or Practical Reason? In *Key Issues in Hunter-Gatherer Research*,
edited by E. S. Burch, Jr., and L. J. Ellanna, pp. 189–215. Berg, Oxford.

Bogin, B., and B. H. Smith
1996 Evolution of the Human Lifecycle. *American Journal of Human Biology* 8:703–716.

Bogin, B., and J. Loucky
1997 Plasticity, Political Economy, and Physical Growth Status of Guatemala Maya Children Living in the United States. *American Journal of Physical Anthropology* 102:17–32.

Bolen, K. M.
1992 Prehistoric Construction of Mothering. In *Exploring Gender Through Archaeology: Selected Papers from the 1991 Boone Conference*, edited by C. Claassen, pp. 49–62. Prehistory Press, Madison, Wisconsin.

Bower, B.
2001 Evolution's Youth Movement: Fossil Children May Harbor Clues to Humanity's Origins. *Science News* 159:346–348.

Bradley, B.
1992 Excavations at Sand Canyon Pueblo. In *The Sand Canyon Archaeological Project: A Progress Report*, edited by W. Lipe, pp. 79–97. Crow Canyon Archaeological Center, Cortez, Colorado.
1993 Planning, Growth, and Functional Differentiation at a Prehistoric Pueblo: A Case Study from Southwest Colorado. *Journal of Field Archaeology* 20:23–42.
1996 Pitchers to Mugs: Chacoan Revival at Sand Canyon Pueblo. *The Kiva* 61:241–255.

Bradley, B., and M. Churchill
1995 *Annual Report of the 1993 Excavations at Sand Canyon Pueblo (5MT765)*. Crow Canyon Archaeological Center, Cortez, Colorado.

Bradley, Candice
1987 Children's Work and Women's Work: A Cross-Cultural Study. *Anthropology of Work Review* 8(1): 2–5.
1993 Women's Power, Children's Labor. *Cross-Cultural Research* 27:70–96.

Bradley, Cynthia S.
1998 Obligation and Children: Attitudes of Obligation in the Nurturing and Interpretation of Children. Unpublished Master's thesis, Vermont College of Norwich University, Montpelier.

Braun, D. P.
1983 Pots as Tools. In *Archaeological Hammers and Theories*, edited by J. Moore and A. Keene, pp. 108–134. Academic Press, New York.

Brody, J. J.
1977 *Mimbres Painted Pottery*. School of American Research, Santa Fe, and University of New Mexico Press, Albuquerque.
1990 *The Anasazi: Ancient Indian People of the American Southwest*. Rizzoli, New York.

Brown, B. A.
1983 Seen but Not Heard: Women in Aztec Ritual: The Sahagún Texts. In *Text and Image in Pre-Columbian Art: Essays on the Interrelationship of the Verbal and Visual Arts*, edited by J. C. Berlo, pp. 119–153. BAR International Series, Oxford.

Brown, E. V.
1975 Developmental Characteristics of Clay Figures Made by Children from Age Three Through Eleven. *Studies in Art Education* 16(3):45–53.

Brown, J. A.
1989 The Beginnings of Pottery as an Economic Process. In *What's New? A Closer Look at the Process of Innovation*, edited by S. E. van der Leeuw and R. Torrence, pp. 203–224. Unwin Hyman, London.

Brown, J. K.
1970 A Note on the Division of Labor by Sex. *American Anthropologist* 72(5):1073–1078.

Buff, M., and C. Buff
1956 *Hah-nee of the Cliff Dwellers*. Houghton Mifflin, Boston.

Buikstra, J. E.
1981 *Prehistoric Tuberculosis in the Americas*. Northwestern University Archaeological Program, Scientific Papers No. 5. Northwestern University, Evanston, Illinois.

Buikstra, J. E., and D. H. Ubelaker
1994 *Standards for Data Collection from Human Skeletal Remains*. Arkansas Archaeological Survey Research Series No. 44. Fayetteville.

Bullock, P. Y. (editor)
1998 *Deciphering Anasazi Violence: With Regional Comparisons to Mesoamerican and Woodland Cultures*. HRM Books, Santa Fe.

Bunzel, R. L.
1932 *Introduction to Zuni Ceremonialism*. Forty-Seventh Annual Report of the Bureau of American Ethnology, for 1929–1930, pp. 467–544. Government Printing Office, Washington, D.C.
1972 *The Pueblo Potter: A Study of Creative Imagination in Primitive Art*. Dover, New York.

Burby, L. N.
1994 *The Pueblo Indians*. Chelsea Juniors, New York.

Burtt, F.
1987 "Man the Hunter": Bias in Children's Archaeology Books. *Archaeological Review from Cambridge* 6(2):157–174.

Cajete, G.
2000 *Native Science: Natural Laws of Interdependence*. Clear Light Publishers, Santa Fe.

Canby, T. Y.
1982 The Anasazi: Riddles in the Ruins. *National Geographic* 162:554–592.

Cassels, E. S.
1972 A Test Concerning Artificial Cranial Deformation and Status from the Grasshopper Site, East-Central Arizona. *The Kiva* 37(2):84–92.

Cattanach, G. S., Jr.
1980 *Long House, Mesa Verde National Park, Colorado*. Publications in Archaeology No. 7H. National Park Service, Washington, D.C.

Caywood, L. R., and E. H. Spicer
1935 *Tuzigoot: The Excavation and Repair of a Ruin on the Verde River near Clarkdale, Arizona*. National Park Service, Berkeley, California.

Chagnon, N.
1974 *Studying the Yanomamo*. Holt, Rinehart, and Winston, New York.

Cheek, L. W.
1994 *A.D. 1250: Ancient Peoples of the Southwest*. Arizona Highways, Phoenix.

Clark, G. A.
1967 A Preliminary Analysis of Burial Clusters at the Grasshopper Site, East-

Central Arizona. Unpublished Master's thesis, Department of Anthropology, University of Arizona, Tucson.

Clark, J. J.
1995 The Role of Migration in Social Change. In *The Roosevelt Community Development Study: New Perspectives in Tonto Basin Prehistory*, edited by M. D. Elson, M. T. Stark, and D. A. Gregory, pp. 369–384. Anthropological Papers No. 15. Center for Desert Archaeology, Tucson.

Cohle, S., D. Hawly, K. Berg, E. Keisel, and J. Pless
1995 Homicidal Cardiac Lesions in Children. *Journal of Forensic Sciences* 40:212–228.

Cole, S. J.
1990 *Legacy on Stone: Rock Art of the Colorado Plateau and Four Corners Region*. Johnson Books, Boulder, Colorado.

Coles, R.
1971 *Migrants, Sharecroppers, Mountaineers*. Little, Brown, Boston.

Colton, H. S.
1960 *Black Sand: Prehistory in Northern Arizona*. University of New Mexico Press, Albuquerque.

Conkey, M., and J. Spector
1984 Archaeology and the Study of Gender. In *Advances in Archaeological Method and Theory*, Vol. 7, edited by M. Schiffer, pp. 1–38. Academic Press, New York.

Cordell, L. S.
1984 *Prehistory of the Southwest*. Academic Press, New York.
1985 Why Did They Leave and Where Did They Go? In *Understanding the Anasazi of Mesa Verde and Hovenweep*, edited by D. G. Noble, pp. 35–39. Ancient City Press, Santa Fe.
1994 *Ancient Pueblo Peoples*. Smithsonian Books, Washington, D.C.
1995 Tracing Migration Pathways from the Receiving End. *Journal of Anthropological Archaeology* 14:203–211.

Costin, C. L., and M. B. Hagstrum
1995 Standardization, Labor Investment, Skill, and the Organization of Production in Late Prehistoric Highland Peru. *American Antiquity* 60(4):619–639.

Cox, M. V.
1993 *Children's Drawings of the Human Figure*. Lawrence Erlbaum, Hove, England.
1997 *Drawings of People by the Under-5s*. Falmer Press, London.

Cravioto, R. O., R. K. Anderson, E. E. Lockhart, F. de P. Miranda, and R. S. Harris
1945 Nutritive Value of the Mexican Tortilla. *Science* 101:91–93.

Crown, P. L.
1998 Becoming a Potter: Situated Learning in the Prehistoric American Southwest. Paper presented at the 63rd Annual Meeting of the Society for American Archaeology, Seattle.
1999 Socialization in American Southwest Pottery Decoration. In *Pottery and People: A Dynamic Interaction*, edited by J. M. Skibo and G. M. Feinman, pp. 25–43. University of Utah Press, Salt Lake City.
2000 Women's Role in Changing Cuisine. In *Women and Men in the Prehispanic*

Southwest: Labor, Power, and Prestige, edited by P. L. Crown, pp. 221–266. School of American Research Press, Santa Fe.

2001 Learning to Make Pottery in the Prehispanic American Southwest. *Journal of Anthropological Research* 57:451–469.

Crown, P. L., and W. H. Wills

1995a Economic Incentive and the Origins of Ceramic Containers in the American Southwest. In *The Emergence of Pottery: Technology and Innovation in Ancient Societies*, edited by W. K. Barnett and J. W. Hoopes, pp. 241–254. Smithsonian Institution Press, Washington, D.C.

1995b The Origin of Southwestern Ceramic Containers: Women's Time Allocation and Economic Intensification. *Journal of Anthropological Research* 51(2):173–186.

Crum, S.

1996 *People of the Red Earth: American Indians of Colorado*. Ancient City Press, Santa Fe.

Cummings, B.

1910 *The Ancient Inhabitants of the San Juan Valley*. Bulletin of the University of Utah. University of Utah, Salt Lake City.

Cummings, L. S.

1995 Agriculture and the Mesa Verde Area Anasazi Diet: Description and Nutritional Analysis. In *Soil, Water, Biology, and Belief in Prehistoric and Traditional Southwestern Agriculture*, edited by H. W. Toll, pp. 335–352. Special Publication 2. New Mexico Archaeological Council, Albuquerque.

Cunningham, H.

1995 *Children and Childhood in Western Society Since 1500*. Longman, London.

Cushing, F. H.

1920 *Zuni Breadstuff*. Indian Notes and Monographs No. 8. Museum of the American Indian, Heye Foundation, New York.

Danforth, M. E., D. C. Cook, S. G. Knick III

1994 The Human Remains from Carter Ranch Pueblo, Arizona: Health in Isolation. *American Antiquity* 59(1):88–101.

Darling, J. A.

1999 Mass Inhumation and the Execution of Witches in the American Southwest. *American Anthropologist* 100:732–752.

DeBoer, W. R.

1990 Interaction, Imitation, and Communication as Expressed in Style: The Ucayli Experience. In *The Uses of Style in Archaeology*, edited by M. Conkey and C. Hastorf, pp. 82–104. Cambridge University Press, Cambridge.

Dennis, W.

1940 *The Hopi Child*. John Wiley and Sons, New York.

1942 The Performance of Hopi Children on the Goodenough Draw-a-Man Test. *Journal of Comparative Psychology* 34:341–348.

Dennis, W., and M. G. Dennis

1940 Cradles and Cradling Practices of the Pueblo Indian. *American Anthropologist* 42(1):107–115.

Deregowski, J. B.

1980 *Illusions, Patterns, and Pictures: A Cross-Cultural Perspective*. Academic Press, New York.

Derrick, S. McCormick
1994 Evidence of Association between Cranial Modeling and Supra-Inion De-
     pressions. Poster presented at the 1994 Annual Meetings of the American
     Association of Physical Anthropologists, Denver.
Deverenski, J. S.
1994 Where Are the Children? Accessing Children in the Past. *Archaeological
     Review from Cambridge* 13(2):7–20.
1997 Engendering Children, Engendering Archaeology. In *Invisible People and
     Processes: Writing Gender and Childhood into European Archaeology*,
     edited by J. Moore and E. Scott, pp. 192–202. Leicester University Press,
     London.
2000 Rings of Life: The Role of Early Metalwork in Mediating the Gendered
     Life Course. *World Archaeology* 31(3):389–406.
Deverenski, J. S. (editor)
2000 *Children and Material Culture*. Routledge, London.
DiPeso, C. C.
1958 *The Reeve Ruin of Southeastern Arizona: A Study of a Prehistoric Western
     Pueblo Migration into the Middle San Pedro Valley*. Publication No. 8.
     Amerind Foundation, Dragoon, Arizona.
Dixon, S.
1992 *The Roman Family*. Johns Hopkins University Press, Baltimore.
Dorsey, G. A.
1899 The Hopi Indians of Arizona. *Popular Science Monthly* 55(6):732–750.
Dozier, E. P.
1970 *The Pueblo Indians of North America*. Holt, Rinehart, and Winston, San
     Francisco.
Draper, P.
1976 Social and Economic Constraints on the Child Life among the !Kung. In
     *Kalahari Hunter-Gatherers: Studies of the !Kung San and Their Neigh-
     bors*, edited by R. B. Lee and I. DeVore, pp. 199–217. Harvard University
     Press, Cambridge.
Draper, P., and E. A. Cashdan
1988 Technological Change and Child Behavior among the !Kung. *Ethnology*
     27(4):339–365.
Driver, H. E.
1941 *Girls' Puberty Rites in Western North America: Culture Element Distribu-
     tions: XVI*. Anthropological Records 6(2). University of California Press,
     Berkeley.
Dunn, P.
1974 "The Enemy Is the Baby": Childhood in Imperial Russia. In *The History of
     Childhood*, edited by L. deMause, pp. 383–405. Psychohistory Press, New
     York.
Eggan, F.
1950 *Social Organization of the Western Pueblos*. University of Chicago Press,
     Chicago.
Eickemeyer, C., and L. W. Eickemeyer
1895 *Among the Pueblo Indians*. Merriam, New York.
Ellis, F. H.
1951 Patterns of Aggression and the War Cult in Southwestern Pueblos.
     Southwestern Journal of Anthropology 7:177–220.

El-Najjar, M. Y.

1979 Human Treponematosis and Tuberculosis: Evidence from the New World. *American Journal of Physical Anthropology* 51:599–618.

El-Najjar, M. Y., D. J. Ryan, C. G. Turner II, and B. Lozoff

1976 The Etiology of Porotic Hyperostosis Among the Prehistoric and Historic Anasazi Indians of Southwestern United States. *American Journal of Physical Anthropology* 44:477–488.

Elting, M., and M. Folsom

1963 *The Secret Story of Pueblo Bonito.* Scholastic Book Services, New York.

Ember, C.

1983 The Relative Decline in Women's Contribution to Agriculture with Intensification. *American Anthropologist* 85(2):285–305.

Erdoes, R.

1976 *The Rain Dance People.* Alfred A. Knopf, New York.

1983 *Native Americans: The Pueblos.* Sterling, New York.

Evans-Pritchard, E. E.

1936 The Nuer: Age-Sets. *Sudan Notes and Records* 19(2):233–271.

Ezzo, J. A.

1991 Dietary Change at Grasshopper Pueblo, Arizona: The Evidence from Bone Chemistry Analyses. Unpublished Ph.D. dissertation, Department of Anthropology, University of Wisconsin, Madison.

1993 *Human Adaptation at Grasshopper Pueblo, Arizona: Social and Ecological Perspectives.* International Monographs in Prehistory, Archaeological Series No. 4. Ann Arbor, Michigan.

1997 Analytical Perspectives on Prehistoric Migration: A Case Study from East-Central Arizona. *Journal of Archaeological Science* 24:447–466.

Falkner, F. T., and J. M. Tanner

1986 *Human Growth: A Comprehensive Treatise.* Plenum Press, New York.

Fenton, T. W.

1998 Dental Conditions at Grasshopper Pueblo: Evidence for Dietary Change and Increased Stress. Unpublished Ph.D. dissertation, Department of Anthropology, University of Arizona, Tucson.

Ferguson, C.

1980 Analysis of Skeletal Remains. In *Tijeras Canyon: Analyses of the Past,* edited by L. S. Cordell, pp. 121–148. Maxwell Museum of Anthropology and University of New Mexico Press, Albuquerque.

Ferguson, R. B.

1992 Explaining War. In *The Anthropology of War,* edited by J. Haas, pp. 26–55. Cambridge University Press, New York.

Ferguson, R. B., and N. L. Whitehead (editors)

1992 *War in the Tribal Zone: Expanding States and Indigenous Warfare.* School of American Research, Santa Fe.

Fewkes, J. W.

1898 *Archaeological Expedition to Arizona in 1895.* Seventeenth Annual Report of the Bureau of American Ethnology, Pt. 2. Washington, D.C.

Fink, T. M.

1985 Tuberculosis and Anemia in a Pueblo II–III (ca. A.D. 900–1300) Anasazi Child from New Mexico. In *Health and Disease in the Prehistoric Southwest,* edited by C. F. Merbs and R. J. Miller, pp. 359–379. Anthropological Research Papers No. 34. Arizona State University, Tempe.

Fink, T. M., and C. F. Merbs
1991 Paleonutrition and Paleopathology of the Salt River Hohokam: A Search for Correlates. *The Kiva* 56(3):293–318.

Finlay, N.
1997 Kid-knapping: The Missing Children in Lithic Analysis. In *Invisible People and Processes: Writing Gender and Childhood into European Archaeology*, edited by J. Moore and E. Scott, pp. 203–212. Leicester University Press, London.
2000 Outside of Life and Death: Traditions of Infant Burial in Ireland from Cillin to Cist. *World Archaeology* 31(3):407–422.

Fish, S. K.
2000 Farming, Foraging, and Gender. In *Women and Men in the Prehispanic Southwest: Labor, Power, and Prestige*, edited by P. L. Crown, pp. 169–196. School of American Research Press, Santa Fe.

Fisher, L. E.
1997 *Anasazi.* Atheneum Books for Young Readers, New York.

Flinn, M. V., and B. G. England
1995 Childhood Stress and Family Environment. *Current Anthropology* 36:854–866.

Folsom, F., and M. E. Folsom
1994 *Ancient Treasures of the Southwest: A Guide to Archaeological Sites and Museums in Arizona, Southern Colorado, New Mexico, and Utah.* University of New Mexico Press, Albuquerque.

Foote, C. J., and S. K. Schackel
1986 Indian Women of New Mexico, 1535–1680. In *New Mexico Women: Intercultural Perspectives*, edited by J. M. Jensen and D. A. Miller, pp. 17–40. University of New Mexico Press, Albuquerque.

Forsberg, H.
1935 The Skeletal Remains of Tuzigoot. In *Tuzigoot: The Excavation and Repair of a Ruin on the Verde River near Clarkdale, Arizona*, edited by L. R. Caywood and E. H. Spicer, pp. 112–119. National Park Service, Washington, D.C.

Fortes, M.
1938 Social and Psychological Aspects of Education in Taleland. In *Time and Social Structure and Other Essays,* edited by M. Fortes, pp. 201–259. Athlone, London.
1940 Children's Drawings Among the Tallensi. *Africa* 13:293–295.

Fossum, R., and K. Descheneaux
1991 Blunt Trauma of the Abdomen in Children. *Journal of Forensic Science* 36:47–50.

Fowler, C.
1977 *Daisy Hooee Nampeyo: The Story of an American Indian.* Dillon Press, Minneapolis.

Fratt, L.
1991 A Preliminary Analysis of Gender Bias in the Sixteenth- and Seventeenth-Century Spanish Documents of the American Southwest. In *The Archaeology of Gender: Proceedings of the 22nd Annual Conference of the Archaeological Association of the University of Calgary*, edited by D. Walde and N. D. Willows, pp. 245–251. University of Calgary Archaeological Association, Calgary.

Frawley, L.

1999 Irrigating the Land. *Cobblestone* 20(6):13–15.

Frazier, K.

1986 *People of the Chaco: A Canyon and Its Culture.* W. W. Norton, New York.

Freeman, J., and B. Freeman

1986 *The Old Ones: A Children's Book about the Anasazi Indians.* The Think Shop, Albuquerque.

Fulginiti, L. C.

1993 Discontinuous Morphological Variation at Grasshopper Pueblo, Arizona. Unpublished Ph.D. dissertation, Department of Anthropology, University of Arizona, Tucson.

Fuller, G. E.

1991 *Anasazi: Builders of Wonders.* G. E. Fuller, Salt Lake City.

Furth, C.

1995 From Birth to Birth: The Growing Body in Chinese Medicine. In *Chinese Views of Childhood*, edited by A. B. Kinney, pp. 157–192. University of Hawaii Press, Honolulu.

Gable, E., and R. Handler

1993 Deep Dirt: Messing Up the Past at Colonial Williamsburg. *Social Analysis* 34:3–15.

Garcia-Mason, V.

1979 Acoma Pueblo. In *Handbook of North American Indians, Volume 9, Southwest*, edited by A. Ortiz, pp. 450–466. Smithsonian Institution, Washington, D.C.

Gates, V.

1996 *Journey to Center Place.* Roberts Rinehart, Boulder, Colorado.

Geib, P. R.

1990 A Basketmaker II Wooden Tool Cache from Lower Glen Canyon. *The Kiva* 55(3):265–277.

Genoves, S.

1967 Proportionality of the Long Bones and Their Relation to Stature Among Mesoamericans. *American Journal of Physical Anthropology* 26:67–78.

Gero, J. M.

1991 Genderlithics: Women's Roles in Stone Tool Production. In *Engendering Archaeology: Women and Prehistory*, edited by J. M. Gero and M. W. Conkey, pp. 163–193. Basil Blackwell, Cambridge.

Gerszten, P. C.

1993 An Investigation into the Practice of Cranial Deformation among the Pre-Columbian Peoples of Northern Chile. *International Journal of Osteo-archaeology* 3:87–98.

Gies, F., and J. Gies

1991 *Life in a Medieval Village.* Harper Perennial, New York.

Gifford-Gonzalez, D.

1993 You Can Hide, But You Can't Run: Representation of Women's Work in Illustrations of Paleolithic Life. *Visual Anthropology Review* 9(1):23–41.

Gladwin, H. S.

1957 *A History of the Ancient Southwest.* Bond Wheelwright, Portland, Maine.

Goddard, V.

1985 Child Labour in Naples: The Case of Outwork. *Anthropology Today* 1(5):18–21.

Goldfrank, E. S.
1945 Socialization, Personality, and the Structure of Pueblo Society (with Particular Reference to the Hopi and Zuni). *American Anthropologist* 47:516– 539.

Golomb, C.
1993 Art and the Young Child: Another Look at the Developmental Question. *Visual Arts Research* 19(1):1–15.

Goodman, A. H., D. L. Martin, G. J. Armelagos, and G. Clark
1984 Indications of Stress from Bone and Teeth. In *Paleopathology at the Origins of Agriculture*, edited by M. N. Cohen and G. J. Armelagos, pp. 13–49. Academic Press, New York.

Goodman, A. H., and J. C. Rose
1990 Assessment of Systematic Physiological Perturbations from Dental Enamel Hypoplasias and Associated Histological Structures. *Yearbook of Physical Anthropology* 33:59–110.

Goodnow, J.
1977 *Children's Drawing*. Open Books, London.

Goody, E. N.
1989 Learning, Apprenticeship, and the Division of Labor. In *Anthropological Perspectives on Apprenticeship*, edited by M. Coy, pp. 233–255. SUNY Press, New York.

Goody, J. R.
1962 *Death, Property, and the Ancestors*. Stanford University Press, Stanford.

Gordon, J. E., J. B. Wyon, and W. Ascoli
1967 The Second Year Death Rate in Less Developed Countries. *American Journal of Medical Science* 254:357–380.

Gosselain, O.
1998 Social and Technical Identity in a Clay Crystal Ball. In *The Archaeology of Social Boundaries*, edited by M. Stark, pp. 78–106. Smithsonian Institution Press, Washington, D.C.

Grant, C.
1978 *Canyon de Chelly: Its People and Rock Art*. University of Arizona Press, Tucson.

Green, J. (editor)
1979 *Zuni: Selected Writings of Frank Hamilton Cushing*. University of Nebraska Press, Lincoln.

Griffin, P. B.
1967 A High-Status Burial from Grasshopper Ruin, Arizona. *The Kiva* 33:37–53.
1969 Late Mogollon Readaptation in East-Central Arizona. Unpublished Ph.D. dissertation, Department of Anthropology, University of Arizona, Tucson.

Guernsey, S. J.
1931 *Explorations in Northeastern Arizona*. Papers of the Peabody Museum of American Archaeology and Ethnology. Harvard University, Cambridge.

Guernsey, S. J., and Alfred V. Kidder
1921 *Basket-Maker Caves of Northeastern Arizona: Report on the Explorations, 1916–17*. Papers of the Peabody Museum of American Archaeology and Ethnology, Harvard University, Cambridge.

Gulranji, M.
1994 Child Labour and the Export Sector in the Third World: A Case of the Indian Carpet Industry. *Labour, Capital, and Society* 27(2):192–214.

Gustafson, S.

1997 *Exploring Bandelier National Monument.* Southwest Parks and Monuments Association, Tucson.

Haas, J.

1986 The Evolution of the Kayenta Anasazi. In *Houses Beneath the Rock: The Anasazi of Canyon de Chelly and Navajo National Monument,* edited by D. G. Noble, pp. 14–23. Ancient City Press, Santa Fe.

Haas, J. (editor)

1990 *The Anthropology of War.* Cambridge University Press, Cambridge.

Haas, J., and W. Creamer

1997 Warfare among the Pueblos: Myth, History, and Ethnology. *Ethnohistory* 44:235–261.

Hagstrum, M. B.

1985 Measuring Prehistoric Ceramic Craft Specialization: A Test Case in the American Southwest. *Journal of Field Archaeology* 12:65–75.

Hail, B. A. (editor)

2000 *Gifts of Pride and Love: Kiowa and Comanche Cradles.* Haffenreffer Museum of Anthropology, Brown University, Bristol, Rhode Island.

Hampsten, E.

1991 *Settlers' Children: Growing Up on the Great Plains.* University of Oklahoma Press, Norman.

Harrington, R. J.

1981 Analysis of the Human Skeletal Remains from Las Colinas. In *The 1968 Excavations at Mound 8, Las Colinas Ruins Group, Phoenix Arizona,* edited by L. D. Hammack and A. P. Sullivan, pp. 251–256. Archaeological Series No. 154. Cultural Resource Management Section, Arizona State Museum, University of Arizona, Tucson.

Harris, D.

1963 *Children's Drawings as Measures of Intellectual Maturity.* Harcourt, Brace, and World, New York.

Haury, E. W.

1958 Evidence at Point of Pines for a Prehistoric Migration from Northern Arizona. In *Migrations in New World Culture History,* edited by R. H. Thompson, pp. 1–6. Social Science Bulletin No. 27. University of Arizona Press, Tucson.

Havighurst, R. J., M. K. Gunther, and I. E. Pratt

1946 Environment and the Draw-a-Man Test: The Performance of Indian Children. *Journal of Abnormal and Social Psychology* 41:50–63.

Hays, K. A.

1992 Anasazi Ceramics as Text and Tool: Toward a Theory of Ceramic Design "Messaging." Unpublished Ph.D. dissertation, Department of Anthropology, University of Arizona, Tucson.

Hays-Gilpin, K.

2001 Rock-Art and Rites of Passage: Studying Women's Puberty Rituals and Iconography in the Western U.S. In *Rock-Art and Culture Process,* edited by S. Turpin. Special Publication 3, Rock Art Foundation, Inc., San Antonio.

2000 Beyond Mother Earth and Father Sky: Sex and Gender in Ancient Southwestern Visual Arts. In *Reading the Body: Representations and Remains in the Archaeological Record,* edited by A. Rautman, pp. 165–186. University of Pennsylvania Press, Philadelphia.

Hays-Gilpin, K., A. C. Deegan, and E. A. Morris
1998 *Prehistoric Sandals from Northeastern Arizona.* Anthropological Papers of the University of Arizona No. 62. University of Arizona Press, Tucson.

Hays-Gilpin, Kelley, and Jane H. Hill
1999 The Flower World in Material Culture: An Iconographic Complex in the Southwest and Mesoamerica. *Journal of Anthropological Research* 55(1):1–31.

Hays-Gilpin, K. A., and E. van Hartesvelt (editors)
1998 *Prehistoric Ceramics of the Puerco Valley, Arizona.* Museum of Northern Arizona Ceramic Series No. 7. Flagstaff.

Heglar, R.
1974 The Prehistoric Population of Cochiti Pueblo and Selected Inter-Population Biological Comparisons. Unpublished Ph.D. dissertation, Department of Anthropology, University of Michigan, Ann Arbor.

Hegmon, M., and W. Trevathan
1996 Gender, Anatomical Knowledge, and Pottery Production: Implications of an Anatomically Unusual Birth Depicted on Mimbres Pottery from Southwestern New Mexico. *American Antiquity* 61:747–754.

Hewett, E. L.
1906 *Antiquities of the Jemez Plateau, New Mexico.* Smithsonian Institution, Bureau of American Ethnology Bulletin 32. Government Printing Office, Washington, D.C.

Hewlett, B.
1991 Demography and Childcare in Preindustrial Societies. *Journal of Anthropological Research* 47:1–37.

Hill, W. W., edited and annotated by C. H. Lange
1982 *An Ethnography of Santa Clara Pueblo, New Mexico.* University of New Mexico Press, Albuquerque.

Hillson, S.
1986 *Teeth.* Cambridge University Press. New York.

Hinkes, M. J.
1983 Skeletal Evidence of Stress in Subadults: Trying to Come of Age at Grasshopper Pueblo. Unpublished Ph.D. dissertation, Department of Anthropology, University of Arizona, Tucson.

Hohmann, J. W.
1992 Through the Mirror of Death: A View of Prehistoric Social Complexity in Central Arizona. Unpublished Ph.D. dissertation, Department of Anthropology, Arizona State University, Tempe.

Holliday, D. Y.
1993 Occipital Lesions: A Possible Cost of Cradleboards. *American Journal of Physical Anthropology* 90:283–290.

Hooton, E. A.
1930 Nutritional Inference from Paleopathology. *Advances in Archeological Method and Theory* 5:395–474.

Hopi Dictionary Project
1998 *Hopi Dictionary: A Hopi-English Dictionary of the Third Mesa Dialect.* University of Arizona Press, Tucson.

Hoshower, L. M., J. E. Buikstra, P. S. Goldstein, and A. D. Webster

1995 Artificial Cranial Deformation at the Omo M10 Site: A Tiwanaku Complex from the Moquegua Valley, Peru. *Latin American Antiquity* 6(2):145–164.

Hough, W.
1907 *Antiquities of the Upper Gila and Salt River Valleys in Arizona and New Mexico.* Government Printing Office, Washington, D.C.
1915 *The Hopi Indians.* Torch Press, Cedar Rapids, Iowa.

Hubbard-Brown, J.
1992 *The Disappearance of the Anasazi.* Avon, New York.

Hunter, A., K. Kamp, and J. Whittaker
1999 Plant Use. In *Surviving Adversity: The Sinagua of Lizard Man Village*, pp. 139–151. University of Utah Anthropological Papers No. 21. University of Utah Press, Salt Lake City.

Huss-Ashmore, R., A. H. Goodman, and G. J. Armelagos
1982 Nutritional Inference from Paleopathology. *Advances in Archeological Method and Theory* 5:395–474.

Ivanhoe, F.
1985 Elevated Orthograde Skeletal Plasticity of Some Archaeological Populations from Mexico and the American Southwest: Direct Relation to Maize Phytate Nutritional Lode. In *Health and Disease in the Prehistoric Southwest*, edited by C. Merbs and R. Miller, pp. 165–176. Anthropological Research Papers No. 34. Arizona State University, Tempe.

Iwaniec, U. T.
1989 Nuvakwewtaqa: An Analysis of Pathology in a Sinagua Population. Unpublished Master's thesis, Arizona State University, Tempe.

Jacobs, S., W. Thomas, and S. Long (editors)
1997 *Two-Spirit People: Native American Gender Identity, Sexuality, and Spirituality.* University of Illinois Press, Urbana.

James, B.
1994 *The Mud Family.* G. P. Putnam and Sons, New York.

Jameson, J. H., Jr., and W. J. Hunt, Jr.
1999 Reconstruction versus Preservation-in-Place in the U.S. National Park Service. In *the Constructed Past: Experimental Archaeology, Education, and the Public*, edited by P. G. Stone and P. G. Planel, pp. 35–62. Routledge, London.

Jennings, J. D.
1968 *Prehistory of North America.* McGraw-Hill, New York.

Jett, S. C., and P. B. Moyle
1986 The Exotic Origins of Fishes Depicted on Prehistoric Mimbres Pottery from New Mexico. *American Antiquity* 51:688–720.

John-Steiner, V.
1975 *Learning Styles Among Pueblo Children.* Final report. U.S. Department of Health, Education, and Welfare National Institute of Education. College of Education, University of New Mexico, Albuquerque.

Jones, A. T., and R. C. Euler
1979 *A Sketch of Grand Canyon Prehistory.* Grand Canyon Natural History Association, Flagstaff, Arizona.

Jones, D., and L. S. Cordell
1985 *Anasazi World.* Graphic Arts Center, Portland, Oregon.

Jones, D. L., and S. G. Sheridan
1994 Reconstruction of Hohokam Diet Utilizing Trace-Element Variation. In *The Pueblo Grande Project, Vol. 6: The Bioethnography of a Classic Period Hohokam Population*, edited by D. P. Van Gerven and S. G. Sheridan, pp. 75–85. Publications in Archaeology No. 20. Soil Systems, Phoenix.

Jones, O. L., Jr.
1966 *Pueblo Warriors and Spanish Conquest*. University of Oklahoma Press, Norman.

Jorgensen, J. G.
1980 *Western Indians: Comparative Environments, Languages, and Cultures of 172 Western American Indian Tribes*. W. H. Freeman, San Francisco.

Joyce, R. A.
2000 Girling the Girl and Boying the Boy: The Production of Adulthood in Ancient Mesoamerica. *World Archaeology* 31(3):473–483.

Judd, N.
1954 *The Material Culture of Pueblo Bonito*. Smithsonian Miscellaneous Collections, Vol. 124. Washington, D.C.

Judge, W. J.
1989 Chaco Canyon–San Juan Basin. In *Dynamics of Southwest Prehistory*, edited by L. S. Cordell and G. J. Gumerman, pp. 209–261. Smithsonian Institution Press, Washington, D.C.

Jurmain, R.
1999 *Stories from the Skeleton*. Gordon and Breach, Amsterdam.

Kamp, K. A.
1998 *Life in the Pueblo: Understanding the Past Through Archaeology*. Waveland Press, Prospect Heights, Illinois.
2001a   Prehistoric Children Working and Playing: A Southwestern Case Study in Learning Ceramics. *Journal of Anthropological Research* 57:427–450.
2001b   Where Have All the Children Gone? The Archaeology of Childhood. *Journal of Archaeological Method and Theory* 8(1):1–34.

Kamp, K., N. Timmerman, G. Lind, J. Graybill, and I. Natowsky
1999 Discovering Childhood: Using Fingerprints to Find Children in the Archaeological Record. *American Antiquity* 64:309–315.

Kamp, K. A., and J. C. Whittaker
1999 *Surviving Adversity: The Sinagua of Lizard Man Village*. University of Utah Anthropological Papers No. 120. University of Utah Press, Salt Lake City.

Karhu, S. L., and J. Amon
1994 Childhood Stress Recorded in the Enamel Defects of the Hohokam of Pueblo Grande. In *The Pueblo Grande Project, Vol. 6: The Bioethnography of a Classic Period Hohokam Population*, edited by D. P. Van Gerven and S. G. Sheridan, pp. 25–45. Publications in Archaeology No. 20. Soil Systems, Phoenix.

Katzenberg, M. A.
1992 Human Skeletal Remains from Sand Canyon Pueblo Excavated from 1988 to 1991. Ms. on file, Crow Canyon Archaeological Center, Cortez, Colorado.

Kehoe, A. B.
1991 No Possible, Probable Shadow of Doubt. *Antiquity* 65(1991):129–131.

Kelley, M. A.
1980 Disease and Environment: A Comparative Analysis of Three Early American Indian Skeletal Collections. Unpublished Ph.D. dissertation, Department of Anthropology, Case Western Reserve University, Cleveland.

Kenagy, S. G.
1986 Ritual Pueblo Ceramics: Symbolic Stylistic Behavior as a Medium of Information Exchange. Unpublished Ph.D. dissertation, Department of Anthropology, University of New Mexico, Albuquerque.

Kensinger, K.
1975 Studying the Cashinahua. In *The Cashinahua of Eastern Peru*, edited by J. P. Dwyer, pp. 9–85. Studies in Anthropology and Material Culture No. 1. Haffenreffer Museum of Anthropology, Brown University, Bristol, Rhode Island.

Khan, A. D., D. G. Schroeder, R. Martorell, J. D. Haas, and J. Rivera
1996 Early Childhood Determinants of Age at Menarche in Rural Guatemala. *American Journal of Physical Anthropology* 8:717–723.

Kidder, A. V.
1924 *An Introduction to the Study of Southwestern Archaeology with a Preliminary Account of the Excavations at Pecos*. Yale University Press, New Haven.
1927 Southwestern Archeological Conference. *Science* 64:489–491.
1932 *The Artifacts of Pecos*. Yale University Press, New Haven.

Kidder, A. V., and S. J. Guernsey
1919 *Archaeological Explorations in Northeastern Arizona*. Bureau of American Ethnography Bulletin 65. Smithsonian Institution, Washington, D.C.

Kidder, A. V., and A. O. Shepard
1936 *The Pottery of Pecos, Volumes 1 and 2*. Yale University Press, New Haven.

King, D.
1951 Pageant of the Pueblos. *Arizona Highways* 27(5):6–35.

Kinney, A. B. (editor)
1995 *Chinese Views of Childhood*. University of Hawaii Press, Honolulu.

Knauft, B. M.
1987 Reconsidering Violence in Simple Human Societies. *Current Anthropology* 28:457–500.

Kramer, C.
1985 Ceramic Ethnoarchaeology. *Annual Review of Anthropology* 14:77–102.
1997 *Pottery in Rajasthan: Ethnoarchaeology in Two Indian Cities*. Smithsonian Institution Press, Washington, D.C.

Krampen, M.
1991 *Children's Drawings: Iconic Coding of the Environment*. Plenum Press, New York.

Kroeber, A. L.
1925 *Handbook of California Indians*. Bureau of American Ethnology 78. Washington, D.C.

Krogman, W. M., and M. Y. Isçan
1986 *The Human Skeleton in Forensic Medicine*. 2nd edition. Charles C Thomas, Springfield, Illinois.

Kuckelman, K. A., R. R. Lightfoot, and D. L. Martin
2000 Changing Patterns of Violence in the Northern San Juan Region. *The Kiva* 66:146–165.

Lackey, L.
1982 *The Pottery of Acatlan.* University of Oklahoma Press, Norman.

Lahr, M. M., and J. E. Bowman
1992 Palaeopathology of the Kechipawan Site: Health and Disease in a Southwestern Pueblo. *Journal of Archaeological Science* 19:639–654.

Lallo, J. W., G. Armelagos, and R. P. Mensforth
1977 The Role of Diet, Disease, and Physiology in the Origin of Porotic Hyperostosis. *Human Biology* 49:471–483.

Lange, F. W.
1998 *Cortez Crossroads: A Guide to the Anasazi Heritage and Scenic Beauty of the Four Corners Region.* Johnson Books, Boulder, Colorado.

Lange, R. W., D. Snow, and J. Habicht-Mauche
1989 New Mexico Archaeological Council, Rio Grande Pottery Field Identification Seminar. Ms. on file, Archaeological Records Management Section, Museum of New Mexico, Santa Fe.

Larsen, C. S.
1997 *Bioarchaeology: Interpreting Behavior from the Human Skeleton.* Cambridge University Press, New York.

Lave, J., and E. Wenger
1991 *Situated Learning: Legitimate Peripheral Participation.* Cambridge University Press, Cambridge.

Lavender, D.
1998 *Mother Earth, Father Sky: Pueblo Indians of the American Southwest.* Holiday House, New York.

Leach, P.
1974 *Babyhood: Infant Development from Birth to Age Two.* Penguin Books, Harmondsworth, Middlesex.

LeBlanc, S. A.
1999 *Prehistoric Warfare in the American Southwest.* University of Utah Press, Salt Lake City.

Lewis, Lucy, Emma Lewis Mithcell, and Delores Lewis Garcia
1990 Daughters of the Anasazi. (Video) Film Projects. Interpark, Farmington, New Mexico.

Lewis-Williams, J. D., and T. Dowson
1988 The Signs of All Times: Entoptic Phenomena and Upper Palaeolithic Art. *Current Anthropology* 29:201–245.

Lightfoot, R., and K. Kuckelman
1994 Warfare and the Pueblo Abandonment of the Mesa Verde Region. Paper presented at the 59th Annual Meeting of the Society for American Archaeology, Anaheim.

Lillehammer, G.
1989 A Child Is Born: The Child's World in an Archaeological Perspective. *Norwegian Archaeological Review* 22(2):91–105.

Lillie, M. C.
1997 Women and Children in Prehistory: Resource Sharing and Social Strati-

fication at the Mesolithic-Neolithic Transition in Ukraine. In *Invisible People and Processes: Writing Gender and Childhood into European Archaeology,* edited by J. Moore and E. Scott, pp. 213–228. Leicester University Press, London.

Lipe, W. D.

1960 *1958 Excavations, Glen Canyon Area* 44. Department of Anthropology, University of Utah, Salt Lake City.

1995 The Depopulation of the Northern San Juan: Conditions in the Turbulent 1200s. *Journal of Anthropological Research* 14:143–169.

Lipe, W. (editor)

1992 *The Sand Canyon Archaeological Project: A Progress Report.* Occasional Papers No. 2. Crow Canyon Archaeological Center, Cortez, Colorado.

Lipe, W. D., M. D. Varien, and R. H. Wilshusen

1999 *Colorado Prehistory: A Context for the Southern Colorado River Basin.* Colorado Council of Professional Archaeologists, Denver.

Lister, R. H., and F. C. Lister

1978 *Anasazi Pottery.* Maxwell Museum and University of New Mexico Press, Albuquerque.

1987 *Aztec Ruins on the Animas: Excavated, Preserved, and Interpreted.* University of New Mexico Press, Albuquerque.

London, G.

1986 Response to Melissa Hagstrum, "Measuring Prehistoric Ceramic Craft Specialization: A Test Case in the American Southwest." *Journal of Field Archaeology* 13:510–511.

Longacre, W.

1981 Kalinga Pottery: An Ethnoarchaeological Study. In *Pattern of the Past: Studies in Honor of David Clarke,* edited by I. Hodder, G. Isaac, and N. Hammond, pp. 49–66. Cambridge University Press, Cambridge.

Longacre, W. A., and J. J. Reid

1974 The University of Arizona Archaeological Field School at Grasshopper: Eleven Years of Multidisciplinary Research and Teaching. *The Kiva* 40:3–38.

Lotrich, V. F.

1941 Indian Terms for the Cradle and the Cradleboard. *Colorado Magazine* 18(3):81–109.

Lowrey, G. H.

1974 *Growth and Development of Children.* Year Book Medical Publishers, Chicago.

Lupher, M.

1995 Revolutionary Little Red Devils: The Social Psychology of Rebel Youth. In *Chinese Views of Childhood,* edited by A. B. Kinney, pp. 321–343. University of Hawaii Press, Honolulu.

Lutz, C. A., and J. L. Collins

1993 *Reading National Geographic.* University of Chicago Press, Chicago.

Lyon, E. L.

1993 *Dreamplace.* Orchard Books, New York.

Mack, M. E.

1995 Pathologies Affecting Children in the African Burial Ground Population. *Newsletter of the African Burial Ground and Five Points Archaeological Projects* 1(7):3–4.

Mails, T. E.
1983 *Pueblo Children of the Earth Mother*. Marlowe, New York.
Malotki, E. (editor, compiler, and translator)
1993 *Hopi Ruin Legends*. Michael Lomatuway'ma, Lorena Lomatuway'ma, and Sidney Namingha, Narrators. University of Nebraska Press, Lincoln.
Marango, Christina
1991 Social Differentiation in the Early Bronze Age: Miniature Metal Tools and Child Burials. *Journal of Mediterranean Studies* 1(2):211–225.
Marek, M.
1990 Long Bone Growth of Mimbres Subadults from the NAN Ranch (LA15049), New Mexico. Unpublished Master's thesis, Texas A&M University, College Station.
Margolis, M. M.
2000 Warriors, Witches, and Cannibals: Violence in the Prehistoric American Southwest. *Southwestern Lore* 66:3–21.
Marinsek, E. A.
1958 The Effect of Cultural Difference in the Education of Pueblo Indians. Ms. prepared for the University of New Mexico Research Study, The Adjustment of Indian and Non-Indian Children in the Public Schools of New Mexico, Albuquerque.
Marriott, A.
1952 *Indians of the Four Corners*. Thomas Y. Crowell, New York.
Martell, H. M.
1993 *Native Americans and Mesa Verde*. Dillon Press, New York.
Martin, D. L.
1994 Patterns of Health and Disease. In *Themes in Southwest Prehistory,* edited by G. J. Gumerman, pp. 87–108. School of American Research Press, Santa Fe.
2000 Bodies and Lives: Biological Indicators of Health Differentials and Division of Labor by Sex. In *Women and Men in the Prehispanic Southwest: Labor, Power, and Prestige,* edited by P. L. Crown, pp. 267–300. School of American Research Press, Santa Fe.
Martin, D. L., N. J. Akins, A. H. Goodman, and A. C. Swedlund
2001 *Harmony and Discord: Bioarchaeology of the La Plata Valley*. Museum of New Mexico Press, Santa Fe (in press).
Martin, D. L., A. H. Goodman, and G. J. Armelagos
1985 Skeletal Pathologies as Indicators of Quality and Quantity of Diet. In *The Analysis of Prehistoric Diets,* edited by R. I. Gilbert, Jr., and J. H. Mielke, pp. 227–280. Academic Press, New York.
Martin, D. L., C. Piacentini, and G. J. Armelagos
1985 Paleopathology of the Black Mesa Anasazi: A Biocultural Approach. In *Health and Disease in the Prehistoric Southwest,* edited by C. F. Merbs and R. J. Miller, pp. 104–114. Anthropological Research Papers No. 34. Arizona State University, Tempe.
Martin, D. L., A. H. Goodman, G. J. Armelagos, and A. L. Magennis
1991 *Black Mesa Anasazi Health: Reconstructing Life from Patterns of Death and Disease*. Center for Archaeological Investigations, Occasional Paper No. 14. Southern Illinois University, Carbondale.

Martin, P. S., G. I. Quimby, and D. Collier
1947 *Indians before Columbus: Twenty Thousand Years of North American History Revealed by Archaeology.* University of Chicago Press, Chicago.

Martin, P. S., J. B. Rinaldo, E. Bluhm, H. C. Cutler, and J. R Grange
1952 *Mogollon Cultural Continuity and Change: The Stratigraphic Analysis of Tularosa and Cordova Caves.* Field Museum of Natural History Anthropological Series 40. Chicago.

Mason, O. T.
1889 *Cradles of the American Aborigines.* Government Printing Office, Washington, D.C.

Matson, R. G.
2001 Basketmaker II Origins: The Evidence for Migration. Paper presented at the 66th Annual Meeting of the Society for American Archaeology, New Orleans.

May, R. L., A. H. Goodman, and R. S. Meindl
1993 Response of Bone and Enamel Formation to Nutritional Supplementation and Morbidity Among Malnourished Guatemalan Children. *American Journal of Physical Anthropology* 92:37–51.

McCafferty, S. D., and G. G. McCafferty
1988 Powerful Women and the Myth of Male Dominance in Aztec Society. *Archaeological Review from Cambridge* 7:45–59.

McClelland, D. C.
1981 Child Rearing versus Ideology and Social Structures as Factors in Personality Development. In *Handbook of Cross-Cultural Human Development,* edited by R. H. Munroe, R. L. Munroe, and B. B. Whiting, pp. 73–90. Garland STPM Press, New York.

McDermott, G.
1974 *Arrow to the Sun.* Puffin Books, New York.

McGuire, R. H.
1992 *Death, Society, and Ideology in a Hohokam Community.* Westview Press, Boulder.

McLaughlin, M. M.
1974 Survivors and Surrogates: Children and Parents from the Ninth to Thirteenth Centuries. In *The History of Childhood,* edited by L. deMause, pp. 101–181. Psychohistory Press, New York.

Mehra-Kempelman, K.
1996 Children at Work: How Many and Where? *World of Work: The Magazine of the ILO*: 15:8–9.

Mensforth, R. P., C. O. Lovejoy, J. W. Lallo, and G. J. Armelagos
1978 The Role of Constitutional Factors, Diet, and Infectious Disease in the Etiology of Porotic Hyperostosis and Periosteal Reactions in Prehistoric Infants and Children. *Medical Anthropology* 2(1):1–59.

Merbs, C. F., and E. M. Vestergaard
1985 The Paleopathology of Sundown, a Prehistoric Site near Prescott, Arizona. In *Health and Disease in the Prehistoric Southwest,* edited by C. F. Merbs and R. J. Miller, pp. 85–103. Anthropological Research Papers No. 34. Arizona State University, Tempe.

Meskell, L.
1994 Dying Young: The Experience of Death at Deir el Medina. *Archaeological Review from Cambridge* 13(2):35–45.

1999 *Archaeologies of Social Life: Age, Sex, Class et cetera in Ancient Egypt.* Blackwell, Oxford.

2000 Cycles of Life and Death: Narrative Homology and Archaeological Realities. *World Archaeology* 31(3):423–441.

Mike, Jan

1991 *Chana, an Anasazi Girl: Historical Paper Doll Book to Read, Color, and Cut.* Treasure Chest, Tucson.

Miles, J. S.

1966 Diseases Encountered at Mesa Verde, Colorado. II. Evidence of Disease. In *Human Paleopathology*, edited by S. Jarcho, pp. 91–98. Yale University Press, New Haven.

Miller, R. J.

1985 Lateral Epicondylitis in the Prehistoric Indian Population from Nuvakwew-taqa (Chavez Pass), Arizona. In *Health and Disease in the Prehistoric Southwest*, edited by C. F. Merbs and R. J. Miller, pp. 391–399. Arizona State University Anthropological Papers No. 34. Arizona State University, Tempe.

Mills, B. J.

1995 Gender and the Reorganization of Historic Zuni Craft Production: Implications for Archaeological Interpretation. *Journal of Anthropological Research* 51(2):149–172.

1997 Gender, Labor, and Inequality: Dynamics of Craft Production in the American Southwest. Paper presented at the School of American Research Advanced Seminar, Sex Roles and Gender Hierarchies in Middle-Range Societies: Engendering Southwestern Prehistory. Santa Fe.

2000 Gender, Craft Production, and Inequality. In *Women and Men in the Prehispanic Southwest: Labor, Power, and Prestige*, edited by P. L. Crown, 301–343. School of American Research Press, Santa Fe.

Mills, B. J., and P. L. Crown

1995 Ceramic Production in the American Southwest: An Introduction. In *Ceramic Production in the American Southwest*, edited by B. J. Mills and P. L. Crown, pp. 1–29. University of Arizona Press, Tucson.

Mills, B. J., and P. L. Crown (editors)

1995 *Ceramic Production in the American Southwest.* University of Arizona Press, Tucson.

Mitchell, D. R. (editor)

1994 *The Pueblo Grande Project, Volume 7: An Analysis of Classic Period Mortuary Patterns.* Publications in Archaeology No. 20. Soil Systems, Phoenix.

Mittler, D. M., and D. P. Van Gerven

1994 Porotic Hyperostosis and Diploic Thickening at Pueblo Grande. In *The Pueblo Grande Project, Volume 6: The Bioethnography of a Classic Period Hohokam Population*, edited by D. P. Van Gerven and S. G. Sheridan, pp. 55–73. Publications in Archaeology No. 20. Soil Systems, Phoenix.

Moore, J.

1997 Conclusion: The Visibility of the Invisible. In *Invisible People and Processes: Writing Gender and Childhood into European Archaeology*, edited by J. Moore and E. Scott, pp. 251–257. Leicester University Press, London.

Moore, J., A. Swedlund, and G. J. Armelagos
1975 The Use of Life Table in Paleodemography. In *Population Studies in Archaeology and Biological Anthropology: A Symposium*, edited by A. Swedlund. Society for American Archaeology Memoir No. 30.

Morris, E. A.
1980 *Basketmaker Caves in the Prayer Rock District, Northeastern Arizona*. Anthropological Papers of the University of Arizona No. 35. University of Arizona Press, Tucson.

Morris, E. H.
1925 Exploring in the Canyon of Death. *National Geographic* 48(September): 263–300.
1939 *Archaeological Studies in the La Plata District, Southwestern Colorado and Northwestern New Mexico*. Carnegie Institution of Washington, Washington, D.C.

Morris, E. H., and R. F. Burgh
1954 *Basket Maker II Sites near Durango, Colorado*. Carnegie Institution of Washington, Washington, D.C.

Morss, N.
1927 *Archaeological Explorations on the Middle Chinlee, 1925*. Memoirs of the American Anthropological Association No. 34. American Anthropological Association, New York.

Muir, R.
1999 Zooarchaeology of Sand Canyon Pueblo, Colorado. Unpublished Ph.D. dissertation, Department of Archaeology, Simon Fraser University, Burnaby, British Columbia.

Mukherjee, M., B. Ganguly, and M. Sen
1987 Child Labour and Fertility. *Bulletin of the Cultural Research Institute* 17:35–38.

Nagata, Shuichi
1970 *Modern Transformations of Moenkopi Pueblo*. University of Illinois Press, Urbana.

Nagy, B. L., and D. E. Hawkey
1993 Correspondence of Osteoarthritis and Muscle Use in Reconstructing Prehistoric Activity Patterns. Paper presented at the 20th Annual Meeting of the Paleopathology Association, April 13–14, Toronto.

Naranjo, T.
1992 Social Change and Pottery-Making at Santa Clara Pueblo. Unpublished Ph.D. dissertation, Department of Sociology, University of New Mexico, Albuquerque.
1993 *Native Americans of the Southwest: A Journey of Discovery*. Running Press, Philadelphia.

National Park Service
1999 *Walnut Canyon: Official Map and Guide*. Government Printing Office, Washington, D.C.

New York State
1855 Census Records.

Nusbaum, J. L.
1922 *Basket-maker Cave in Kane County, Utah*. Indian Notes and Monographs,

a Series of Publications Relating to the American Aborigines. Museum of the American Indian, Heye Foundation, New York.

Ortiz, A.

1969 *The Tewa World: Space, Time, Being, and Becoming in a Pueblo Society.* University of Chicago Press, Chicago.

Ortman, S.

2000 Castle Rock Pueblo Artifacts. In *The Archaeology of Castle Rock Pueblo: A Thirteenth-Century Village in Southwestern Colorado.* [HTML title]. Available: http://crowcanyon.org/ResearchReports/CastleRock/Text/crpw_home.htm.

Osborne, D.

1964 Solving the Riddles of Wetherill Mesa. *National Geographic* 125:155–195.

Otterbein, K. F.

2000 Killing of Captured Enemies: A Cross-Cultural Study. *Current Anthropology* 41:439–443.

Paget, G. W.

1932 Some Drawings of Men and Women Made by Children of Certain Non-European Races. *Journal of the Royal Anthropological Institute of Great Britain and Ireland* 62:127–144.

Palkovich, A. M.

1980 *Pueblo Population and Society: The Arroyo Hondo Skeletal and Mortuary Remains.* Arroyo Hondo Archaeological Series, Vol. 3. School of American Research Press, Santa Fe.

1982 Disease and Mortality Patterns in the Burial Rooms of Pueblo Bonito: Preliminary Considerations. In *Recent Research on Chaco Prehistory*, edited by W. J. Judge and J. D. Schelberg, pp. 103–114. Division of Cultural Research, U.S. Department of the Interior, National Park Service, Albuquerque.

1984 Agriculture, Marginal Environments, and Nutritional Stress in the Prehistoric Southwest. In *Paleopathology at the Origins of Agriculture*, edited by M. N. Cohen and G. J. Armelagos, pp. 425–462. Academic Press, New York.

Parsons, E. C.

1925 *The Pueblo of Jemez.* Yale University Press, New Haven.

1936a *Hopi Journals of Alexander M. Stephen, Parts I and II.* Columbia University Contributions to Anthropology Vol. 23. Columbia University Press, New York.

1936b *Taos Pueblo.* George Banta, Menasha, Wisconsin.

1939 *Pueblo Indian Religion.* University of Chicago Press, Chicago.

Patrick, S. S.

1988 Description and Demographic Analysis of a Mimbres Mogollon Population from LA15049 (NAN Ruin). Unpublished Master's thesis, Texas A&M University, College Station.

Pepper, G. H.

1902 The Ancient Basket Makers of Southeastern Utah. *American Museum Journal* 2:3–26.

Petersen, D.

1991 *The Anasazi.* Children's Press, Chicago.

1999 *Chaco Culture National Park.* Children's Press, New York.

Pettit, G. A.
1946 *Primitive Education in North America.* University of California Publications in American Archaeology and Ethnology No. 43. Berkeley.

Pilles, P. J., Jr.
1976 The Field House and Sinagua Demography. In *Limited Activity and Occupation Sites: A Collection of Conference Papers,* edited by A. E. Ward, pp. 119–133. Center for Anthropological Studies, Albuquerque.
1993 The Sinagua: Ancient People of the Flagstaff Region. In *Wupatki and Walnut Canyon: New Perspectives on History, Prehistory, and Rock Art,* edited by D. G. Noble. Ancient City Press, Santa Fe.

Polgar, S.
1972 Population History and Population Policies from an Anthropological Perspective. *Current Anthropology* 13:203–267.

Potter, J.
2000 Pots, Parties, and Politics: Communal Feasting in the American Southwest. *American Antiquity* 65:471–492.

Powell, M. L.
1991 Ranked Status and Health in the Mississippian Chiefdom at Moundville. In *What Means These Bones?* edited by M. L. Powell, P. S. Bridges, and A. M. W. Mires, pp. 22–51. University of Alabama Press, Tuscaloosa.

Powell, S. I.
1993 *The Pueblos.* Franklin Watts, New York.

Powell, S., and G. J. Gumerman
1987 *People of Black Mesa: the Archaeology of Black Mesa, Arizona.* Southwest Parks and Monuments Association, Tucson, and Southern Illinois University Press, Carbondale.

Prout, A., and A. James
1990 A New Paradigm for the Sociology of Childhood: Provenance, Promise, and Problems. In *Constructing and Reconstructing Childhood: Contemporary Issues in the Sociological Study of Childhood,* edited by A. James and A. Prout, pp. 7–34. Falmer Press, London.

Provinzano, J.
1968 The Osteological Remains of the Galaz Mimbres Amerinds. Unpublished Master's thesis, Department of Anthropology, University of Minnesota, Minneapolis.

Puffer, R., and C. Serrano
1973 *Patterns of Mortality in Childhood.* Pan American Health Organization, Scientific Publication No. 22. Washington, D.C.

Qvortup, J.
1990 A Voice for Children in Statistical and Social Accounting: A Plea for Children's Rights to Be Heard. In *Constructing and Reconstructing Childhood: Contemporary Issues in the Sociological Study of Childhood,* edited by A. James and A. Prout, pp. 78–98. Falmer Press, London.

Rappaport, R. A.
1968 *Pigs for the Ancestors: Ritual in the Ecology of a New Guinea People.* Yale University Press, New Haven.

Rasmussen, R. K.
2001 *Native American Homes: Pueblo.* Rourke Book Co., Vero Beach, Florida.

Redman, C. H.

1993 *People of the Tonto Rim: Archaeological Discovery in Prehistoric Arizona.* Smithsonian Institution Press, Washington, D.C.

Reed, E. K.

1949 The Significance of Skull Deformation in the Southwest. *El Palacio* (April):106–119.

1965 Human Skeletal Material from Site 34, Mesa Verde National Park. *El Palacio* 72:31–45.

1981 Human Skeletal Material from the Gran Quivira District. In *Contributions to Gran Quivira Archeology: Gran Quivira National Monument, New Mexico,* edited by Alden C. Hayes, pp. 75–118. Publication in Archeology No. 17. National Park Service, Washington, D.C.

Reed, P. F.

2000 Introduction: Fundamental Issues in Basketmaker Archaeology. In *Foundations of Anasazi Culture: The Basketmaker-Pueblo Transition,* edited by P. F. Reed, pp. 3–16. University of Utah Press, Salt Lake City.

Reid, J. J.

1973 Growth and Response to Stress at Grasshopper Pueblo, Arizona. Unpublished Ph.D. dissertation, Department of Anthropology, University of Arizona, Tucson.

1989 A Grasshopper Perspective on the Mogollon of the Arizona Mountains. In *Dynamics of Southwest Prehistory,* edited by L. S. Cordell and G. J. Gumerman, pp. 65–97. Smithsonian Institution Press, Washington, D.C.

Reid, J. J., and S. M. Whittlesey

1982 Households at Grasshopper Pueblo. *American Behavioral Scientist* 25:687–703.

1997 *The Archaeology of Ancient Arizona.* University of Arizona Press, Tucson.

1999 *Grasshopper Pueblo: A Story of Archaeology and Ancient Life.* University of Arizona Press, Tucson.

Reiley, D. E.

1969 *Two Pueblo III Cradle Burials from Upper Glen Canyon, Utah.* Museum of Northern Arizona. Report No. 14.354. Submitted to the National Park Service. Copies available from the Museum of Northern Arizona, Flagstaff.

Reinhard, K. J.

1985 Recovery of Helminths from Prehistoric Feces: The Cultural Ecology of Ancient Parasitism. Unpublished Master's thesis, Department of Anthropology, Northern Arizona University, Flagstaff.

Rice, P. M.

1987 *Pottery Analysis: A Sourcebook.* University of Chicago Press, Chicago.

Riggs, C. R., Jr.

1999 The Architecture of Grasshopper Pueblo: Dynamics of Form, Function, and Use of Space in a Prehistoric Community. Unpublished Ph.D. dissertation, Department of Anthropology, University of Arizona, Tucson.

Ritchie, J., and Ritchie, J.

1979 *Growing Up in Polynesia.* George Allen and Unwin, Sydney.

Robarchek, C.

1990 Motivations and Material Causes: On the Explanation of Conflict and War. In *The Anthropology of War,* edited by J. Haas, pp. 56–76. Cambridge University Press, Cambridge.

Roberts, F. H.
1929 *Shabik'eshchee Village: A Late Basket Maker Site in the Chaco Canyon, New Mexico.* Smithsonian Institution, Bureau of American Ethnology. Government Printing Office, Washington, D.C.
1931 *The Ruins at Kiatuthlanna.* Bureau of American Ethnology Bulletin 100. Smithsonian Institution, Washington, D.C.

Robins, M. R., and K. Hays-Gilpin
2000 The Bird in the Basket: Gender and Social Change in Basketmaker Iconography. In *Foundations of Anasazi Culture: The Basketmaker-Pueblo Transition*, edited by P. F. Reed. University of Utah Press, Salt Lake City.

Robinson, C. K.
1976 Human Skeletal Remains from 1975 Archaeological Excavations in Mancos Canyon, Colorado. Unpublished Master's thesis, Department of Anthropology, University of Colorado, Boulder.

Roe, P. G.
1995 Style, Society, Myth, and Structure. In *Style, Society, and Person: Archaeological and Ethnological Perspectives*, edited by C. Carr and J. Neitzel, pp. 27–76. Plenum Press, New York.

Rogers, S. L.
1975 *Artificial Deformation of the Head: New World Examples of Ethnic Mutilation and Notes on Its Consequences.* San Diego Museum Papers No. 8. San Diego Museum of Man, San Diego.

Rohn, A. H.
1971 *Wetherill Mesa Excavations: Mug House.* National Park Service, Washington, D.C.
1977 *Cultural Change and Continuity on Chapin Mesa.* Regents Press of Kansas, Lawrence.
1989 *Rock Art of Bandelier National Monument.* University of New Mexico Press, Albuquerque.

Roscoe, W.
1998 *Changing Ones: Third and Fourth Genders in Native North America.* St. Martin's Press, New York.

Rothschild, N. A.
1990 *Prehistoric Dimensions of Status: Gender and Age in Eastern North America.* Garland Publishing, New York.

Roveland, B. E.
1992 Child the Creator: Children as Agents of Change in Juvenile Prehistoric Literature. *Visual Anthropology Review* 9(1):147–153.

Russell, R. W.
1943 The Spontaneous and Instructed Drawings of Zuni Children. *Journal of Comparative Psychology* 35:11–15.

Ryan, D. J.
1977 The Paleopathology and Paleoepidemiology of the Kayenta Anasazi Indians in Northeastern Arizona. Unpublished Ph.D. dissertation, Department of Anthropology, Arizona State University.

Rye, O. S.
1981 *Pottery Technology: Principles and Reconstruction.* Taraxacum, Washington, D.C.

Sagan, E.
1985 *At the Dawn of Tyranny*. Alfred A. Knopf, New York.
Sancho-Liao, N.
1994 Child Labour in the Philippines: Exploitation in the Process of Global-
    ization of the Economy. *Labour, Capital, and Society* 27(2):270–281.
Sando, J. S.
1992 *Pueblo Nations: Eight Centuries of Pueblo Indian History*. Clear Light
    Publishers, Santa Fe.
Santrock, J. W.
1998 *Adolescence*. 7th edition. McGraw-Hill, Dallas.
Sattler, H. N.
1993 *The Earliest Americans*. Clarion Books, New York.
Saunders, C. F.
1973 *The Indians of the Terraced Houses*. Putnam, New York.
Schaafsma, P.
1980 *Indian Rock Art of the Southwest*. School of American Research, Santa Fe.
Schiffer, M. B., and J. M. Skibo
1987 Theory and Experiment in the Study of Technological Change. *Current
    Anthropology* 28:595–622.
1989 A Provisional Theory of Ceramic Abrasion. *American Anthropologist*
    91(1):101–115.
Schlegal, A.
1973 The Adolescent Socialization of the Hopi Girl. *Ethnology* 12:449–462.
Schroeder, A. H., and H. F. Hastings
1958 *Montezuma Castle National Monument*. National Park Service,
    Washington, D.C.
Schwartz, D. W.
1980 Foreword. In *The Arroyo Hondo Skeletal and Mortuary Remains,* by
    A. M. Palkovich, pp. ix–xix. School of American Research Press, Santa Fe.
Scott, G. R.
1981 A Stature Reconstruction of the Gran Quivira Skeletal Population. In
    *Contributions to Gran Quivira Archeology: Gran Quivira National Monu-
    ment, New Mexico*, edited by Alden C. Hayes, pp. 129–138. Publication in
    Archeology No. 17. National Park Service, Washington D.C.
Sekaquaptewa, H.
1969 *Me and Mine: The Life Story of Helen Sekaquaptewa as Told to Louise
    Udall*. University of Arizona Press, Tucson.
Seltzer, C. C.
1944 *Racial Prehistory in the Southwest and the Hawikuh Zunis*. Papers of the
    Peabody Museum of American Archaeology and Ethnology 23. Harvard
    University, Cambridge.
Shanks, M., and C. Tilley
1987 *Reconstructing Archaeology*. Cambridge University Press, Cambridge.
Shepard, A. O.
1956 *Ceramics for the Archaeologist*. Carnegie Institution of Washington,
    Washington, D.C.
Shipman, J. H.
1982 Biological Relationships Among Prehistoric Western Pueblo Indian Groups
    Based on Metric and Disease Traits of the Skeleton. Unpublished Ph.D.
    dissertation, Department of Anthropology, University of Arizona, Tucson.

Shostak, M.

1976 A !Kung Woman's Memories of Childhood. In *Kalahari Hunter-Gatherers: Studies of the !Kung San and Their Neighbors*, edited by R. B. Lee and I. DeVore, pp. 246–278. Harvard University Press, Cambridge.

Shufeldt, R. W.

1891 Head-Flattening Among the Navajos. *Popular Science Monthly* 39:535– 539.

Shulamith, S.

1990 *Childhood in the Middle Ages*. Routledge, New York.

Shuter, J.

2000 *Visiting the Past: Mesa Verde*. Heinemann Library, Chicago.

Sillar, B.

1994 Playing with God: Cultural Perceptions of Children, Play, and Miniatures in the Andes. *Archaeological Review from Cambridge* 13(2):47–63.

Smilansky, S., J. Hagan, and H. Lewis

1988 *Clay in the Classroom: Helping Children Develop Cognitive and Affective Skills for Learning*. Peter Lang, New York.

Smith, M.

1983 Toward an Economic Interpretation of Ceramics: Relating Vessel Size and Shape to Use. In *Decoding Prehistoric Ceramics*, edited by B. Nelson, pp. 254–309. Southern Illinois University Press.

1988 Function from Whole Vessel Shape: A Method and an Application to Anasazi Black Mesa, Arizona. *American Anthropologist* 90:912–923.

Snow, D. H.

1990 Tener comal y metate: Protohistoric Rio Grande Maize Use and Diet. In *Perspectives in Southwestern Prehistory*, edited by P. E. Minnis and C. L. Redman, pp. 289–300. Westview Press, Boulder.

Spector, J.

1983 Male/Female Task Differentiation Among the Hidatsa: Toward the Development of an Archaeological Approach to the Study of Gender. In *The Hidden Half: Studies of Plains Indian Women*, edited by P. Albers and B. Medicine, pp. 77–99. University Press of America, Washington, D.C.

1993 *What This Awl Means: Feminist Archaeology at a Wahpeton Dakota Village*. Minnesota Historical Society Press, St. Paul.

Spencer, F. C.

1899 *Education of the Pueblo Child: A Study in Arrested Development*. Columbia University Contributions to Philosophy, Psychology, and Education Vol. 7(1). Macmillan, New York.

Spicer, E. H.

1962 *Cycles of Conquest: The Impact of Spain, Mexico, and the United States on Indians in the Southwest, 1533–1960*. University of Arizona Press, Tucson.

Spielmann, K. A.

1995 Glimpses of Gender in the Prehistoric Southwest. *Journal of Anthropological Research* 51(2):91–102.

Stanislawski, M. B., and B. B. Stanislawski

1978 Hopi and Hopi-Tewa Ceramic Tradition Networks. In *The Spatial Organization of Culture*, edited by I. Hodder, pp. 61–76. University of Pittsburgh Press, Pittsburgh.

Stark, B. L.

1995 Problems in Analysis of Standardization and Specialization in Pottery. In

Ceramic Production in the Southwest, edited by B. Mills and P. Crown, pp. 142–166. University of Arizona Press, Tucson.

Steinbock, R. T.

1976 *Paleopathological Diagnosis and Interpretation.* Charles C Thomas, Springfield, Illinois.

Stephens, S.

1998 Children and the Politics of Culture in "Late Capitalism." In *Children and the Politics of Culture,* edited by S. Stephens, pp. 3–48. Princeton University Press, Princeton.

Steward, J. H.

1933 *Archaeological Problems of the Northern Periphery of the Southwest.* Museum of Northern Arizona Bulletin No. 5. Northern Arizona Society of Science and Art, Flagstaff.

Stewart, T. D.

1936 Skeletal Remains from Chaco Canyon. *American Journal of Physical Anthropology* 21(supplement to No. 2):17.

1940 *Skeletal Remains from the Whitewater District, Eastern Arizona.* Bureau of American Ethnology Bulletin No. 121. Smithsonian Institution, Washington, D.C.

1973 *The People of America.* Scribner's, New York.

1976 Are Supra-Inion Depressions Evidence of Prophylactic Trephination? *Bulletin of the History of Medicine* 50:414–434.

Stillman, K.

1993 *The First Apartment Houses.* CPI Group, New York.

Stini, W. A.

1985 Growth Rates and Sexual Dimorphism in Evolutionary Perspective. In *The Analysis of Prehistoric Diets*, edited by R. I. Gilbert, Jr., and J. H. Mielke, pp. 191–226. Academic Press, New York.

Stodder, A. L. W.

1984 Paleoepidemiology of the Mesa Verde Region Anasazi: Demography, Stress, Migration. Unpublished Master's thesis, University of Colorado, Boulder.

1987 The Physical Anthropology and Mortuary Practice of the Dolores Anasazi: An Early Pueblo Population in Local and Regional Context. In *Dolores Archaeological Program: Supporting Studies: Settlement and Environment*, compiled by K. L. Petersen and J. D. Orcutt, pp. 339–504. U.S. Department of the Interior, Bureau of Reclamation, Engineering and Research Center, Denver.

1990 Paleoepidemiology of Eastern and Western Pueblo Communities in Protohistoric New Mexico. Unpublished Ph.D. dissertation, Department of Anthropology, University of Colorado, Boulder.

Stodder, A. L. W., and D. L. Martin

1992 Health and Disease in the Southwest Before and After Spanish Contact. In *Disease and Demography in the Americas*, edited by J. W. Verano and D. H. Ubelaker, pp. 55–74. Smithsonian Institution Press, Washington, D.C.

Stone, Lawrence

1979 *The Family, Sex, and Marriage in England, 1500–1800.* Harper Torchbooks, New York.

Stoodley, N.

2000 From the Cradle to the Grave: Age, Organization, and the Early Anglo-Saxon Burial Rite. *World Archaeology* 31(3):456–472.

Strauss, W., and N. Howe

1991 *Generations: The History of America's Future, 1584 to 2069.* William Morrow, New York.

Surovell, T. A.

2000 Early Paleoindian Women, Children, Mobility, and Fertility. *American Antiquity* 65(3):493–508.

Swedlund, A. C.

1969 Human Skeletal Material from the Yellowjacket Canyon Area, Southwestern Colorado. Unpublished Master's thesis, Department of Anthropology, University of Colorado, Boulder.

Swedlund, A. C., and G. J. Armelagos

1976 *Demographic Anthropology.* Wm. C. Brown, Dubuque, Iowa.

Swentzell, R.

1992 Book Review. *American Indian Quarterly* 16:277–278.

Talayesva, D., and L. W. Simmons

1942 *Sun Chief: The Autobiography of a Hopi Indian.* Yale University Press, New Haven.

Tanner, L.

2000 Flat-Headed Babies Linked to SIDS Effort. *Des Moines Register*, July 31, 2000.

Taylor, M. G.

1985 The Paleopathology of a Southern Sinagua Population from Oak Creek Pueblo, Arizona. In *Health and Disease in the Prehistoric Southwest*, edited by C. F. Merbs and R. J. Miller, pp. 115–118. Anthropological Research Papers No. 34. Arizona State University, Tempe.

Telkkä, A.

1950 On the Prediction of Human Stature from the Long Bones. *Acta Anatomica* 9:103–117.

Thomas, G. V.

1995 The Role of Drawing Strategies and Skills. In *Drawing and Looking*, edited by C. Lange-Kuttner and G. V. Thomas, pp. 107–122. Harvester Wheatsheaf, New York.

Thompson, L., and A. Joseph

1944 *The Hopi Way.* Russell and Russell, New York.

Titche, L. L., S. W. Coulthard, R. D. Wachter, A. Thies, and L. L. Harries

1981 Prevalence of Mastoid Infection in Prehistoric Arizona Indians. *American Journal of Physical Anthropology* 56:269–273.

Titiev, M.

1944 *Old Oraibi: A Study of the Hopi Indians of Third Mesa.* Papers of the Peabody Museum of American Archaeology and Ethnology No. 22. Harvard University, Cambridge.

Triadan, D.

1997 *Ceramic Commodities and Common Containers: Production and Distribution of White Mountain Redware in the Grasshopper Region, Arizona.* Anthropological Papers of the University of Arizona No. 61. University of Arizona Press, Tucson.

Trimble, S.

1990 *The Village of Blue Stone*. Macmillan, New York.

Trotter, M., and G. C. Gleser

1958 A Re-evaluation of Estimation of Stature Based on Measurements of Stature Taken During Life and of Long Bones After Death. *American Journal of Physical Anthropology* 16:79–123.

Turk, A. E., J. G. McCarthy, C. H. M. Thorne, and J. H. Wisoff

1996 The "Back to Sleep Campaign" and Deformational Plagiocephaly: Is There Cause for Concern? *Journal of Craniofacial Surgery* 7(1):13–18.

Turner, C., II, and J. Turner

1999 *Man Corn: Cannibalism and Violence in the Prehistoric American Southwest*. University of Utah Press, Salt Lake City.

Ubelaker, D.

1989 *Human Skeletal Remains: Excavation, Analysis, Interpretation*. 2nd edition. Taraxacum, Washington, D.C.

van Gennep, A.

1960 [1909]   *The Rites of Passage*. University of Chicago Press, Chicago.

Van Gerven, D. P., and S. G. Sheridan

1994a   A Biocultural Reconstruction of a Classic Period Hohokam Community. In *The Pueblo Grande Project, Volume 6: The Bioethnography of a Classic Period Hohokam Population*, edited by D. P. Van Gerven and S. G. Sheridan, pp. 123–128. Publications in Archaeology No. 20. Soil Systems, Phoenix.

1994b   Bone Growth and Cortical Bone Maintenance at Pueblo Grande. In *The Pueblo Grande Project, Volume 6: The Bioethnography of a Classic Period Hohokam Population*, edited by D. P. Van Gerven and S. G. Sheridan, pp. 47–54. Publications in Archaeology No. 20. Soil Systems, Phoenix.

1994c   Life and Death at Pueblo Grande: The Demographic Context. In *The Pueblo Grande Project, Volume 6: The Bioethnography of a Classic Period Hohokam Population*, edited by D. P. Van Gerven and S. G. Sheridan, pp. 5–24. Publications in Archaeology No. 20. Soil Systems, Phoenix.

Van Keuren, S.

1999 *Ceramic Design Structure Variation and the Organization of Cibola White Ware Production in the Grasshopper Region, Arizona*. Arizona State Museum Archaeological Series No. 191. University of Arizona, Tucson.

Vivian, R. G.

2000 Conclusion: Basketmaker Archaeology at the Millennium: New Answers to Old Questions. In *Foundations of Anasazi Culture: The Basketmaker-Pueblo Transition*, edited by P. F. Reed, pp. 251–257. University of Utah Press, Salt Lake City.

von Bonin, G.

1936 The Skeletal Material from the Lowry Area. In *Lowry Ruin in Southwestern Colorado*, edited by P. S. Martin, pp. 143–179. Anthropology Series. Field Museum of Natural History, Chicago.

Voth, H. R.

1912 *Brief Miscellaneous Hopi Papers I. Notes on Modern Burial Customs of the Hopi of Arizona*. Publication No. 157, Anthropology Series No. 11. Field Museum of Natural History, Chicago.

Wade, W. D.

1970 Skeletal Remains of a Prehistoric Population from the Puerco Valley, Eastern Arizona. Unpublished Ph.D. dissertation, Department of Anthropology, University of Colorado, Boulder.

Walker, P. L.

1985 Anemia Among Prehistoric Indians of the American Southwest. In *Health and Disease in the Prehistoric Southwest*, edited by C. F. Merbs and R. J. Miller, pp. 139–164. Anthropological Research Papers No. 34. Arizona State University, Tempe.

Wallaert-Pêtre, H.

2001 Learning How to Make the Right Pots: Apprenticeship Strategies Serving Style Duplication: A Case Study in Handmade Pottery from Cameroon. *Journal of Anthropological Research* 57(4).

Watson, D.

1961 *Indians of the Mesa Verde*. Mesa Verde Museum Association, Mesa Verde National Park, Colorado.

Weiss, K. M.

1973 *Demographic Models for Anthropology*. Memoir No. 27. *American Antiquity* 38(2), Pt. 2. Society for American Archaeology, Washington, D.C.

Wenger, G. R.

1991 *The Story of Mesa Verde National Park*. Mesa Verde Museum Association, Mesa Verde National Park, Colorado.

West, B.

1988 The Making of the English Working Past: A Critical View of the Ironbridge Gorge Museum. In *The Museum Time Machine*, edited by R. Lumley, pp. 36–62. Routledge, London.

West, E.

1989 *Growing Up with the Country: Childhood on the Far Western Frontier*. University of New Mexico Press, Albuquerque.

Wetterstrom, W.

1986 *Food, Diet, and Population at Prehistoric Arroyo Hondo Pueblo, New Mexico*. School of American Research Press, Santa Fe.

Wheeler, R. L.

1985 Pathology in Late Thirteenth Century Zuni from the El Morro Valley, New Mexico. In *Health and Disease in the Prehistoric Southwest*, edited by C. F. Merbs and R. J. Miller, pp. 79–84. Anthropological Research Papers No. 34. Arizona State University, Tempe.

White, L. A.

1942 *The Pueblo of Santa Ana, New Mexico*. Memoirs No. 60. *American Anthropologist* 44(4), Pt. 2. American Anthropological Association, Menasha, Wisconsin.

White, T. D.

1992 *Prehistoric Cannibalism at Mancos 5MTUR-2346*. Princeton University Press, Princeton.

Whiteley, P. M.

1988 *Deliberate Acts: Changing Hopi Culture Through the Oraibi Split*. University of Arizona Press, Tucson.

Whiting, B. B., and C. P. Edwards
1988 *Children of Different Worlds: The Formation of Social Behavior*. Harvard University Press, Cambridge.

Whiting, B., and J. Whiting
1975 *Children of Six Cultures*. Harvard University Press, Cambridge.

Whitley, D. S.
1994 Ethnography and Rock Art in the Far West: Some Archaeological Implications. In *New Light on Old Art: Recent Advances in Hunter-Gatherer Rock Art Research*, edited by D. S. Whitley and L. L. Loendorf, pp. 81–93. Institute of Archaeology, Monograph No. 36. University of California, Los Angeles.

1998 Finding Rain in the Desert: Landscape, Gender, and Far Western North American Rock-Art. In *The Archaeology of Rock-Art*, edited by C. Chippendale and P. S. C. Taçon, pp. 11–29. Cambridge University Press, Cambridge.

2000 *The Art of the Shaman: Rock Art of California*. University of Utah Press, Salt Lake City.

Whitman, W.
1947 *The Pueblo Indians of San Ildefonso*. Columbia University Press, New York.

Whittaker, J., K. Kamp, M. Krouse, and M. Regan
1999 Human Burials. In *Surviving Adversity: The Sinagua of Lizard Man Village*, by K. A. Kamp and J. C. Whittaker, pp. 163–184. University of Utah Anthropological Papers No. 120. University of Utah Press, Salt Lake City.

Whittlesey, S. M.
1978 Status and Death at Grasshopper Pueblo: Experiments Toward an Archaeological Theory of Correlates. Unpublished Ph.D. dissertation, Department of Anthropology, University of Arizona, Tucson.

1989 The Individual, the Community, and Social Organization: Issues of Evidence and Inference Justification. In *Households and Communities*, edited by S. MacEachern, D. Archer, and R. Garvin, pp. 227–234. University of Calgary, Calgary.

1999 Engendering the Mogollon Past: Theory and Mortuary Data from Grasshopper Pueblo. In *Sixty Years of Mogollon Archaeology: Papers from the Ninth Mogollon Conference, Silver City, New Mexico, 1996*, edited by S. M. Whittlesey, pp. 39–48. SRI Press, Tucson.

Whittlesey, S. M., and J. J. Reid
1982 Cholla Perspectives on Salado. In *Introduction and Special Studies*, edited by J. J. Reid, pp. 63–80. Cholla Project Archaeology, Vol. 1. Archaeological Series No. 161. Arizona State Museum, University of Arizona, Tucson.

2001 Mortuary Ritual and Organizational Inferences at Grasshopper Pueblo, Arizona. In *Ancient Burial Practices in the American Southwest: Archaeology, Physical Anthropology, and Native American Perspectives*, edited by D. R. Mitchell and J. L. Brunson-Hadley, pp. 68–96. University of New Mexico Press, Albuquerque.

Wiener, A. L.
1984 Human Skeletal Remains. In *Dolores Archaeological Program: Synthetic Report, 1978–1981*, edited by D. A. Breternitz, pp. 239–248. U.S.

Department of the Interior, Bureau of Reclamation, Engineering and Research Center, Denver.

Wilcox, D. R., and J. Haas

1994 The Scream of the Butterfly: Competition and Conflict in the Prehistoric Southwest. In *Themes in Southwest Prehistory*, edited by G. J. Gumerman, pp. 211–238. School of American Research Press, Santa Fe.

Wilkinson, P., and M. Pollard

1994 *Mysterious Places of the Master Builders*. Chelsea House, New York.

Wills, V. G., and J. C. Waterloo

1958 The Death Rate in Age Group 1–4 Years as an Index of Malnutrition. *Journal of Tropical Pediatrics* 3:167–170.

Wilshusen, R. H., and E. Blinman

1992 Pueblo I Village Formation: A Reevaluation of Sites Recorded by Earl Morris on Ute Mountain Tribal Lands. *The Kiva* 57:251–269.

Wilshusen, R. H., and S. G. Ortman

1999 Rethinking the Pueblo I Period in the San Juan Drainage: Aggregation, Migration, and Cultural Diversity. *The Kiva* 64(3):369–399.

Wilson, B., and Ligtvoet, J.

1992 Across Time and Cultures: Stylistic Changes in the Drawings of Dutch Children. In *Drawing Research and Development*, edited by D. Thistlewood, pp. 75–88. Longman, London.

Wilson, B., and Wilson, M.

1984 Children's Drawings in Egypt: Cultural Style Acquisition as Graphic Development. *Visual Arts Research* 10:13–26.

Wobst, H. M.

1977 Stylistic Behavior and Information Exchange. *Anthropological Papers of the University of Michigan* 16:317–342. University of Michigan, Ann Arbor.

Woodson, M. K.

1995 The Goat Hill Site: A Western Anasazi Pueblo in the Safford Valley of Southeastern Arizona. Unpublished Master's thesis, Department of Anthropology, University of Texas, Austin.

Wright, R. P.

1991 Women's Labor and Pottery Production. In *Engendering Archaeology: Women and Prehistory*, edited by J. M. Gero and M. W. Conkey, pp. 194–223. Basil Blackwell, Cambridge, Massachusetts.

Wulff, H.

1995 Introducing Youth Culture in Its Own Right. In *Youth Cultures: A Cross-Cultural Perspective*, edited by V. Amit-Talal and H. Wulff, pp. 1–18. Routledge, London.

Wyaco, V.

1998 *A Zuni Life: A Pueblo Indian in Two Worlds*. University of New Mexico Press, Albuquerque.

Wyckoff, L. L.

1985 *Designs and Factions: Politics, Religion, and Ceramics on the Hopi Third Mesa*. University of New Mexico Press, Albuquerque.

Yava, A.

1978 *Big Falling Snow: A Tewa-Hopi Indian's Life and Times and the History and Traditions of His People*. Crown, New York.

Young, R.
1999 *A Personal Tour of Mesa Verde*. Lerner Publications, Minneapolis.
Yue, C., and D. Yue
1986 *The Pueblo*. Houghton Mifflin, Boston.
Zelizer, V. A.
1985 *Pricing the Priceless Child: The Changing Social Value of Children*. Princeton University Press, Princeton.
Zeller, A. C.
1987 A Role for Women in Hominid Evolution. *Man* (N.S.) 22(2):528–557.

Contributors

ELIZABETH A. BAGWELL
Department of Anthropology
University of New Mexico
Albuquerque, New Mexico 87131

CYNTHIA S. BRADLEY
Primitive Tech Enterprises, Inc.
Cortez, Colorado 81321

PATRICIA L. CROWN
Department of Anthropology
University of New Mexico
Albuquerque, New Mexico 87131

KELLEY HAYS-GILPIN
Department of Anthropology
Northern Arizona University
Flagstaff, Arizona 86011–5200

KATHRYN A. KAMP
Department of Anthropology
Grinnell College
Grinnell, Iowa 50112

CLAUDETTE PIPER
4410 S. Lance Road
Flagstaff, Arizona 86001

NAN A. ROTHSCHILD
Department of Anthropology
Barnard College
New York, New York 10027

KRISTIN D. SOBOLIK
Department of Anthropology
Institute for Quaternary Studies
University of Maine
Orono, Maine 04469

JOHN C. WHITTAKER
Department of Anthropology
Grinnell College
Grinnell, Iowa 50112

STEPHANIE M. WHITTLESEY
Statistical Research, Inc.
Tucson, Arizona 85751